名著名译
英汉对照
读本

VANITY FAIR

名利场

〔英〕萨克雷 著
杨必 译

2019年·北京

图书在版编目(CIP)数据

名利场/(英)萨克雷著;杨必译.—北京:商务印书馆,2019
(名著名译英汉对照读本)
ISBN 978-7-100-17158-8

Ⅰ.①名… Ⅱ.①萨…②杨… Ⅲ.①英语—汉语—对照读物②长篇小说—英国—近代 Ⅳ.①H319.4:I

中国版本图书馆CIP数据核字(2019)第039123号

名著名译英汉对照读本
名 利 场
〔英〕萨克雷 著
杨 必 译

商 务 印 书 馆 出 版
(北京王府井大街36号 邮政编码100710)
商 务 印 书 馆 发 行
北 京 冠 中 印 刷 厂 印 刷
ISBN 978-7-100-17158-8

2019年4月第1版 开本850×1168 1/32
2019年4月北京第1次印刷 印张8¾
定价:28.00元

前　　言

这套丛书的名字比较长：名著名译英汉对照读本。还应该长一点儿才更准确，比如叫做“名著名译英汉对照翻译教程读本”，因为这更接近我们费尽周折编出这套书的全部用意和目的。下面简单地说明一下。

名著。外国文学名著成千上万，按说选出十种八种，做成英汉对照读物，奉献给读者，不应该是难事。但凡事怕讲条件。英汉对照读物不宜太长，最好在八九万字的篇幅；体裁要丰富，至少戏剧、长篇和短篇小说要照顾到；英语难易要兼顾，各个时期尽量不漏，写作风格多样化；译文优秀，确实可以作为翻译教程式的读本……这么多条件相加，名著挑选起来就有相当难度了。多亏了各家老字号出版社几十年来出版的外国文化和文学翻译作品十分丰厚，虽然花费了不少力气，但结果相当令人满意。且看我们所选作品的书目：剧本有《哈姆莱特》、《凯撒和克莉奥佩特拉》和《理想丈夫》；长篇小说有《名利场》和《简·爱》；中篇小说有《伊坦·弗洛美》和《黑暗的心》；随笔有《一间自己的房间》；短篇小说有《马克·吐温短篇小说选》和《欧·亨利短篇小说选》。

三个戏剧。流传下来的优秀戏剧作品是西方文学的重要组成部分。阅读西方文学作品，必须阅读优秀的戏剧作品。另外，戏剧是西方文学的重要形式之一。在小说形式没有出现之前，戏剧是文艺创作中最具包容量的形式。小说出现后，戏剧除了不断丰富自己，仍然保持着所有文艺创作形式所无法取代的优势，那就是舞台演出。小说可以朗读，但是无法在舞台上演出。要想登台演出，还得改编成剧本。因此，戏剧仍然是阅读的一个重要对象。《哈姆莱特》不仅是莎士比亚的扛鼎之作，也是所有剧本中公认的代表之作，其深度、广度和厚度，只有亲自阅读才能领会。莎士比亚是戏剧发展史上的一座山，后来者只有仰望的，没有叫板的，偏偏出了个萧伯纳要与他试比高低。萧伯纳发愤读书（包括不列颠百科全书的全部），勤奋写作（共写了五十余部），还创办“费边社”。莎士比亚有个名剧叫《安东尼与克莉奥佩特拉》，写古罗马人的人性和爱情。萧伯纳说，不，古人更喜欢政治，不信你看我写的《凯撒和克莉奥佩特拉》。后者也成了名剧，还拍成了电影，成为电影经典。才子作家奥斯卡·王尔德却说，爱情和政治都重要，唯美主义更重要，我来写一出唯美剧本《理想丈夫》让你们看看。于是，《理想丈夫》集爱情、政治讽刺与社会风俗于一体，上演时轰动一时，也成了名剧。

两个长篇。为了适合英汉对照，我们只能选长篇小说名著的若干章节。萨克雷的《名利场》和夏洛特·勃朗特的《简·爱》我们各选了其中的八九万字，首先是因为这两部作品在西方文学史上具有独一无二的地位，其次是因为这个译本已经成了翻译外国文学作品的范本。所选的几章当然是其中最精彩的，完全可以当做短篇小说看，却又大体上窥见了全书中的几个主人公。萨克雷生前十分走红，许多后起作家都对他十分仰慕，夏洛特·勃朗特就是他的追星族，醉心文学，终写出一部《简·爱》献给他，勃朗特也从此成名。

别。但是读者在对照英文和中文的时候，一定要琢磨一下，消化一下，发现有“对不上的”也切不要立即下结论，最好回头看看书前的那篇千把字的“翻译谈”，然后再下结论。你这样做了，无论发现什么结果，都会获得一种意想不到的飞跃，英文的和中文的。

读本。既然是读本，首先考虑的是为读者服务。无论英文中文，均有难易之分。按我们的设想，先读短篇，而后中篇，然后长篇，最后是戏剧。但是如果你只读英语，参考译文，那么先读戏剧中的对话倒是一个提高英语理解的有效捷径。

另外，前边说过，我们的这套书应该叫做“翻译教程读本”才更尽其意。我们知道，许多优秀的译家都承认他们从优秀的译本中获益颇多，翻译的经验和感受很重要，例如，“关键是‘信’‘达’”，“务使作者之命意豁然呈露”，“一仆二主”，“五点谈”，“首要原则是忠实，并力求神似”，“学会表达”，“拉住两个朋友的手”，等等，在每一读本的前面都作了具体而珍贵的详述。如果有什么东西可以称为翻译教程的话，这些类似“翻译谈”的东西才当之无愧。

苏福忠

《名利场》翻译谈

"一仆二主"

1949年后的翻译界,《名利场》译本的出现,是一件大事。这件大事的出现好像是水到渠成的。杨绛在她的《记杨必》里有这样一段话:

> 傅雷曾请杨必教傅聪英文。傅雷鼓励她翻译。阿必就写信请教默存指导她翻一本比较短而容易翻的书,试试笔。默存尽老师之责,为她找了玛丽亚·埃杰窝斯的一本小说。建议她译为《剥削世家》。阿必很快译完,也很快就出版了。傅雷以翻译家的经验,劝杨必不要翻名家小说,该翻译大作家的名著。阿必又求教老师。默存想到了萨克雷名著的旧译本不够理想,建议她重译,题目改为《名利场》。阿必欣然准备翻译这部名作,随即和人民文学出版社订下合同。

在翻译圈子里,谈翻译总会谈到《名利场》的译文;认真做翻译的人,没有不认真研读《名利场》的译本的;高校外文系上英译中的课,也没有不拿中译本《名利场》中的章节做范译的。读别的译本,读者需要有心理准备,遇上疙疙瘩瘩别别扭扭的欧化句子和用词,得私下宽慰:唉,译文嘛,凑合着看吧。但是,读《名利场》,如读传统的白话文小说,通俗清新、美丽流畅的译文一下子拉近了读者与原著的距离,让人感到亲切、和蔼,欢欢喜喜地读下去。我们不妨随便从书中举一个例子来看看:

"Dear little innocent lamb, you want one," said the Marquis, and his jaw thrust out, and he began go grin hideously, his little eyes leering towards Rebecca. 勋爵道:"亲爱的小羔羊,你多么纯洁,真需要一只看羊狗来保护你。"他伸出下巴涎着脸儿笑起来,乜斜着一双小眼睛对她一溜,那样子难看极了。

加几个字,减几个字,颠倒一点点句序,一段译文不仅生动,译文中的人物形象一下子丰富起来。难能可贵的是,杨必的《名利场》译本里,全是这样的段与句。真让人忍不住想亲自聆听杨必说说她是如何把萨克雷老辣而冗长的英文句子,翻译成这么地道的中国话。然而,很遗憾,由于译者英年早逝,没有什么关于翻译的文字留下来。幸运的是,身为姐姐的杨绛有一篇《失败的经验——试谈翻译》,我们不妨摘一段,看看能否看出与杨必的翻译有一些相通的东西:

> 谈失败的经验,不免强调翻译的困难。至少,这是一项苦差,因为一切得听从主人,不能自作主张。而且一仆二主,同时伺候着两个主人:一是原著,二是译文的读者。译者一方面得彻底了解原著;不仅了解字句的意义,还须领会字句之间的含蕴,字句之外的语气声调。另一方面,译文的读者要求从译文里领略原文。译者得用读者的语言,把原作的内容按原样表达;内容不可有所增删,语气声调也不可走样。原文的弦外之音,只从弦上传出;含蕴未吐的意思,也只附着在字句上。译者只能在译文的句子上用功夫表达,不能插入自己的解释或擅用自己的说法。译者必须对原著彻底

了解，方才能够贴合着原文，照模照样地向读者表达。可是尽管了解彻底，未必就能照样表达。彻底了解不易，贴合着原著照模照样表达更难。

从这段精彩的翻译谈中，我们不难感觉到，尽管杨必不可否认具有翻译方面的天赋与灵气，但美好的译文背后绝少不了译者的心血。在《记杨必》一文里，杨绛这样写到："杨必翻译的《名利场》如期交卷，出版社评给她最高的稿酬。她向来体弱失眠，工作紧张了失眠更厉害，等她赶完《名利场》，身体就垮了。"

文　心

CONTENTS 目录

（本书节选了原书如下章节）

VANITY FAIR

名 利 场

Before the Curtain

As the Manager of the Performance sits before the curtain on the boards, and looks into the Fair, a feeling of profound melancholy comes over him in his survey of the bustling place. There is a great quantity of eating and drinking, making love and jilting, laughing and the contrary, smoking, cheating, fighting, dancing, and fiddling: there are bullies pushing about, bucks ogling the women, knaves picking pockets, policemen on the look-out, quacks (*other* quacks, plague take them!) bawling in front of their booths, and yokels looking up at the tinselled dancers and poor old rouged tumblers, while the light-fingered folk are operating upon their pockets behind. Yes, this is VANITY FAIR; not a moral place certainly; nor a merry one, though very noisy. Look at the faces of the actors and buffoons when they come off from their business; and Tom Fool washing the paint off his cheeks before he sits down to dinner with his wife and the little Jack Puddings behind the canvas. The curtain will be up presently, and he will be turning over head and heels, and crying, "How are you?"

A man with a reflective turn of mind, walking through an exhibition of this sort, will not be oppressed, I take it, by his own or other people's hilarity. An episode of humour or kindness touches and amuses him here and there;—a pretty child looking at a gingerbread stall; a pretty girl blushing whilst her lover talks to her and chooses her fairing; poor Tom Fool, yonder behind the waggon, mumbling his bone with the honest family

开幕以前的几句话

领班的坐在戏台上幔子前面，对着底下闹哄哄的市场，瞧了半晌，心里不觉悲惨起来。市场上的人有的在吃喝，有的在调情，有的得了新宠就丢了旧爱；有在笑的，也有在哭的，还有在抽烟的，打架的，跳舞的，拉提琴的，诓骗哄人的。有些是到处横行的强梁汉子，有些是对女人飞眼儿的花花公子，也有扒儿手和到处巡逻的警察，还有走江湖吃十方的，在自己摊子前面扯起嗓子嚷嚷（这些人偏和我同行，真该死！），跳舞的穿着浑身发亮的衣服，可怜的翻斤斗老头儿涂着两腮帮子胭脂，引得那些乡下佬睁着眼瞧，不提防后面就有三只手的家伙在掏他们的口袋。是了，这就是我们的名利场。这里虽然是个热闹去处，却是道德沦亡，说不上有什么快活。你瞧瞧戏子们丑角们下场以后的脸色——譬如那逗人发笑的傻小子汤姆回到后台洗净了脸上的油彩，准备和老婆儿子（一群小傻小子）坐下吃饭时候的情景，你就明白了。不久开场做戏，汤姆又会出来连连翻斤斗，嘴里叫唤着说："您好哇？"

我想，凡是有思想的人在这种市场上观光，不但不怪人家兴致好，自己也会跟着乐。他不时的会碰上一两件事，或是幽默得逗人发笑，或是显得出人心忠厚的一面，使人感动。这儿有一个漂亮的孩子，眼巴巴的瞧着卖姜汁面包的摊儿；那儿有一个漂亮的姑娘，脸红红的听她的爱人说话，瞧他给自己挑礼物；再过去是可怜的小丑汤姆躲在货车后

which lives by his tumbling; but the general impression is one more melancholy than mirthful. When you come home, you sit down, in a sober, contemplative, not uncharitable frame of mind, and apply yourself to your books or your business.

I have no other moral than this to tag to the present story of "Vanity Fair". Some people consider Fairs immoral altogether, and eschew such, with their servants and families; very likely they are right. But persons who think otherwise, and are of a lazy, or a benevolent, or a sarcastic mood, may perhaps like to step in for half an hour, and look at the performances. There are scenes of all sorts; some dreadful combats, some grand and lofty horse-riding, some scenes of high life, and some of very middling indeed; some love-making for the sentimental, and some light comic business; the whole accompanied by appropriate scenery, and brilliantly illuminated with the Author's own candles.

What more has the Manager of the Performance to say? —To acknowledge the kindness with which it has been received in all the principal towns of England through which the Show has passed, and where it has been most favourably noticed by the respected conductors of the Public Press, and by the Nobility and Gentry. He is proud to think that his Puppets have given satisfaction to the very best company in this empire. The famous little Becky Puppet has been pronounced to be uncommonly flexible in the joints, and lively on the wire: the Amelia Doll, though it has had a smaller circle of admirers, has yet been carved and dressed with the greatest care by the artist: the Dobbin Figure, though apparently clumsy, yet dances in a very amusing and natural man-

头带着一家老小啃骨头，这些老实人就靠他翻斤斗赚来的钱过活。可是话又说回来，大致的印象还是使人愁而不是逗人乐的。等你回到家里坐下来读书做事的时候，玩味着刚才所见的一切，就会冷静下来，对于别人的短处也不太苛责了。

我这本小说《名利场》就只有这么一点儿教训。有人认为市场上人口混杂，是个下流的地方，不但自己不去，连家眷和用人也不准去。大概他们的看法是不错的。不过也有人生就懒散的脾气，或是仁慈的心肠，或是爱取笑讽刺的性格，他们看法不同一些，倒愿意在市场里消磨半个钟头，看看各种表演，像激烈的格斗，精彩的骑术，上流社会的形形色色，普通人家生活的情形，专为多情的看客预备的恋爱场面，轻松滑稽的穿插等等。这场表演每一幕都有相称的布景，四面点着作者自己的蜡烛，满台照得雪亮。

领班的还有什么可说的呢？他带着戏班子在英国各大城市上演，多承各界惠顾，各报的编辑先生们也都有好评，又蒙各位大人先生提拔，真是不胜感激。他的傀儡戏被英国最高尚的人士所赏识，使他觉得面上很有光彩。那个叫蓓基的木偶人儿非常有名，大家一致称赞她的骨节特别的灵活，线一牵就活泼泼的手舞足蹈。那个叫爱米丽亚的洋娃娃虽然没有这么叫座，卖艺的倒也费了好些心血刻画她的面貌，设计她的服装。还有一个叫都宾的傀儡，看着笨手笨脚的，跳起舞来却很有趣，很自然。也有人爱看男孩子们

ner:the Little Boys' Dance has been liked by some;and please to remark the richly dressed figure of the Wicked Nobleman, on which no expense has been spared, and which Old Nick will fetch away at the end of this singular performance.

And with this, and a profound bow to his patrons, the Manager retires, and the curtain rises.

LONDON, June 28, 1848

跳的一场舞。请各位观众注意那“黑心的贵人”，他的服饰非常华丽，我们筹备的时候真是不惜工本；这次表演完毕以后，它马上会给“魔鬼老爹”请去。

领班的说到这儿，向各位主顾深深的打了一躬退到后台，接下去就开幕了。

一八四八年六月二十八日于伦敦

Quite a Sentimental Chapter

We must now take leave of Arcadia, and those amiable people practising the rural virtues there, and travel back to London, to inquire what has become of Miss Amelia. "We don't care a fig for her," writes some unknown correspondent with a pretty little handwriting and a pink seal to her note. "She is fade and insipid," and adds some more kind remarks in this strain, which I should never have repeated at all, but that they are in truth prodigiously complimentary to the young lady whom they concern.

Has the beloved reader, in his experience of society, never heard similar remarks by good-natured female friends; who always wonder what you *can* see in Miss Smith that is so fascinating; or what *could* induce Major Jones to propose for that silly insignificant simpering Miss Thompson, who has nothing but her wax-doll face to recommend her? What is there in a pair of pink cheeks and blue eyes forsooth? these dear Moralists ask, and hint wisely that the gifts of genius, the accomplishments of the mind, the mastery of Mangnall's questions, and a ladylike knowledge of botany and geology, the knack of making poetry, the power of rattling sonatas in the Herz manner, and so forth, are far more valuable endowments for a female, than those fugitive charms which a few years will inevitably tarnish. It is quite edifying to hear women speculate upon the worthlessness and the duration of beauty.

很多情的一章

现在我们应该离开田园乐土，和当地那些纯朴可爱的好人告别，回到伦敦去探听探听爱米丽亚小姐的消息了。一位隐名的读者写给我一封信，她的字迹娟秀，信封用粉红的火漆封了口。信上说："我们一点儿不喜欢她，这个人没有意思，乏味得很。"此外还有几句别的话，也是这一类好意的评语。这些话对于被批评的小姐实在是一种了不起的赞扬，要不然我也不会说给大家听。

亲爱的读者，当你在交际场里应酬的时候，难道没有听见过好心的女朋友们说过同样的话吗？她们常常怀疑斯密士小姐究竟有什么引人的地方。她们认为汤姆生小姐又蠢又没意思，只会傻笑；脸蛋儿长得像蜡做的洋娃娃，其他一无好处；为什么琼斯少佐偏要向她求婚呢？亲爱的道学先生们说："粉红脸蛋儿和蓝眼珠子有什么了不起？"她们很有道理的点醒大家，说是一个女人有天赋的才能和灵智方面的成就；能够明了曼格耐尔的《问题》[1]；掌握上等女人应有的地质学植物学的智识；会作诗；会学赫滋[2]派的手法，在琴上叮叮咚咚弹奏鸣曲等等，比好看的相貌有价值得多，因为红颜难保，不过几年便消退了。听得女人批评美貌不值钱不耐久，倒使我长进了不少。

---

① 曼格耐尔(Mangnall，1769—1820)，英国女教师，所著《历史问题及其他》在1800年出版，是风行的女校教本。

② 赫滋(Heinrich Herz，1806—1888)，奥国作曲家，在法国教琴出名。

But though virtue is a much finer thing, and those hapless creatures who suffer under the misfortune of good looks ought to be continually put in mind of the fate which awaits them; and though, very likely, the heroic female character which ladies admire is a more glorious and beautiful object than the kind, fresh, smiling, artless, tender little domestic goddess, whom men are inclined to worship—yet the latter and inferior sort of women must have this consolation—that the men *do* admire them after all; and that, in spite of all our kind friends' warnings and protests, we go on in our desperate error and folly, and shall to the end of the chapter. Indeed, for my own part, though I have been repeatedly told by persons for whom I have the greatest respect, that Miss Brown is an insignificant chit, and Mrs. White has nothing but her *petit minois chiffonné*, and Mrs. Black has not a word to say for herself; yet I know that I have had the most delightful conversations with Mrs. Black (of course, my dear Madam, they are inviolable): I see all the men in a cluster round Mrs. White's chair: all the young fellows battling to dance with Miss Brown; and so I am tempted to think that to be despised by her sex is a very great compliment to a woman.

The young ladies in Amelia's society did this for her very satisfactorily. For instance, there was scarcely any point upon which the Miss Osbornes, George's sisters, and the Mesdemoiselles Dobbin agreed so well as in their estimate of her very trifling merits: and their wonder that their brothers could find any charms in her. "We are kind to her," the Misses Osborne said, a pair of fine black-browed young ladies who had had the best of governesses, masters, and milliners; and they treated her with

当然，德行比容貌要紧得多，我们应该时常提醒不幸身为美人的女子，叫她们时常记着将来的苦命。还有一层，男人们虽然把那些眉开眼笑、脸色鲜嫩、脾气温和、心地良善、不明白世事的小东西当神明似的供奉在家里，太太小姐们却佩服女中的豪杰；而且两相比较起来，女中豪杰的确更值得颂扬和赞美。不过话虽这么说，前面一种次一等的女人也有可以聊以自慰的地方，因为归根结底，男人还是喜欢她们的。我们的好朋友白费了许多唇舌，一会儿警告，一会儿劝导，我们却至死不悟，荒唐糊涂到底。就拿我来说吧，有几位我向来尊敬的太太小姐曾经几次三番告诉我，说白朗小姐身材瘦小，没有什么动人的去处；又说忽爱德太太除了脸蛋儿还算讨人喜欢，没有什么了不起；又说勃拉克太太最没有口齿，一句话都不会说。可是我明明跟勃拉克太太谈得津津有味（亲爱的太太，我们说的话当然是无可訾议的）；忽爱德太太椅子旁边明明挤满了男人；说到白朗小姐呢，所有的小伙子都在你抢我夺的要和她跳舞。这样看起来，一个女人给别的女人瞧不起，倒是一件非常值得骄傲的事。

和爱米丽亚来往的小姐们把这一套儿做得很到家。譬如说，乔治的姊妹，那两位奥斯本小姐，还有两位都宾小姐，一说起爱米丽亚种种没出息的地方，意见完全相同，大家都不明白自己的兄弟看着她哪一点上可爱。两位奥斯本小姐生得不错，都长着漆黑的眉毛。讲到教育，家里一向请着第一流的男女家庭教师；讲到穿着，又是雇的最讲究的裁缝。她们说："我们待爱米丽亚很好。"她们竭力俯就她，对她非常客气，那种降低了身份抬举她的样子实在叫人受不了，弄

such extreme kindness and condescension, and patronised her so insufferably, that the poor little thing *was* in fact perfectly dumb in their presence, and to all outward appearance as stupid as they thought her. She made efforts to like them, as in duty bound, and as sisters of her future husband. She passed "long mornings" with them—the most dreary and serious of forenoons. She drove out solemnly in their great family coach with them and Miss Wirt their governess, that raw-boned Vestal. They took her to the ancient concerts by way of a treat, and to the oratorio, and to St. Paul's to see the charity children, where in such terror was she of her friends, she almost did not dare be affected by the hymn the children sang. Their house was comfortable; their papa's table rich and handsome; their society solemn and genteel; their self-respect prodigious; they had the best pew at the Foundling; all their habits were pompous and orderly, and all their amusements intolerably dull and decorous. After every one of her visits (and oh how glad she was when they were over!) Miss Osborne and Miss Maria Osborne, and Miss Wirt, the vestal governess, asked each other with increased wonder, "What could George find in that creature?"

How is this? some carping reader exclaims. How is it that Amelia, who had such a number of friends at school, and was so beloved there, comes out into the world and is spurned by her discriminating sex? My dear sir, there were no men at Miss Pinkerton's establishment except the old dancing-master; and you would not have had the girls fall out about *him*? When George, their handsome brother, ran off directly after breakfast, and dined from home half-a-dozen times a week, no wonder

得可怜的爱米在她们面前一句话都说不出来，活像个呆子，竟和小姐们对于她的估计吻合了。爱米丽亚因为她们是未来丈夫的姊妹，努力叫自己喜欢她们，觉得这是她的责任。她往往整个上午陪着她们，挨过多少沉闷没有趣味的时光。她和她们一块儿出去，一本正经的坐在奥斯本家的大马车里，旁边还有个瘦骨嶙峋的女教师——那个叫乌德小姐的老姑娘，相陪着。奥斯本小姐们款待爱米的法子，就是带她去听枯燥无味的音乐会，或是去听圣乐，或是到圣·保罗教堂去看那些靠施主养活的穷苦孩子。她对于新朋友们怕得厉害，甚至于在教堂里听了孩子们唱的圣诗，也不大敢表示感动。奥斯本家里很舒服，他的爸爸讲究吃喝，菜蔬做得十分精致，排场又阔。他们待人接物的态度严肃而又文雅；他们的自尊心强得与众不同；他们在孤儿教堂的包座是全堂第一；他们做事有条有理，最讲面子；连他们取乐儿的时候，也只挑规规矩矩、沉闷不堪的事干。爱米丽亚每去拜访一次（拜访完了之后她心里多轻松啊！）奥斯本大小姐、玛丽亚·奥斯本小姐，还有女教师乌德小姐那个老姑娘，总免不了你问我我问你的说："乔治究竟瞧着她哪点儿好啊？"她们越看越不明白了。

有些爱找错儿的读者叫起来说："怎么的？爱米丽亚在学校里朋友那么多，人缘那么好，怎么出来以后碰见的奶奶姑娘们倒会不喜欢她呢？她们又不是辨不出好歹的人。"亲爱的先生，别忘了在平克顿小姐的学校里，除了一个上了年纪的跳舞教师之外一个男人都没有，女孩子们难道为着这老头儿吵架不成？乔治的姊妹们瞧着漂亮的兄弟一吃完早饭就往外跑，一星期里头倒有五六天不在家吃饭，难怪她们

the neglected sisters felt a little vexation. When young Bullock (of the firm of Hulker, Bullock & Co., Bankers, Lombard Street), who had been making up to Miss Maria the last two seasons, actually asked Amelia to dance the cotillon, could you expect that the former young lady should be pleased? And yet she said she was, like an artless, forgiving creature. "I'm so delighted you like dear Amelia," she said quite eagerly to Mr. Bullock after the dance. "She's engaged to my brother George; there's not much in her, but she's the best-natured and most unaffected young creature: at home we're all *so* fond of her." Dear girl! who can calculate the depth of affection expressed in that enthusiastic *so*?

Miss Wirt and these two affectionate young women so earnestly and frequently impressed upon George Osborne's mind the enormity of the sacrifice he was making, and his romantic generosity in throwing himself away upon Amelia, that I'm not sure but that he really thought he was one of the most deserving characters in the British army, and gave himself up to be loved with a good deal of easy resignation.

Somehow, although he left home every morning, as was stated, and dined abroad six days in the week, when his sisters believed the infatuated youth to be at Miss Sedley's apron-strings: he was *not* always with Amelia, whilst the world supposed him at her feet. Certain it is that on more occasions than one, when Captain Dobbin called to look for his friend, Miss Osborne (who was very attentive to the Captain, and anxious to hear his military stories, and to know about the health of his dear Mamma,) would laughingly point to the opposite side of the square, and say, "Oh, you must go to the Sedleys to ask

觉得受了怠慢,心里不高兴。朗白街上赫尔格和白洛克合营银行里的小白洛克最近两年本来在追求玛丽亚小姐,哪知道有一回跳八人舞的时候竟然挑了爱米丽亚做舞伴,你想玛丽亚会喜欢吗?亏得这位小姐生来不工心计,器量也大,表示她瞧着很喜欢。跳完舞以后,她很热心地对白洛克先生说:“你喜欢亲爱的爱米丽亚,我瞧着真高兴。她是我哥哥的未婚妻。她没有什么本事,可是脾气真好,也不会装腔作势。我们家里的人真喜欢她。”好姑娘!她那热心热肠的“真”字儿里面包含的情义,有谁量得出它的深浅?

乌德小姐和两位热心肠的女孩儿常常很恳切地点醒乔治,说他委屈自己错配了爱米丽亚,真是绝大的牺牲,过度的慷慨。乔治把这些话听熟了,大概到后来真心以为自己是英国军队里面数一数二的大好佬,便死心塌地等人家爱他,反正这也并不是难事。

我刚才说他每天早上出门,一星期在外吃六餐饭。他的姊妹们想他准是昏了头,只在赛特笠小姐左右侍奉她,其实大家以为他拜倒在爱米丽亚脚边的时候,他往往到别处去了。有好几次,都宾上尉走来拜访他的朋友,奥斯本大小姐(她很关心上尉,爱听他说军队里的故事,常常打听他亲爱的妈妈身体好不好)——奥斯本大小姐就指着广场对面的屋子笑着说:“唷,你要找乔治,就得到赛特笠家里去呀,

for George; *we* never see him from morning till night." At which kind of speech the Captain would laugh in rather an absurd constrained manner, and turn off the conversation, like a consummate man of the world, to some topic of general interest, such as the Opera, the Prince's last ball at Carlton House, or the weather—that blessing to society.

"What an innocent it is, that pet of yours," Miss Maria would then say to Miss Jane, upon the Captain's departure. "Did you see how he blushed at the mention of poor George on duty?"

"It's a pity Frederick Bullock hadn't some of his modesty, Maria," replies the elder sister, with a toss of her head.

"Modesty! Awkwardness you mean, Jane. I don't want Frederick to trample a hole in my muslin frock, as Captain Dobbin did in yours at Mrs. Perkins'."

"In *your* frock, he, he! How could he? Wasn't he dancing with Amelia?"

The fact is, when Captain Dobbin blushed so, and looked so awkward, he remembered a circumstance of which he did not think it was necessary to inform the young ladies, viz., that he had been calling at Mr. Sedley's house already, on the pretence of seeing George, of course, and George wasn't there, only poor little Amelia, with rather a sad wistful face, seated near the drawing-room window, who, after some very trifling stupid talk, ventured to ask, was there any truth in the report that the regiment was soon to be ordered abroad; and had Captain Dobbin seen Mr. Osborne that day?

The regiment was not ordered abroad as yet; and Captain Dobbin had not seen George. "He was with his

我们从早到晚都见不着他的面。”上尉听她这么一说，脸上非常尴尬，勉强笑了一笑。还亏得他熟晓人情世故，立刻把话锋转到大家爱谈的题目上去，像歌剧啊，亲王最近在卡尔登大厦①开的跳舞会啊，天气啊，——在应酬场中，天气真是有用，没话说的时候就可以把它做谈话资料。

上尉走掉之后，玛丽亚小姐便对吉恩小姐说道：“你那心上人儿可真傻气。你瞧见没有？咱们说起乔治到对门上班儿，他就脸红了。”

她的姐姐扬着脸儿回答说：“玛丽亚，可惜弗莱特立克·白洛克没有他这点儿虚心。”

“虚心！还不如说他笨手笨脚，吉恩。那一回在潘金家跳舞，他把你的纱衣服踩了一个洞，我可不愿意弗莱特立克在我细纱袍子上踩个洞。”

“你的纱袍子？呵呵！怎么的？他不是在跟爱米丽亚跳舞吗？”

都宾上尉脸上发烧，样子局促不安，为的是他心里想着一件事情，不愿意让小姐们知道。原来他假托找寻乔治，已经到过赛特笠家里，发现乔治不在那里，只有可怜的爱米丽亚闷闷的坐在客厅窗口。她扯了几句淡话之后，鼓起勇气向上尉说：听说联队又要外调，是真的吗？还有，上尉那天可曾看见奥斯本先生吗？

联队还不准备外调，都宾上尉也没有看见乔治。他说：“大概他跟姊妹们在一块儿。要我去把那游手好闲的家伙

① 指后来的乔治第四，他登极之前住在卡尔登大厦，时常招待宾客，连房子也出了名。

sister, most likely," the Captain said. "Should he go and fetch the truant?" So she gave him her hand kindly and gratefully: and he crossed the square; and she waited and waited, but George never came.

Poor little tender heart! and so it goes on hoping and beating, and longing and trusting. You see it is not much of a life to describe. There is not much of what you call incident in it. Only one feeling all day—when will he come? Only one thought to sleep and wake upon. I believe George was playing billiards with Captain Cannon in Swallow Street at the time when Amelia was asking Captain Dobbin about him; for George was a jolly sociable fellow, and excellent in all games of skill.

Once, after three days of absence, Miss Amelia put on her bonnet, and actually invaded the Osborne house. "What! leave our brother to come to us?" said the young ladies. "Have you had a quarrel, Amelia? Do tell us!" No, indeed, there had been no quarrel. "Who could quarrel with him?" says she, with her eyes filled with tears. She only came over to—to see her dear friends; they had not met for so long. And this day she was so perfectly stupid and awkward, that the Miss Osbornes and their governess, who stared after her as she went sadly away, wondered more than ever what George could see in poor little Amelia.

Of course they did. How was she to bare that timid little heart for the inspection of those young ladies with their bold black eyes? It was best that it should shrink and hide itself. I know the Miss Osbornes were excellent critics of a Cashmere shawl, or a pink satin slip; and when Miss Turner had hers died purple, and made into a spencer; and when Miss Pickford had her ermine tippet

叫过来吗?”爱米丽亚心里感激,很客气地跟都宾握手告别,他就穿过广场找到乔治家里来。可是她等了又等,总不见乔治的影子。

可怜这温柔的小姑娘,一颗心抖簌簌的跳个不停,她左盼右盼,一直在想念情人,对于他深信不疑。你看,这种生活没什么可描写的,因为里面没有多大变化。她从早到晚想着:“他什么时候来啊?”不论睡着醒着,只挂念这一件事。照我猜想起来,爱米丽亚向都宾上尉打听乔治的行止的时候,他正在燕子街跟加能上尉打弹子,因为他是个爱热闹会交际的家伙,而且对一切赌技巧的玩艺儿全是内行。

有一次,乔治连着三天不见,爱米丽亚竟然戴上帽子找到奥斯本家里去,小姐们问她说:“怎么的?你丢了我们的兄弟到这儿来了?说吧,爱米丽亚,你们拌过嘴了吗?”没有,他们没有拌过嘴。爱米丽亚眼泪汪汪的说:“谁还能跟他拌嘴呢?”她迟迟疑疑的说她过来望望朋友,因为大家好久没见面了。那天她又呆又笨,两位小姐和那女教师瞧着她怏怏的回家,都瞪着眼在她后头呆看,她们想到乔治竟会看上可怜的爱米丽亚,就觉得纳闷。

这也难怪她们纳闷。爱米丽亚怎么能把自己颤抖的心掏出来给这两个睁着黑眼睛瞪人的姑娘看呢?还是退后一步把感情埋藏起来吧。两位奥斯本小姐对于细绒线披肩和粉红缎子衬裙是内行。泰纳小姐把她的衬裙染了紫色改成

twisted into a muff and trimmings, I warrant you the changes did not escape the two intelligent young women before mentioned. But there are things, look you, of a finer texture than fur or satin, and all solomon's glories, and all the wardrobe of the Queen of Sheba;—things whereof the beauty escapes the eyes of many connoisseurs. And there are sweet modest little souls on which you light, fragrant, and blooming tenderly in quiet shady places; and there are garden-ornaments, as big as brass warming-pans, that are fit to stare the sun itself out of countenance. Miss Sedley was not of the sun-flower sort; and I say it is out of the rules of all proportion to draw a violet of the size of a double dahlia.

No, indeed; the life of a good young girl who is in the paternal nest as yet, can't have many of those thrilling incidents to which the heroine of romance commonly lays claim. Snares or shot may take off the old birds foraging without—hawks may be abroad, from which they escape or by whom they suffer; but the young ones in the nest have a pretty comfortable unromantic sort of existence in the down and the straw, till it comes to their turn, too, to get on the wing. While Becky Sharp was on her own wing in the country, hopping on all sorts of twigs, and amid a multiplicity of traps, and pecking up her food quite harmless and successful, Amelia lay snug in her home of Russell Square; if she went into the world, it was under the guidance of the elders; nor did it seem that any evil could befall her or that opulent cheery comfortable home in which she was affectionately sheltered. Mamma had her morning duties, and her daily drive, and the delightful round of visits and shopping which forms the amusement or the profession as you may

短披风；毕克福小姐把银鼠肩衣改成手笼和衣服上的镶边；都逃不过这两个聪明女孩子的眼睛。可是世界上有些东西比皮毛和软缎更精美；任是苏罗门的财富，希巴皇后的华裳艳服，也望尘莫及，只可惜它们的好处连许多鉴赏家都看不出来。有些羞缩的小花儿，开在偏僻阴暗的地方，细细的发出幽香；全凭偶然的机缘才见得着。也有些花儿，大得像铜脚炉，跟它们相比，连太阳都显得腼腆怕羞。赛特笠小姐不是向日葵的一类。而且我认为假如把紫罗兰画得像重瓣大理菊一般肥大，未免不相称。

说真话，一个贞静的姑娘出阁以前的生活非常单调，不像传奇里的女主角那样有许多惊心动魄的遭遇。老鸟儿在外面打食，也许会给人一枪打死，也许会自投罗网，况且外头又有老鹰，它们有时候侥幸躲过，有时候免不了遭殃。至于在窝里的小鸟呢，在飞出老窝另立门户之前，只消蹲在软软的绒毛和干草上，过着舒服而平淡的日子。蓓基·夏泼已经张开翅膀飞到了乡下，在树枝上跳来跳去，虽然前后左右布满了罗网，她倒是很平安很得意的在吃她的一份食料。这一向，爱米丽亚只在勒塞尔广场安稳过日子。凡是和外面人接触的时候，都有长辈指引。她家里又阔，又舒服，又快乐，而且人人疼她，照顾她，哪里会有不幸的事情临到她头上来呢？她妈妈早上管管家事，每天坐了马车出去兜一圈，应酬应酬，买买东西。伦敦的阔太太们借此消遣，也可

call it, of the rich London lady. Papa conducted his mysterious operations in the city—a stirring place in those days, when war was raging all over Europe, and empires were being staked; when the "Courier" newspaper had tens of thousands of subscribers; when one day brought you a battle of Vittoria, another a burning of Moscow, or a newsman's horn blowing down Russell Square about dinner-time, announced such a fact as—"Battle of Leipsic—six hundred thousand men engaged—total defeat of the French —two hundred thousand killed." Old Sedley once or twice came home with a very grave face; and no wonder, when such news as this was agitating all the hearts and all the Stocks of Europe.

Meanwhile matters went on in Russell Square, Bloomsbury, just as if matters in Europe were not in the least disorganized. The retreat from Leipsic made no difference in the number of meals Mr. Sambo took in the servants' hall; the allies poured into France, and the dinner-bell rang at five o'clock just as usual. I don't think poor Amelia cared anything about Brienne and Montmirail, or was fairly interested in the war until the abdication of the Emperor; when she clapped her hands and said prayers,—oh, how grateful! and flung herself into George Osborne's arms with all her soul, to the astonishment of everybody who witnessed that ebullition of sentiment. The fact is, peace was declared, Europe was going to be at rest; the Corsican was overthrown, and Lieutenant Osborne's regiment would not be ordered on service. That was the way in which Miss Amelia reasoned. The fate of Europe was Lieutenant George Osborne to her. His dangers being over, she sang Te Deum. He was her Europe: her emperor: her allied monarchs and august

以说就把这种事情当做自己的职业。她爹在市中心做些很奥妙的买卖。当年市中心是个热闹的所在,因为那时候整个欧洲在打仗,有好些皇国存亡未卜。《驿差报》有成千累万的订户。报上的消息惊心动魄,第一天报道威多利的战役,第二天又登载莫斯科的大火。往往到晚饭时分,卖报的拿着号筒,在勒塞尔广场高声叫喊:"莱比锡战役[①]! 六十万大军交战! 法军大败! 伤亡二十万人!"有一两回,赛特笠老先生回到家里,一脸心事重重的样子。这一类的消息闹得人心惶惑,欧洲的交易所里也有波动,怪不得他着急。

在白鲁姆斯贝莱区的勒塞尔广场,一切照常,仿佛欧洲仍旧风平浪静没出乱子。三菩先生每天在下房吃饭的次数不会因为莱比锡退军而有所变更;尽管联军大批涌进法国,每天五点钟他们照常打铃子开饭。白利安也罢,蒙密拉依[②]也罢,可怜的爱米丽亚都不放在心上,直到拿破仑退位,她才起始关心战局。她一听这个消息,快乐得拍起手来,诚心感谢上苍,热烈地搂着乔治不放。旁边的人看见她这样感情奔放,全觉得诧异。原来现在各国宣告停战,欧洲太平,那科西嘉人下了台,奥斯本中尉的联队也就不必派出去打仗了。这是爱米丽亚小姐的估计。在她看来,欧洲的命运所以重要,不过是因为它影响乔治·奥斯本中尉。他脱离了危险,她就唱圣诗赞美上帝。他是她的欧洲,她的皇帝,抵得过联军里所有的君主和本国权势赫赫的摄政王。

① 1813年10月,拿破仑在德国境内和普、奥、俄联军交战,大败。

② 1814年1月,拿破仑与联军在法国白利安开战,2月又与联军在法国蒙密拉依开战,两次都大胜。

prince regent. He was her sun and moon; and I believe she thought the grand illumination and ball at the Mansion House, given to the sovereigns, were especially in honour of George Osborne.

We have talked of shift, self, and poverty, as those dismal instructors under whom poor Miss Becky Sharp got her education. Now, love was Miss Amelia Sedley's last tutoress, and it was amazing what progress our young lady made under that popular teacher. In the course of fifteen or eighteen months' daily and constant attention to this eminent finishing governess, what a deal of secrets Amelia learned, which Miss Wirt and the black-eyed young ladies over the way, which old Miss Pinkerton of Chiswick herself had no cognizance of! As, indeed, how should any of those prim and reputable virgins? With Misses P. and W. the tender passion is out of the question: I would not dare to breathe such an idea regarding them. Miss Maria Osborne, it is true, was "attached" to Mr. Frederick Augustus Bullock, of the firm of Hulker, Bul-lock & Bullock; but hers was a most respectable attachment, and she would have taken Bullock Senior just the same, her mind being fixed—as that of a well-bred young woman should be,—upon a house in Park Lane, a country house at Wimbledon, a handsome chariot, and two prodigious tall horses and footmen, and a fourth of the annual profits of the eminent firm of Hulker & Bullock, all of which advantages were represented in the person of Frederick Augustus. Had orange blossoms been invented then (those touching emblems of female purity imported by us from France, where people's daughters are universally sold in marriage), Miss Maria, I say, would have assumed the spotless wreath, and stepped into

乔治是她的太阳，她的月亮。政府公廨里招待各国君王，大开跳舞会，点得灯烛辉煌，没准她也觉得大家是为了乔治·奥斯本才那么忙碌。

我们已经说过，教育利蓓加成人的是三个叫人扫兴的教师：人事的变迁，贫苦的生活，连上她自己本人。新近爱米丽亚也有了一位老师，那就是她自己的一片痴情。在这个怪得人心的教师手下，她有了惊人的进步。这一年半以来，爱米丽亚日夜受这位有名望的教师点化，学得了许多秘密。关于这方面的知识，不但对面房子里的乌德小姐和两个黑眼睛姑娘十分缺乏，连平克顿小姐也不在行。这几位拘谨体面的小姐怎么会懂得这里面的奥妙呢？平克顿小姐和乌德小姐当然跟痴情恋慕这些事情无缘，一说到她们俩，我这话根本不敢出口。就拿玛丽亚·奥斯本小姐来说吧，她算是跟白洛克父子以及赫克尔合营公司的弗莱特立克·奥克斯德·白洛克有情有义的。可是她这人非常大方，嫁给白洛克先生，或是嫁给白洛克先生的父亲，在她都无所谓。她像一切有教养的小姐一般，一心只要在派克街有一所房子，在温勃尔顿有一所别墅，再要一辆漂亮的马车，两匹高头大马，许多听差，连上有名的赫尔格和白洛克的公司里每年四分之一的利润。弗莱特立克·奥克斯德·白洛克就代表这些好处。假如新娘戴橘子花的习惯在当年已经风行的话（这风气是从盛行买卖婚姻的法国传进来的，这童贞的象征多么令人感动啊！）——如果当年已经风行戴橘子花的话，那么玛丽亚小姐准会戴上这种洁白的花圈，紧靠着那

the travelling carriage by the side of gouty, old, bald-headed, bottle-nosed Bullock Senior; and devoted her beautiful existence to his happiness with perfect modesty,—only the old gentleman was married already; so she bestowed her young affections on the junior partner. Sweet, blooming, orange flowers! The other day I saw Miss Trotter (that was), arrayed in them, trip into the travelling carriage at St. George's, Hanover Square, and Lord Methuselah hobbled in after. With what an engaging modesty she pulled down the blinds of the chariot—the dear innocent! There were half the carriages of Vanity Fair at the wedding.

This was not the sort of love that finished Amelia's education: and in the course of a year turned a good young girl into a good young woman—to be a good wife presently, when the happy time should come. This young person (perhaps it was very imprudent in her parents to encourage her, and abet her in such idolatry and silly romantic ideas) loved, with all her heart, the young officer in his Majesty's service with whom we have made a brief acquaintance. She thought about him the very first moment on waking; and his was the very last name mentioned in her prayers. She never had seen a man so beautiful or so clever: such a figure on horseback: such a dancer: such a hero in general. Talk of the Prince's bow! what was it to George's? She had seen Mr. Brummell, whom everybody praised so. Compare such a person as that to her George! Not amongst all the beaux at the Opera (and there were beaux in those days with actual opera hats) was there any one to equal him. He was only good enough to be a fairy prince; and oh, what magnanimity to stoop to such a humble Cinderella! Miss Pink-

又老又秃、鼻子像酒瓶、浑身风湿的白洛克老头儿在大马车里坐下来，准备跟他出门度蜜月。她一定甘心情愿，把自己美丽的一生奉献给他，使他快乐。可惜老头儿已经有了妻子，所以她只好把纯洁的爱情献给公司里的下级股东了。香喷喷娇滴滴的橘子花啊！前些日子我看见特洛德小姐(她现在当然不用这名字了)，戴着这花儿从汉诺佛广场的圣·乔治礼拜堂里轻快地出来，踏上了马车，接着玛土撒拉老勋爵拐着腿也跟了进去。好个天真可爱的姑娘！她把马车里的窗帘拉下来，那端庄的样子多么讨人喜欢！他们这次结婚，名利场里的马车来了一半。

熏陶爱米丽亚的痴情却是各别另样的。它在一年里面完成了她的教育，把品性优美的小姑娘训练成品性优美的妇人，到喜事一来，便准备做贤惠的妻子。女孩子一心一意爱她的年轻军官——就是我们新近认识的那一位。只怪她爹娘不小心，不该奖励她崇拜英雄的心理，让这种糊涂不切实际的观念在她心里滋长。她早上一醒过来，第一件事就想着他，晚上祷告的时候，末了一句话还是提到他。她从来没有看见过这么漂亮聪明的人。他骑马骑得好，跳舞跳得好；各方面说起来都是个英雄豪杰。大家称赞摄政王鞠躬的仪态，可是跟乔治一比，他就望尘莫及。人人都夸奖白鲁美尔先生，这个人她也见过，在她看来，无论如何赶不上乔治。在歌剧院里看见的花花公子们(当年的公子哥儿真有戴了大高帽子去听戏的)，没有一个可以与他相提并论。他这人出众得配做神话里的王子，竟然肯纡尊降贵爱上她这么一个寒碜的灰姑娘，这份恩宠太了不起了。平克顿小姐

erton would have tried to check this blind devotion very likely, had she been Amelia's confidante; but not with much success, depend upon it. It is in the nature and instinct of some women. Some are made to scheme, and some to love; and I wish any respected bachelor that reads this may take the sort that best likes him.

While under this overpowering impression, Miss Amelia neglected her twelve dear friends at Chiswick most cruelly, as such selfish people commonly will do. She had but this subject, of course, to think about; and Miss Saltire was too cold for a confidante, and she couldn't bring her mind to tell Miss Swartz, the woolly-haired young heiress from St. Kitt's. She had little Laura Martin home for the holidays; and my belief is, she made a confidante of her, and promised that Laura should come and live with her when she was married, and gave Laura a great deal of information regarding the passion of love, which must have been singularly useful and novel to that little person. Alas, alas! I fear poor Emmy had not a well-regulated mind.

What were her parents doing, not to keep this little heart from beating so fast? Old Sedley did not seem much to notice matters. He was graver of late, and his City affairs absorbed him. Mrs. Sedley was of so easy and uninquisitive a nature, that she wasn't even jealous. Mr. Jos was away, being besieged by an Irish widow at Cheltenham. Amelia had the house to herself—ah! too much to herself sometimes—not that she ever doubted; for, to be sure, George must be at the Horse Guards; and he can't always get leave from Chatham; and he must see his friends and sisters, and mingle in society when in town (he, such an ornament to every society!); and when he is

假如知道爱米丽亚的心事，准会想法子阻止她盲目地崇拜乔治，不过我看她的劝导未见得有效，因为对于有些女人说来，崇拜英雄的本能是与生俱来的。女人里面有的骨子里爱耍手段，有的却是天生的痴情种子。可敬的读者之中如果有单身汉子的话，希望他们都能挑选到适合自己脾胃的妻子。

在这样不可抗拒的大力量影响之下，爱米丽亚硬硬心肠不理会契息克的十二个朋友了。这也是自私的人的通病。她当然心心念念只惦记着爱人，可是她这衷肠话儿不能向赛尔泰小姐这么冷冰冰的人倾诉。对于圣·葛脱来的那头上一窝子卷毛的女财主呢，这话也难出口。放假的时候，她把罗拉·马丁接到家里来住，大概就把心事吐露给小孩儿听了。她答应罗拉结婚以后接她去住。还讲给她听许多关于爱情的知识。这些话儿小孩儿听来一定觉得新鲜，而且很有用处。可怜！可怜！我看爱米的心地不大明白。

她的爹妈是干什么的？怎么不加提防，任她这样感情奔放呢？赛特笠老头儿仿佛不大关心家事。近来他愁眉不展，市中心的事情又多，因此分不出心来。赛特笠太太是随和脾气，百事不问，连妒忌别人的心思都没有。乔斯先生在契尔顿纳姆给一个爱尔兰寡妇缠住了，也不在家。家里只有爱米丽亚一个人，所以有的时候她真觉得寂寞。她倒不是信不过乔治。他准是在骑兵营里，不能常常请假离开契顿姆。就算他到伦敦来，也少不得看望姊妹朋友，跟大家应酬一番（因为在无论哪个圈子里，都数他是个尖儿）。再说，

with the regiment, he is too tired to write long letters. I know where she kept that packet she had—and can steal in and out of her chamber like Iachimo—like Iachimo? No—that is a bad part. I will only act Moonshine, and peep harmless into the bed where faith and beauty and innocence lie dreaming.

But if Osborne's were short and soldierlike letters, it must be confessed, that were Miss Sedley's letters to Mr. Osborne to be published, we should have to extend this novel to such a multiplicity of volumes as not the most sentimental reader could support; that she not only filled sheets of large paper, but crossed them with the most astonishing perverseness; that she wrote whole pages out of poetry-books without the least pity: that she underlined words and passages with quite a frantic emphasis; and, in fine, gave the usual tokens of her condition. She wasn't a heroine. Her letters were full of repetition. She wrote rather doubtful grammar sometimes, and in her verses took all sorts of liberties with the metre. But oh, mesdames, if you are not allowed to touch the heart sometimes in spite of syntax, and are not to be loved until you all know the difference between trimeter and tetrameter, may all Poetry go to the deuce, and every schoolmaster perish miserably.

在营里的时候，他太累了，自然不能写长信。我知道爱米丽亚的一包信藏在什么地方，而且能像依阿器莫[①]一般人不知鬼不觉的在她的房里出出进进。依阿器莫？不行，他是戏里的坏蛋，我还是做月光[②]吧。月光是不害人的，只不过在忠诚、美丽、纯洁的爱米丽亚睡着的时候，偷眼看看她罢了。

奥斯本的信很短，不失他兵士的本色，可是爱米丽亚写给他的信呢，不瞒你说，如果印出来的话，我这本小说得写好几年才能写完，连最多情的读者也会觉得不耐烦。她不但把一大张一大张的信纸都写得满满的，而且有的时候闹起刁钻古怪的脾气来，把写好的句子重新画掉。她不顾看信的人，把整页的诗句抄下来。在有些句子底下，她发狠画了一条条道儿加重语气。总而言之，在她心境下常有的征象，统统显现出来了。她不是个特出的人才。她信里面的确有许多颠倒重复的句子，有的时候连文法也不大通。她写的诗，音节错得厉害。太太小姐们啊，假如你们写错了句子就打不动男人的心，分不清三节韵脚和四节韵脚就得不到男人的爱——那么我宁愿一切诗歌都遭殃，所有的教书先生都不得好死。

---

① 莎士比亚《辛白林》一剧里的反角，曾经潜入女主角的房间里去偷东西。

② 莎士比亚《仲夏夜之梦》第三幕第一景及第五幕第一景中，月光照见比拉默斯和底斯贝幽会，这角色由一个村夫举着灯扮演，灯便算月光。

In Which Jos Takes Flight, and the War Is Brought to a Close

We of peaceful London City have never beheld—and please God never shall witness—such a scene of hurry and alarm, as that which Brussels presented. Crowds rushed to the Namur gate, from which direction the noise proceeded, and many rode along the level *chaussée*, to be in advance of any intelligence from the army. Each man asked his neighbour for news; and even great English lords and ladies condescended to speak to persons whom they did not know. The friends of the French went abroad, wild with excitement, and prophesying the triumph of their Emperor. The merchants closed their shops, and came out to swell the general chorus of alarm and clamour. Women rushed to the churches, and crowded the chapels, and knelt and prayed on the flags and steps. The dull sound of the cannon went on rolling, rolling. Presently carriages with travellers began to leave the town, galloping away by the Ghent barrier. The prophecies of the French partisans began to pass for facts. "He has cut the armies in two," it was said. "He is marching straight on Brussels. He will overpower the English, and be here to-night." "He will overpower the English," shrieked Isidor to his master, "and will be here to-night." The man bounded in and out from the lodgings to the street, always returning with some fresh particulars of disaster. Jos's face grew paler and paler. Alarm began to take entire possession of the stout civilian. All the

乔斯逃难，战争也结束了

布鲁塞尔那天人心慌乱，到处乱哄哄的，我们平安住在伦敦城里的人从来没有见过这场面。天可怜见，希望永远不用见这场面才好！炮声是从那摩门传来的，一群群的人都往那边挤。好些人骑着马从平坦的马路上赶到那儿去，希望早些得到军队里的准信。大家互相探问，连了不起的英国爵爷和英国太太也都降低了身份和陌生人攀谈。亲法派的人兴奋得差点儿没发狂，满街跑着，预言他们的皇帝准打胜仗。做买卖的关了铺子，也走出来闹闹嚷嚷，给本来的慌乱和喧哗更添了声势。女人们都赶到教堂里去祈祷，不管新教旧教的教堂都挤满了人，有的人只能跪在石板上和台阶上。重浊的炮声继续轰隆轰隆的响着。不久，就有载着旅客的马车离开布鲁塞尔急急的向甘德的边境跑。大家把亲法派的预言渐渐信以为真。谣言说："他已经把军队割成两半了，他的军队正在往布鲁塞尔推进。他快要把英国人打垮了，今儿晚上就要到了。"伊息多向主人尖声叫道："他快要把英国人打垮了，今儿晚上就要到了！"他跳跳蹦蹦地从屋里走到街上，又从街上走到屋里。每出一趟门，就带些新的坏消息回来；乔斯的脸蛋儿也跟着越来越灰白。这

champagne he drank brought no courage to him. Before sunset he was worked up to such a pitch of nervousness as gratified his friend Isidor to behold, who now counted surely upon the spoils of the owner of the laced coat.

The women were away all this time. After hearing the firing for a moment, the stout Major's wife bethought her of her friend in the next chamber, and ran in to watch, and if possible to console, Amelia. The idea that she had that helpless and gentle creature to protect, gave additional strength to the natural courage of the honest Irishwoman. She passed five hours by her friend's side, sometimes in remonstrance, sometimes talking cheerfully, oftener in silence, and terrified mental supplication. "I never let go her hand once," said the stout lady afterwards, "until after sunset, when the firing was over." Pauline, the *bonne*, was on her knees at church hard by, praying for *son homme à elle*.

When the noise of the cannonading was over, Mrs. O'Dowd issued out of Amelia's room into the parlour adjoining, where Jos sate with two emptied flasks, and courage entirely gone. Once or twice he had ventured into his sister's bed-room, looking very much alarmed, and as if he would say something. But the Major's wife kept her place, and he went away without disburthening himself of his speech. He was ashamed to tell her that he wanted to fly.

But when she made her appearance in the dining-room, where he sate in the twilight in the cheerless company of his empty champagne bottles, he began to open his mind to her.

"Mrs. O'Dowd," he said, "hadn't you better get Amelia ready?"

大胖子印度官儿急得没了主意，虽然喝下去许多香槟酒，仍旧鼓不起勇气来。不到太阳下山，他已给吓得六神无主，连他的朋友伊息多瞧着也觉得称心合意，因为那穿花边外套的东家所有的财产稳稳都是他的了。

两位太太一直不露脸。少佐的那位胖太太听见炮声以后不久，就想起隔壁房里的朋友爱米丽亚，连忙跑进去看她，想法子安慰她。这厚道的爱尔兰女人本来有胆量；她一想起这个无能的、温柔的小东西需要她来保护，越发添了勇气。她在朋友身旁整整守了五点钟，一会儿劝慰她，一会儿说些高兴的话给她开心，不过大半的时候害怕得只会心里祷告，话也说不上来。胖太太后来对人说起当时的情形道："我一直拉着她的手，直到太阳下山，炮声停了以后才松手。"女用人宝林也在附近教堂里跪着求天保佑她的心上人儿。

炮声停止以后，奥多太太从爱米丽亚的房里走到隔壁的起坐间，看见乔斯坐在两只空酒瓶旁边，泄了气了。他曾经到妹妹的卧房瞧了一两次，那样子心慌意乱的好像要想说话。可是少佐的太太不动，他也拉不下脸来告诉她打算逃难，只好憋着一肚子话又回来。奥多太太走出来的时候，见他没情没绪地坐在朦胧的饭间里，旁边搁着两个空酒瓶子。乔斯见了她，便把自己的心事说了出来。

他说："奥多太太，我看你还是叫爱米丽亚准备一下吧！"

"Are you going to take her out for a walk?"said the Major's lady;"sure she's too weak to stir."

"I—I've ordered the carriage," he said, "and—and post-horses;Isidor is gone for them,"Jos continued.

"What do you want with driving to-night?"answered the lady."Isn't she better on her bed? I've just got her to lie down."

"Get her up,"said Jos;"she must get up,I say:"and he stamped his foot energetically."I say the horses are ordered —yes, the horses are ordered. It's all over. and—"

"And what?"asked Mrs.O'Dowd.

"I'm off for Ghent,"Jos answered."Everybody is going;there's a place for you! We shall start in half-an-hour."

The Major's wife looked at him with infinite scorn. "I don't move till O'Dowd gives me the route,"said she. "You may go if you like, Mr. Sedley; but, faith, Amelia and I stop here."

"She *shall* go,"said Jos, with another stamp of his foot. Mrs. O'Dowd put herself with arms akimbo before the bed-room door.

"Is it her mother you're going to take her to?"she said;"or do you want to go to Mamma yourself,Mr.Sedley? Good marning—a pleasant journey to ye, sir. *Bon voyage*,as they say, and take my counsel, and shave off them mustachios,or they'll bring you into mischief."

"D—n!" yelled out Jos, wild with fear, rage, and mortification;and Isidor came in at this juncture, swearing in his turn."*Pas de chevaux, sacre bleu*!"hissed out the furious domestic. All the horses were gone. Jos was not the only man in Brussels seized with panic that day.

少佐的太太答道:“你要带她出去散步吗?她身体不好,不能动。”

他道:“我——我已经叫他们准备车了。还有——还有马。我叫伊息多去找马去了。”

那位太太答道:“今天晚上你还坐什么马车?还是让她睡吧。我刚刚服侍她躺下。”

乔斯道:“叫她起来。我说呀,她非起来不可!”他使劲跺着脚接下去说道:“我已经去找马了——已经去找马了。什么都完了,以后——”

奥多太太问道:“以后什么?”

乔斯答道:“我打算上甘德。人人都准备走了。车里也有你的位子。半小时以后我们就动身。”

少佐的妻子脸上那份儿轻蔑真是形容不出,望着他说道:“除非奥多叫我走,我是不动身的。赛特笠先生,你要走的话,就请便,可是我和爱米丽亚是留在这儿的。”

乔斯又跺了一跺脚,说道:“我偏要她走。”奥多太太叉着腰站在房门口答道:“你还是要送她回娘家呢,还是你自己着急要找妈妈去呢,赛特笠先生?望你路上愉快,再见了!就像他们说的,望你一路顺风。听我的话,把胡子剃掉吧,省得给你找上麻烦。”

乔斯又怕又急又气,差点儿发疯,直着脖子骂了一句粗话。刚在这当儿,伊息多进来了,嘴里也在咒骂。这当差的气得咬牙切齿说道:“混蛋吗,竟没有马!”所有的马都卖掉了。原来布鲁塞尔城里着急的人不止乔斯一个。

But Jos's fears, great and cruel as they were already, were destined to increase to an almost frantic pitch before the night was over. It has been mentioned how Pauline, the *bonne*, had *son homme à elle* also in the ranks of the army that had gone out to meet the Emperor Napoleon. This lover was a native of Brussels, and a Belgian hussar. The troops of his nation signalised themselves in this war for anything but courage, and young Van Cutsum, Pauline's admirer, was too good a soldier to disobey his Colonel's orders to run away. Whilst in garrison at Brussels young Regulus (he had been born in the revolutionary times) found his great comfort, and passed almost all his leisure moments in Pauline's kitchen; and it was with pockets and holsters crammed full of good things from her larder, that he had taken leave of his weeping sweetheart, to proceed upon the campaign a few days before.

As far as his regiment was concerned, this campaign was over now. They had formed a part of the division under the command of his Sovereign apparent, the Prince of Orange, and as respected length of swords and mustachios, and the richness of uniform and equipments, Regulus and his comrades looked to be as gallant a body of men as ever trumpet sounded for.

When Ney dashed upon the advance of the allied troops, carrying one position after the other, until the arrival of the great body of the British army from Brussels changed the aspect of the combat of Quatre Bras, the squadrons among which Regulus rode showed the greatest activity in retreating before the French, and were dislodged from one post and another which they occupied with perfect alacrity on their part. Their movements

乔斯虽然已经给吓得够瞧的，不幸他命里注定，那天夜里还得担惊受怕，差点儿没把他吓糊涂了。前面已经说过，女用人宝林的心上人也在军中，一起开拔出去和拿破仑皇帝打仗。她的爱人是布鲁塞尔根生土长的，编在比利时骑兵队里。那次战争中，他们国家的军队在别方面出人头地，就是缺些勇气。对宝林倾倒的雷古鲁斯·范·葛村，是个好兵丁，他的统领命令他逃走，他当然服从。雷古鲁斯这小子（他是在大革命时候出生的①）驻扎在布鲁塞尔的时候，大半的光阴都消磨在宝林的厨房里，过得非常舒服。几天之前他奉命出征，和哭哭啼啼的爱人分别，口袋里和枪套里还塞满了她储藏间里面的好东西。

单就他的联队来说，战争已经算结束了。他的一师是储君奥兰奇王子统领的。雷古鲁斯和他的伙伴们全留着大胡子，带着长剑，服饰和配备富丽得很，外表看来并不输似任何给军号催上战场的军士。

当年耐将军②和各国联军交战，法军接连着打胜仗，直到英国军队从布鲁塞尔出发，两方面的军队在加德白拉交手，才把局面挽回过来。雷古鲁斯所属的骑兵队碰上了法国兵，来不及地直往后退，接连着从他们占领的据点上给驱逐出来，一些儿也不迟疑，直到英国军队从后面向前推进，

---

① 大革命时的风气崇拜罗马，那时候的人生了孩子，不照往常的习惯取个圣人的名字，却喜欢用罗马名字。

② 耐将军（Ney，1769—1815），拿破仑手下大将。

were only checked by the advance of the British in their rear. Thus forced to halt, the enemy's cavalry (whose bloodthirsty obstinacy cannot be too severely reprehended) had at length an opportunity of coming to close quarters with the brave Belgians before them; who preferred to encounter the British rather than the French, and at once turning tail rode through the English regiments that were behind them, and scattered in all directions. The regiment in fact did not exist any more. It was nowhere. It had no head-quarters. Regulus found himself galloping many miles from the field of action, entirely alone; and whither should he fly for refuge so naturally as to that kitchen and those faithful arms in which Pauline had so often welcomed him?

At some ten o'clock the clinking of a sabre might have been heard up the stair of the house where the Osbornes occupied a storey in the continental fashion. A knock might have been heard at the kitchen door; and poor Pauline, come back from church, fainted almost with terror as she opened it and saw before her her haggard hussar. He looked as pale as the midnight dragoon who came to disturb Leonora. Pauline would have screamed, but that her cry would have called her masters, and discovered her friend. She stifled her scream, then, and leading her hero into the kitchen, gave him beer, and the choice bits from the dinner, which Jos had not had the heart to taste. The hussar showed he was no ghost by the prodigious quantity of flesh and beer which he devoured—and during the mouthfuls he told his tale of disaster.

His regiment had performed prodigies of courage, and had withstood for a while the onset of the whole

才阻碍了他们的去路。这样他们不得不停下来，敌人的骑兵（这些人的不放手爱杀人的劲儿真该好好儿处治一下子）才有机会跟勇敢的比利时兵碰在一块儿。比利时军队宁可和英国人冲突，不愿意和法国人对打，立刻转身向后面的英军各联队当中穿过去，四散逃走。这么一来，他们的联队不知到哪里去了，又没有司令部，只好算从此不存在了。雷古鲁斯单人匹马，一口气从战场逃走，跑了好几英里路。可叫他投奔谁呢？当然只能回到宝林的厨房里，宝林的怀抱里来了。她以前不总是欢迎他吗？

奥斯本夫妇按照欧洲大陆的习惯，只住一层楼。约莫十点钟光景，在他家楼梯上就能听见底下钢刀叮叮当当的声音。厨房那里有人敲门。宝林刚从教堂里回家，一开门瞧见她的骑兵脸无人色的站在面前，吓得几乎晕过去。他脸色灰白，和那半夜里来打搅莉奥诺拉[①]的骑士不相上下。宝林若不是怕惊吵了主人，连累爱人藏不住身，准会尖声大叫。她掩住口，把她的英雄领到厨房里，给他啤酒喝；乔斯那天没有心绪吃饭，剩下的好菜也给骑兵受用了。他吃喝的分量真是惊人，足见他不是个鬼。他一方面大口吃喝，一方面就把遭到的灾难讲给宝林听。

据说他联队里的兵士以惊人的勇气挡住整个法国军队，总算使法军的进展慢了一步。可是到后来寡不敌众，直

① 莉奥诺拉（Leonora）是德国诗人毕格尔（Gottfried August Bürger，1747—1794）著名诗中的女主角。她爱人的鬼魂半夜出现，把她放在马背上带到坟墓旁边举行婚礼。

French army. But they were overwhelmed at last, as was the whole British army by this time. Ney destroyed each regiment as it came up. The Belgians in vain interposed to prevent the butchery of the English. The Brunswickers were routed and had fled—their Duke was killed. It was a general *debâcle*. He sought to drown his sorrow for the defeat in floods of beer.

Isidor, who had come into the kitchen, heard the conversation and rushed out to inform his master. "It is all over," he shrieked to Jos. "Milor Duke is a prisoner; the Duke of Brunswick is killed; the British army is in full flight; there is only one man escaped, and he is in the kitchen now—come and hear him." So Jos tottered into that apartment where Regulus still sate on the kitchen table, and clung fast to his flagon of beer. In the best French which he could muster, and which was in sooth of a very ungrammatical sort, Jos besought the hussar to tell his tale. The disasters deepened as Regulus spoke. He was the only man of his regiment not slain on the field. He had seen the Duke of Brunswick fall, the black hussars fly, the Ecossais pounded down by the cannon.

"And the —th?" gasped Jos.

"Cut in pieces." said the hussar—upon which Pauline crying out, "O my mistress, *ma bonne petite dame*," went off fairly into hysterics, and filled the house with her screams.

Wild with terror, Mr. Sedley knew not how or where to seek for safety. He rushed from the kitchen back to the sitting-room, and cast an appealing look at Amelia's door, which Mrs. O'Dowd had closed and locked in his face; but he remembered how scornfully the latter had

败下来，大概此刻英国军队也给打退了。耐将军反正是来一联队，杀一联队。比利时人原想把英国人救出来，使他们不至于给法国人杀个罄净，可是也没有用。白伦息克[1]的兵士已经溃退，他们的大公爵也已经战死。四面八方都打败仗。雷古鲁斯伤心得很，只好没命地喝啤酒解闷。

伊息多进来听见他们说话，急忙赶上去报告主人。他对乔斯尖声呼喊道："什么都完了，公爵大人做了俘虏；白伦息克大公爵已经战死；英国军队里的人全在逃命。只有一个人活着回来，——他就在楼下。来听听他说的话！"乔斯跌跌撞撞地跟到厨房里；那时雷古鲁斯仍旧坐在厨房桌子上，紧紧地抱着啤酒瓶子。乔斯使出全副本事，用不合文法的法文求骑兵把刚才的话再说一遍。雷古鲁斯一开口，方才的大祸好像更可怕了。他说他联队里面只有他一人活着回家，其余的都死在战场上。他眼看着白伦息克大公爵被杀，黑骑兵[2]逃命，苏格兰龙骑兵死在炮火之下。

乔斯气喘吁吁的问道："第×联队呢？"

骑兵答道："剁成肉酱啦！"宝林一听这话，叫道："嗳哟，我的太太呀，我那小不点儿的好太太呀！"她大哭大叫，屋子里闹成一片。

赛特笠先生吓得人也糊涂了，不知该往哪里躲，也不知怎么办。他从厨房冲到起坐间，求救似的瞧着爱米丽亚的房门。不久以前奥多太太冲着他的脸把房门关上锁好，他记得奥多太太的样子多么瞧不起他，所以在房门口听了一

① 指德国白伦息克亲王（Duke of Brunswick，1771—1815），他在比利时加德白拉战死。

② 黑骑兵是白伦息克带领的，因为在奥斯德里兹一役损失惨重，所以穿上黑衣服，表示哀悼的意思。

received him, and after pausing and listening for a brief space at the door, he left it, and resolved to go into the street, for the first time that day. So, seizing a candle, he looked about for his gold-laced cap, and found it lying in its usual place, on a console-table, in the ante-room, placed before a mirror at which Jos used to coquet, always giving his side-locks a twirl, and his cap the proper cock over his eye, before he went forth to make appearance in public. Such is the force of habit, that even in the midst of his terror he began mechanically to twiddle with his hair, and arrange the cock of his hat. Then he looked amazed at the pale face in the glass before him, and especially at his mustachios, which had attained a rich growth in the course of near seven weeks, since they had come into the world. They *will* mistake me for a military man, thought he, remembering Isidor's warning, as to the massacre with which all the defeated British army was threatened; and staggering back to his bed-chamber, he began wildly pulling the bell which summoned his valet.

Isidor answered that summons. Jos had sunk in a chair—he had torn off his neckcloths, and turned down his collars, and was sitting with both his hands lifted to his throat.

"*Coupez-moi*, Isidor," shouted he; "*vite! Coupez-moi!*"

Isidor thought for a moment he had gone mad, and that he wished his valet to cut his throat.

"*Les moustaches*," gasped Jos; "*les moustaches—coupy, rasy, vite!*"—his French was of this sort—voluble, as we have said, but not remarkable for grammar.

Isidor swept off the mustachios in no time with the razor, and heard with inexpressible delight his master's

听就走掉了。他决定上街去瞧瞧，反正那天他还没有出去过呢。他拿了一支蜡烛，到处找他的金箍帽子，结果发现仍旧搁在老地方，就在后房的小桌子上。小桌子前面是一面镜子；乔斯出门见人之前，总爱照着镜子装模作样，捻捻连鬓胡子，整整帽子，叫它不太正，不太歪，恰到好处。他已经习惯成自然，虽然吓得那样，不知不觉的伸出手来摸头发，整帽子。正在那时候，他一眼看见镜子里那张灰白的脸，不由得吃了一惊。尤其叫他心慌的是上唇的胡子，已经留了七个星期，长得又厚又密。他想，他们真的要把我当做军人了；转念记得伊息多警告过他，说凡是英国军队里的败兵一律都得死，急得一步一跌地走到卧房里，没命地拉铃子叫听差。

伊息多听见铃响走来，乔斯已经倒在椅子里了。他扯掉了领巾，把领子翻下来，两手捧着脖子用法文叫道："伊息多，割我。快！割我！"

伊息多一怔，以为他神经错乱，要人家替他抹脖子。

乔斯喘着气说道："胡子，胡子，——割，剃，快！"他的法文就是这样。前面已经说过，他说得很流利，可就是文法不大高明。

伊息多拿了剃刀，一会儿就把胡子刮个干净。他听得主人叫他把便装的外套和帽子拿来，心里说不出多少欢喜。

orders that he should fetch a hat and a plain coat. "*Ne porty ploo—habit militair—bonn—bonny a voo, prenny dehors*"—were Jos's words,—the coat and cap were at last his property.

This gift being made, Jos selected a plain black coat and waistcoat from his stock, and put on a large white neckcloth, and a plain beaver. If he could have got a shovel-hat he would have worn it. As it was, you would have fancied he was a flourishing, large parson of the Church of England.

"*Venny maintenong*," he continued, "*sweevy—ally—party—dong la roo.*" And so having said, he plunged swiftly down the stairs of the house, and passed into the street.

Although Regulus had vowed that he was the only man of his regiment or of the allied army, almost, who had escaped being cut to pieces by Ney, it appeared that his statement was incorrect, and that a good number more of the supposed victims had survived the massacre. Many scores of Regulus's comrades had found their way back to Brussels, and—all agreeing that they had run away—filled the whole town with an idea of the defeat of the allies. The arrival of the French was expected hourly; the panic continued, and preparations for flight went on everywhere. No horses! thought Jos, in terror. He made Isidor inquire of scores of persons, whether they had any to lend or sell, and his heart sank within him, at the negative answers returned everywhere. Should he take the journey on foot? Even fear could not render that ponderous body so active.

Almost all the hotels occupied by the English in Brussels face the Parc, and Jos wandered irresolutely

乔斯说："兵衣——不穿了——我给你——拿出去。"外套和帽子终究到手了。

乔斯把这份礼送掉以后，挑了一套便装穿上，外套和背心都是黑的，领巾是白的，头上戴一只海狸皮的便帽。如果他找得着教士带的宽边帽子，准会往头上戴。照他当时的打扮，很像英国国教教会里长得肥胖、过得舒服的牧师。

他接下去说道："现在来，跟我，去，走，到街上。"说完，他快快地下楼，走到街上。

虽然雷古鲁斯赌神发誓说他是他联队里唯一活着回来的人，甚至可以说是整个同盟国军队里唯一没有给耐将军剁成肉酱的人，看来他的话并不可靠。除他以外，许多别的人也从大屠杀中逃回来了。好几十好几百和雷古鲁斯同一联队的兵丁回到布鲁塞尔，众口一词说他们是逃回来的。全城的人一听这话，都以为同盟国的军队已经打败。大家随时准备法国人进城；人心继续慌乱，到处看见有人逃难。乔斯满心害怕，想道："没有马！"他叫伊息多逢人便问：有马出租吗？有马出卖吗？每次都没有结果，急得他一颗心直往下沉。他想，要不，就用脚走吧。可惜他身子笨重，虽然怕得紧，还是活动不起来。

英国人住的旅馆差不多全对着公园。乔斯在这一带踌躇不决地踱来踱去，挤在街上一大群跟他一样又害怕又想

about in this quarter, with crowds of other people, oppressed as he was by fear and curiosity. Some families he saw more happy than himself, having discovered a team of horses, and rattling through the streets in retreat; others again there were whose case was like his own, and who could not for any bribes or entreaties procure the necessary means of flight. Amongst these would-be fugitives, Jos remarked the Lady Bareacres and her daughter, who sate in their carriage in the *porte-cochère* of their hotel, all their imperials packed, and the only drawback to whose flight was the same want of motive power which kept Jos stationary.

Rebecca Crawley occupied apartments in this hotel; and had before this period had sundry hostile meetings with the ladies of the Bareacres family. My Lady Bareacres cut Mrs. Crawley on the stairs when they met by chance; and in all places where the latter's name was mentioned, spoke perseveringly ill of her neighbour. The Countess was shocked at the familiarity of General Tufto with the aide-de-camp's wife. The Lady Blanche avoided her as if she had been an infectious disease. Only the Earl himself kept up a sly occasional acquaintance with her, when out of the jurisdiction of his ladies.

Rebecca had her revenge now upon these insolent enemies. It became known in the hotel that Captain Crawley's horses had been left behind, and when the panic began, Lady Bareacres condescended to send her maid to the Captain's wife with her Ladyship's compliments, and a desire to know the price of Mrs. Crawley's horses. Mrs. Crawley returned a note with her compliments, and an intimation that it was not her custom to transact bargains with ladies' maids.

打听消息的人里面。他看见有几家运气比他好，找到了几匹马，轰隆隆的驾着车子走了。有些人和他一样，花钱和求情都得不到逃难少不了的脚力。在这些想走而走不掉的人里头，乔斯看见贝亚爱格思夫人母女两个也在。她们坐在车子里，歇在旅馆门口，细软都已经包扎停当，只可惜没有拉车的，跟乔斯一般动不得身。

利蓓加·克劳莱也住在那家旅馆里，并且已经和贝亚爱格思母女两个见过几面，两方面竟像是对头冤家。贝亚爱格思夫人偶然在楼梯上碰到克劳莱太太，总是不瞅不睬，而且每逢有人提起她邻舍的名字，老说她的坏话。伯爵夫人觉得德夫托将军和副官太太那么不避嫌疑，简直不成话说。白朗茜小姐呢，看着她就像传染病，来不及地躲开。只有伯爵是例外，碰上有妻子女儿管不着他的当儿，就偷偷摸摸地来找利蓓加。

如今利蓓加有机会对这些混账的冤家报仇了。旅馆里的人都知道克劳莱上尉的马没有带走，到人心慌乱的时候，贝亚爱格思夫人竟降低了身份打发她的女用人去问候上尉的妻子，打听她的两匹马究竟卖多少钱。克劳莱太太回了个便条给伯爵夫人问好，说她向来不惯和丫头老妈子做买卖。

This curt reply brought the Earl in person to Becky's apartment; but he could get no more success than the first ambassador. "Send a lady's maid to *me*!" Mrs. Crawley cried in great anger; "why didn't my Lady Bareacres tell me to go and saddle the horses! Is it her Ladyship that wants to escape, or her Ladyship's *femme de chambre*?" And this was all the answer that the Earl bore back to his Countess.

What will not necessity do? The Countess herself actually come to wait upon Mrs. Crawley on the failure of her second envoy. She entreated her to name her own price; she even offered to invite Becky to Bareacres House, if the latter would but give her the means of returning to that residence. Mrs. Crawley sneered at her.

"I don't want to be waited on by bailiffs in livery," she said; "you will never get back though most probably—at least not you and your diamonds together. The French will have those. They will be here in two hours, and I shall be half way to Ghent by that time. I would not sell you my horses, no, not for the two largest diamonds that your Ladyship wore at the ball." Lady Bareacres trembled with rage and terror. The diamonds were sewed into her habit, and secreted in my Lord's padding and boots. "Woman, the diamonds are at the banker's, and I *will* have the horses," she said. Rebecca laughed in her face. The infuriate Countess went below, and sate in her carriage; her maid, her courier, and her husband were sent once more through the town, each to look for cattle; and woe betide those who came last! Her Ladyship was resolved on departing the very instant the horses arrived from any quarter—with her husband or without him.

这斩截的回答把伯爵本人给请到蓓基的房间里来了，可是他跟第一个大使不差什么，也是白走一趟。克劳莱太太大怒，说道："贝亚爱格思夫人竟然使唤她的老妈子来跟我说话！倒亏她没叫我亲自下去备马。是伯爵夫人要逃难还是她的老妈子要逃难？"伯爵带回给她太太的就是这么一句话。

到了这么要紧的关头可有什么法子呢？伯爵夫人眼看第二个使臣又白跑了一趟，只得亲自过来拜会克劳莱太太。她恳求蓓基自己定价钱，她甚至于答应请她到贝亚爱格思公馆里去做客，只要蓓基帮她回家。克劳莱太太听了只是冷笑。

她说："你的听差不过是衙门前的地保穿上了你家的号衣[①]，我可不希罕他们伺候。看来你也回不了家，至少不能够带着你的金刚钻一块儿回家。法国人是不肯放手的。再过两点钟，他们就到这儿来了，那时候我已经在半路，即刻就到甘德。我的马不卖给你，就是你把跳舞会上戴的那两颗最大的金刚钻给我我也不卖。"贝亚爱格思夫人又急又气，浑身打哆嗦。所有的金刚钻首饰，有的缝在她衣服里，有的藏在伯爵的肩衬和靴子里。她说："你这娘儿们，我的金刚钻在银行里。你的马非卖给我不可。"利蓓加冲着她的脸大笑。伯爵夫人只得气呼呼的回到楼下坐在马车里。她的女用人，她的丈夫，她的伺候上路的听差，又一个个给打发到全城去找马。谁回来得晚，谁就倒霉！伯爵夫人打定主意，不管谁找了马来，她就动身，丈夫到底带着还是留下，只能到时候再说。

---

① 这里形容没落贵族的穷形尽相，每逢家里请客，没有听差，便叫催债的地保穿上家里号衣权充听差。

Rebecca had the pleasure of seeing her Ladyship in the horseless carriage, and keeping her eyes fixed upon her, and bewailing, in the loudest tone of voice, the Countess's perplexities. "Not to be able to get horses!" she said, "and to have all those diamonds sewed into the carriage cushions! What a prize it will be for the French when they come! —the carriage and the diamonds, I mean; not the lady!" She gave this information to the landlord, to the servants, to the guests, and the innumerable stragglers about the courtyard. Lady Bareacres could have shot her from the carriage window.

It was while enjoying the humiliation of her enemy that Rebecca caught sight of Jos, who made towards her directly he perceived her.

That altered, frightened, fat face told his secret well enough. He too wanted to fly, and was on the look-out for the means of escape. "*He* shall buy my horses," thought Rebecca, "and I'll ride the mare."

Jos walked up to his friend, and put the question for the hundredth time during the past hour, "Did she know where horses were to be had?"

"What, *you* fly?" said Rebecca, with a laugh. "I thought you were the champion of all the ladies, Mr. Sedley."

"I—I'm not a military man," gasped he.

"And Amelia? —Who is to protect that poor little sister of yours?" asked Rebecca. "You surely would not desert her?"

"What good can I do her, suppose—suppose the enemy arrive?" Jos answered. "They'll spare the women; but my man tells me that they have taken an oath to give no quarter to the men—the dastardly cowards."

利蓓加看见伯爵夫人坐在没有马的马车里，得意之极。她紧紧地瞧着她，扯起嗓子告诉大家说她多么可怜伯爵夫人。她说："唉，找不到马！所有的金刚钻首饰又都缝在车垫里面。法国军队来了以后倒可以大大地受用一下子，我说的是马车和金刚钻，不是说那位太太。"她把这话告诉旅馆主人，告诉跑堂的，告诉住旅馆的客人，告诉好些在院子里闲逛的人。贝亚爱格思夫人恨不得从马车窗口开枪打死她。

利蓓加瞧着冤家倒霉，正在趁愿，一眼看见乔斯也在那儿。乔斯也瞧见她了，急忙走过来。

他的胖脸蛋儿吓得走了样子，他心里的打算一看就知道。他也要逃走，正在找马。利蓓加暗想："我把马卖给他吧，剩下的一匹小母马我自己骑。"

乔斯过来见了朋友，问她知道不知道什么地方有马出卖——最后这一个钟头里面。这问题已经问过一百遍了。

利蓓加笑道："什么？你也逃难吗？赛特笠先生，我还当你要留下保护我们这些女人呢。"

他喘吁吁的说道："我——我不是军人。"

利蓓加问道："那么爱米丽亚呢？谁来招呼你那可怜的小妹妹呢？难道你忍心把她丢了不成？"

乔斯答道："如果——如果敌人来到这儿，我也帮不了她的忙。他们不杀女人。可是我的听差说他们已经起过誓，凡是男人都不给饶命呢。这些没胆子的混蛋！"

"Horrid!"cried Rebecca,enjoying his perplexity.

"Besides, I don't want to desert her," cried the brother. "She *shan't* be deserted. There is a seat for her in my carriage, and one for you, dear Mrs. Crawley, if you will come; and if we can get horses—"sighed he—

"I have two to sell," the lady said. Jos could have flung himself into her arms at the news. "Get the carriage, Isidor," he cried; "we've found them—we have found them."

"My horses never were in harness," added the lady. "Bullfinch would kick the carriage to pieces, if you put him in the traces."

"But he is quiet to ride?"asked the civilian.

"As quiet as a lamb, and as fast as a hare,"answered Rebecca.

"Do you think he is up to my weight?"Jos said. He was already on his back, in imagination, without ever so much as a thought for poor Amelia. What person who loved a horse-speculation could resist such a temptation?

In reply, Rebecca asked him to come into her room, whither he followed her quite breathless to conclude the bargain. Jos seldom spent a half hour in his life which cost him so much money. Rebecca, measuring the value of the goods which she had for sale by Jos's eagerness to purchase, as well as by the scarcity of the article, put upon her horses a price so prodigious as to make even the civilian draw back. "She would sell both or neither,"she said, resolutely. Rawdon had ordered her not to part with them for a price less than that which she specified. Lord Bareacres below would give her the same money—and with all her love and regard for the Sedley family, her dear Mr. Joseph must conceive that poor people must

利蓓加见他为难，觉得有趣，答道："他们可恶极了！"

做哥哥的嚷嚷着说："而且我也不打算丢了她不顾，我无论怎么要照顾她的。我的马车里有她的位子。亲爱的克劳莱太太，如果你愿意同走，我也给你留个位子。只要我们有马就行——"说着，他叹了一口气。

那位太太答道："我有两匹马出卖。"一听这消息，乔斯差点儿倒在她怀里。他嚷道："伊息多，把车准备好。马有了——马有了！"

那位太太又说道："我的马可从没有拉过车子。如果你把勃耳芬却套上笼头，它准会把车踢成碎片儿。"

那印度官儿问道："那么骑上稳不稳呢？"

利蓓加道："它像小羊那么乖，跑得像野兔子那么快。"

乔斯道："它驮得动我吗？"在他脑子里，自己已经骑上了马背，可怜的爱米丽亚完全给忘掉了。喜欢赛马赌输赢的人谁能挡得住这样的引诱呢？

利蓓加的答复，就是请他到她房里去商量。乔斯屏着气跟她进去，巴不得赶快成交。这半点钟以内他花的钱实在可观，真是一辈子少有的经验。利蓓加见市上的马那么少，乔斯又急急的要买，把自己打算脱手的货色估计了一下，说了一个吓死人的大价钱，连这印度官儿都觉得不敢领教。她斩截地说道："你要买就两匹一起买，一匹是不卖的。"她说罗登吩咐过的，这两匹马非要这些钱不可，少一文不卖。楼下贝亚爱格思伯爵就出那么多呢。她虽然敬爱赛特笠一家，可是穷人也得活命，亲爱的乔瑟夫先生非得在这

live—nobody, in a word, could be more affectionate, but more firm about the matter of business.

Jos ended by agreeing, as might be supposed of him. The sum he had to give her was so large that he was obliged to ask for time; so large as to be a little fortune to Rebecca, who rapidly calculated that with this sum, and the sale of the residue of Rawdon's effects, and her pension as a widow should he fall, she would now be absolutely independent of the world, and might look her weeds steadily in the face.

Once or twice in the day she certainly had herself thought about flying. But her reason gave her better counsel. "Suppose the French do come," thought Becky, "what can they do to a poor officer's widow? Bah! the times of sacks and sieges are over. We shall be let to go home quietly, or I may live pleasantly abroad with a snug little income."

Meanwhile Jos and Isidor went off to the stables to inspect the newly-purchased cattle. Jos bade his man saddle the horses at once. He would ride away that very night, that very hour. And he left the valet busy in getting the horses ready, and went homewards himself to prepare for his departure. It must be secret. He would go to his chamber by the back entrance. He did not care to face Mrs. O'Dowd and Amelia, and own to them that he was about to run.

By the time Jos's bargain with Rebecca was completed, and his horses had been visited and examined, it was almost morning once more. But though midnight was long passed, there was no rest for the city; the people were up, the lights in the houses flamed, crowds were still about the doors, and the streets were busy. Rumours of var-

一点上弄个明白。总而言之，她待人比谁都热和，可是办事也比谁都有决断。

结果不出你我所料，还是乔斯让步。他付的价钱那么大，甚至于一次付不清，要求展期。利蓓加可算发了一笔小财。她很快地计算了一下，万一罗登给打死，她还有一笔年金可拿，再把他的动产卖掉，连上卖马所得，她就能独立自主，做寡妇也不怕了。

那天有一两回她也想逃难，可是她的理智给她的劝告更好。蓓基心中忖度道："就算法国兵来到这儿，我是个穷苦的军官老婆，他们能够把我怎么样？呸！什么围攻掳掠，现在是没有这种事的了。他们总会让我们平平安安的回家。要不，我就住在外国，靠我这点小收入舒服过日子。"

乔斯和伊息多走到马房里去看新买的马。乔斯叫用人立刻备上鞍子，因为他当夜就动身——不，立刻就动身。他让用人忙着备马，自己回家准备出发。他觉得这事不可张扬出去，还是从后门上去好。他不愿意碰见奥多太太和爱米丽亚，省得再向她们承认自己打算逃走。

乔斯和利蓓加交易成功，那两匹马看过验过，天也快亮了。可是虽然黑夜已经过了大半，城里的居民却不去歇息。到处屋子里灯烛通明，门口仍是一群群的人，街上也热闹得

ious natures went still from mouth to mouth: one report averred that the Prussians had been utterly defeated; another that it was the English who had been attacked and conquered; a third that the latter had held their ground. This last rumour gradually got strength. No Frenchmen had made their appearance. Stragglers had come in from the army bringing reports more and more favourable: at last: an aide-de-camp actually reached Brussels with despatches for the Commandant of the place, who placarded presently through the town an official announcement of the success of the allies at Quatre Bras, and the entire repulse of the French under Ney after a six hours' battle. The aide-de-camp must have arrived sometime while Jos and Rebecca were making their bargain together, or the latter was inspecting his purchase. When he reached his own hotel, he found a score of its numerous inhabitants on the threshold discoursing of the news; there was no doubt as to its truth. And he went up to communicate it to the ladies under his charge. He did not think it was necessary to tell them how he had intended to take leave of them, how he had bought horses, and what a price he had paid for them.

But success or defeat was a minor matter to them, who had only thought for the safety of those they loved. Amelia, at the news of the victory, became still more agitated even than before. She was for going that moment to the army. She besought her brother with tears to conduct her thither. Her doubts and terrors reached their paroxysm; and the poor girl, who for many hours had been plunged into stupor, raved and ran hither and thither in hysteric insanity—a piteous sight. No man writhing in pain on the hard-fought field fifteen miles off, where

很。大家传说着各种各样的谣言，有的说普鲁士全军覆没，有的说英国军队受到袭击，已经给打败了，有的又说英国人站定脚跟坚持下去了。到后来相信末了一种说法的人渐渐增加。法国兵并没有来，三三两两从军中回来的人带来的消息却越来越好。最后，一个副官到了布鲁塞尔，身边带着给当地指挥官的公文，这才正式发布通告，晓谕居民说同盟军队在加德白拉大捷，经过六小时的战斗，打退耐将军带领的法国军队。看来副官到达城里，离乔斯和利蓓加订约的时候不远，或许刚在他检验那两匹马的一忽儿。他回到自己旅馆门口，就见二十来个人（旅馆里的住客很多）在讨论这事；消息无疑是真的。他上楼把这消息又告诉受他照管的太太们。至于他怎么打算丢了她们一跑，怎么买马，一共花了多少钱，他觉得没有必要告诉她们。

太太们最关心的是心上人的安全，战事的胜败倒是小事。爱米丽亚听说打了胜仗，比先前更加激动，立刻就要上前线，流着泪哀求哥哥带她去。可怜这小姑娘又急又愁，已经到精神失常的程度，先是连着几个钟头神志昏迷，这时又发疯似的跑来跑去，哭哭闹闹，叫人看着心里难受。十五英

lay, after their struggles, so many of the brave—no man suffered more keenly than this poor harmless victim of the war. Jos could not bear the sight of her pain. He left his sister in the charge of her stouter female companion, and descended once more to the threshold of the hotel, where everybody still lingered, and talked, and waited for more news.

It grew to be broad daylight as they stood here, and fresh news began to arrive from the war, brought by men who had been actors in the scene. Wagons and Long country carts laden with wounded came rolling into the town; ghastly groans came from within them, and haggard faces looked up sadly from out of the straw. Jos Sedley was looking at one of these carriages with a painful curiosity—the moans of the people within were frightful—the wearied horses could hardly pull the cart. Stop! stop! a feeble voice cried from the straw, and the carriage stopped opposite Mr. Sedley's hotel.

"It is George, I know it is!" cried Amelia, rushing in a moment to the balcony, with a pallid face and loose flowing hair. It was not George, however, but it was the next best thing: it was news of him.

It was poor Tom Stubble, who had marched out of Brussels so gallantly twenty-four hours before, bearing the colours of the regiment, which he had defended very gallantly upon the field. A French lancer had speared the young ensign in the leg, who fell, still bravely holding to his flag. At the conclusion of the engagement, a place had been found for the poor boy in a cart, and he had been brought back to Brussels.

"Mr. Sedley, Mr. Sedley!" cried the boy, faintly, and Jos came up almost frightened at the appeal. He had not

里路以外的战场上，经过一场大战之后，躺着多少死伤的勇士，可是没一个辗转呻吟的伤兵比这个可怜的、无能的、给战争牺牲的小人儿受苦更深的了。乔斯不忍看她的痛苦，让她那勇敢的女伴陪着她，重新下楼走到门口。所有的人仍旧在那里说话，希望听到别的消息。

他们站着的当儿，天已经大亮，新的消息源源而来，都是亲身战斗过来的人带来的。一辆辆的货车和乡下的大卡车装满了伤兵陆续进城。车子里面发出可怕的呻吟，伤兵们躺在干草上，萎萎缩缩，愁眉苦脸地向外张望。乔斯对其中一辆瞧着，又好奇，又害怕；里面哼哼唧唧的声音真是可怕，拉车的马累得拉不动车。干草上一个细弱的声音叫道："停下来！停下来！"车子就在赛特笠先生的旅馆对面歇下来。

爱米丽亚叫道："是乔治呀！准是乔治！"她脸上发白，披头散发地冲到阳台上去。躺在车子里的并不是乔治，可是带了乔治的消息来，也就差不多了。

来的人原来是可怜的汤姆·斯德博尔。二十四小时以前这小旗手举着联队里的旗子离开布鲁塞尔，在战场上还勇敢地保卫着它。一个法国长枪手把他的腿刺伤了，他倒下地来的时候还拼命地紧握着旗子。战斗完毕之后，可怜的孩子给安置在大车里送回布鲁塞尔。

孩子气短力弱地叫道："赛特笠先生，赛特笠先生！"乔斯听得有人向他求救，心里有些恐慌，只得走近车来。原来

at first distinguished who it was that called him.

Little Tom Stubble held out his hot and feeble hand. "I'm to be taken in here," he said. "Osborne—and—and Dobbin said I was; and you are to give the man two napoleons: my mother will pay you." This young fellow's thoughts, during the long feverish hours passed in the cart, had been wandering to his father's parsonage which he had quitted only a few months before, and he had sometimes forgotten his pain in that delirium.

The hotel was large, and the people kind, and all the inmates of the cart were taken in and placed on various couches. The young ensign was conveyed upstairs to Osborne's quarters. Amelia and the Major's wife had rushed down to him, when the latter had recognised him from the balcony. You may fancy the feelings of these women when they were told that the day was over, and both their husbands were safe; in what mute rapture Amelia fell on her good friend's neck, and embraced her; in what a grateful passion of prayer she fell on her knees, and thanked the Power which had saved her husband.

Our young lady, in her fevered and nervous condition, could have had no more salutary medicine prescribed for her by any physician than that which chance put in her way. She and Mrs. O'Dowd watched incessantly by the wounded lad, whose pains were very severe, and in the duty thus forced upon her, Amelia had not time to brood over her personal anxieties, or to give herself up to her own fears and forebodings after her wont. The young patient told in his simple fashion the events of the day, and the actions of our friends of the gallant —th. They had suffered severely. They had lost very many officers

起先他听不准谁在叫他。

小汤姆·斯德博尔有气无力地把滚热的手伸出来说道："请你收留我。奥斯本，还有——还有都宾说我可以住在这儿。请你给那赶车的两块金洋，我母亲会还你的。"在卡车上一段很长的时间里，这小伙子发着烧，迷迷糊糊的想着几个月以前才离开的老家（他父亲是个副牧师），因为不省人事，也就忘了疼痛。

他们住的旅馆很大，那里的人心地也忠厚，因此所有车子里的伤兵都给运来安放在榻上和床上。小旗手给送到楼上奥斯本家里。少佐太太从阳台上发现是他，便和爱米丽亚赶快跑到楼下。这两位太太打听得当天战事已经结束，两个人的丈夫都安好，心里是什么滋味是不难想象的。爱米丽亚搂住好朋友的脖子吻她，又跪下来诚诚心心感谢上苍救了她丈夫的命。

我们的少奶奶神经过度的兴奋紧张，亏得这次无意之中得到一帖对她大有补益的药，竟比医生开的方子还有效。受伤的孩子疼痛得厉害，她和奥多太太时刻守在旁边服侍他。肩膀上有了责任，爱米丽亚也就没有时候为自己心焦，或是像平常一样幻想出许多不吉利的预兆来吓唬自己。年轻的病人简简单单地把当天的经过说了一遍，描写第×联队里勇敢的朋友们怎么打仗。他们的损失非常惨重，军官

and men. The Major's horse had been shot under him as the regiment charged, and they all thought that O'Dowd was gone, and that Dobbin had got his majority, until on their return from the charge to their old ground, the Major was discovered seated on Pyramus's carcase, refreshing himself from a case-bottle. It was Captain Osborne that cut down the French lancer who had speared the ensign. Amelia turned so pale at the notion, that Mrs. O'Dowd stopped the young ensign in this story. And it was Captain Dobbin who at the end of the day, though wounded himself, took up the lad in his arms and carried him to the surgeon, and thence to the cart which was to bring him back to Brussels. And it was he who promised the driver two louis if he would make his way to Mr. Sedley's hotel in the city; and tell Mrs. Captain Osborne that the action was over, and that her husband was unhurt and well.

"Indeed, but he has a good heart that William Dobbin," Mrs. O'Dowd said, "though he is always laughing at me."

Young Stubble vowed there was not such another officer in the army, and never ceased his praises of the senior captain, his modesty, his kindness, and his admirable coolness in the field. To these parts of the conversation, Amelia lent a very distracted attention: it was only when George was spoken of that she listened, and when he was not mentioned, she thought about him.

In tending her patient, and in thinking of the wonderful escapes of the day before, her second day passed away not too slowly with Amelia. There was only one man in the army for her: and as long as he was well, it must be owned that its movements interested her little.

和兵士阵亡的不在少数。联队冲锋的时候，少佐的坐骑中了一枪。大家都以为奥多这一下完了，都宾要升做少佐了，不料战争结束以后回到老地方，看见少佐坐在比拉密斯的尸首上面，凑着酒瓶喝酒呢。刺伤旗手的法国长枪手是奥斯本上尉杀死的；爱米丽亚听到这里脸色惨白，奥多太太便把小旗手的话岔开去。停火之后，全亏都宾上尉抱起旗手把他送到外科医生那里医治，又把他送到车上运回布鲁塞尔来，其实他自己也受了伤。他又许那车夫两块金洋，叫他找到赛特笠先生的旅馆里，告诉奥斯本上尉太太说战事已经结束，她的丈夫很平安，没有受伤。

奥多太太说道："那个威廉·都宾心肠真好，虽然他老是笑我。"

小斯德博尔起誓说整个军队里没有一个军官比得上他。他称赞上尉的谦虚、忠厚，说他在战场上那不慌不忙的劲儿真了不起。他们说这些话的当儿，爱米丽亚只是心不在焉，提到乔治她才听着，听不见他的名字，她便在心里想他。

爱米丽亚一面伺候病人，一面庆幸前一天的好运气，倒也并不觉得那天特别长。整个军队里，她关心的只有一个

All the reports which Jos brought from the streets fell very vaguely on her ears; though they were sufficient to give that timorous gentleman, and many other people then in Brussels, every disquiet. The French had been repulsed certainly, but it was after a severe and doubtful struggle, and with only a division of the French army. The Emperor, with the main body, was away at Ligny, where he had utterly annihilated the Prussians, and was now free to bring his whole force to bear upon the allies. The Duke of Wellington was retreating upon the capital, and a great battle must be fought under its walls probably, of which the chances were more than doubtful. The Duke of Wellington had but twenty thousand British troops on whom he could rely, for the Germans were raw militia, the Belgians disaffected; and with this handful his Grace had to resist a hundred and fifty thousand men that had broken into Belgium under Napoleon. Under Napoleon! What warrior was there, however famous and skilful, that could fight at odds with him?

Jos thought of all these things, and trembled. So did all the rest of Brussels—where people felt that the fight of the day before was but the prelude to the greater combat which was imminent. One of the armies opposed to the Emperor was scattered to the winds already. The few English that could be brought to resist him would perish at their posts, and the conqueror would pass over their bodies into the city. Woe be to those whom he found there! Addresses were prepared, public functionaries assembled and debated secretly, apartments were got ready, and tricoloured banners and triumphal emblems manufactured, to welcome the arrival of his Majesty the Emperor and King.

人。说老实话，只要他平安，其余的动静都不在她心上。乔斯从街上带了消息回来，她也不过糊里糊涂地听着。胆小的乔斯和布鲁塞尔好些居民都很担忧；法国军队虽然已经败退，可是这边经过一场恶战才勉强打了个胜仗，而且这一回敌人只来了一师。法国皇帝带着大军驻在里尼，已经歼灭了普鲁士军队，正可以把全副力量来对付各国的联军。威灵顿公爵正在向比利时首都布鲁塞尔退却，大约在城墙下不免要有一场大战，结果究竟怎样，一点儿没有把握。威灵顿公爵手下只有两万英国兵是靠得住的，此外，德国兵都是生手，比利时军队又已经叛离了盟军。敌军共有十五万人，曾经跟着拿破仑杀到比利时国境，而他大人却只有那么几个人去抵挡。拿破仑！不管是什么有名望有本领的军人，谁还能够战胜他呢？

乔斯盘算着这些事，止不住发抖。所有布鲁塞尔的人也都这样担心，觉得隔天的战争不过是开端，大战即刻跟着来了。和法国皇帝敌对的军队有一支已经逃得无影无踪，能够打仗的几个英国兵准会死在战场上，然后得胜的军队便跨过他们的尸首向布鲁塞尔进军，留在城里的人就得遭殃。政府官员偷偷地聚会讨论，欢迎词已经准备好，房间也收拾端正，三色旗呀，庆祝胜利用的标识呀，都已经赶做起来，只等皇帝陛下进城。

The emigration still continued, and wherever families could find means of departure, they fled. When Jos, on the afternoon of the 17th of June, went to Rebecca's hotel, he found that the great Bareacres' carriage had at lenght rolled away from the *porte-cochère*. The Earl had procured a pair of horses somehow, in spite of Mrs. Crawley, and was rolling on the road to Ghent. Louis the Desired was getting ready his portmanteau in that city, too. It seemed as if Misfortune was never tired of worrying into motion that unwieldy exile.

Jos felt that the delay of yesterday had been only a respite, and that his dearly bought horses must of a surety be put into requisition. His agonies were very severe all this day. As long as there was an English army between Brussels and Napoleon, there was no need of immediate flight; but he had his horses brought from their distant stables, to the stables in the court-yard of the hotel where he lived; so that they might be under his own eyes, and beyond the risk of violent abduction. Isidor watched the stable-door constantly, and had the horses saddled, to be ready for the start. He longed intensely for that event.

After the reception of the previous day, Rebecca did not care to come near her dear Amelia. She clipped the bouquet which George had brought her, and gave fresh water to the flowers, and read over the letter which he had sent her. "Poor wretch," she said, twirling round the little bit of paper in her fingers, "how I could crush her with this! —and it is for a thing like this that she must break her heart, forsooth—for a man who is stupid—a coxcomb—and who does not care for her. My poor good Rawdon is worth ten of this creature." And then she fell to thinking what she should do if—if anything happened

离城逃难的人仍旧络绎不绝，能够逃走的人都走了。六月十七日下午，乔斯到利蓓加旅馆里去，发现贝亚爱格思家里的大马车总算离开旅馆门口动身了。虽然克劳莱太太作梗，伯爵终究弄来两匹马，驾着车子出发到甘德去。“人民拥戴的路易”[①]也在布鲁塞尔整理行囊。这个流亡在外国的人实在不容易安顿，背运仿佛不怕麻烦似的跟定了他，不让他停留在一个地方。

乔斯觉得隔天的耽搁只是暂时的，他的那两匹出大价钱买来的马儿总还得用一下。那天他真是急得走投无路。拿破仑和布鲁塞尔之间还有一支英国军队。只要英国军队还在，他就不必马上逃难。话虽是这么说，他把两匹马老远地牵来养在自己旅馆院子旁的马槽里，常常照看着，生怕有人行凶把马抢去。伊息多一直守在马房旁边，马鞍子也已经备好，以便随时动身。他迫不及待地希望主人快走。

利蓓加隔天受到冷落，所以不愿走近亲爱的爱米丽亚。她把乔治买给她的花球修剪了一下，换了水，拿出他写给自己的条子又看了一遍。她把那小纸片儿绕着指头旋转，说道：“可怜的孽障！单是这封信就能把她气死。为这么一件小事情，她就能气个心伤肠断。她男人又蠢，又是个纨绔子弟，又不爱她！我可怜的好罗登比他强十倍呢。”接着她心下盘算，万一——万一可怜的好罗登有个失闪，她应该怎么

① 即路易十八，这外号是保皇党人替他取的，当时他流亡在比利时，拿破仑的军队逼近布鲁塞尔，他只能再逃难。

to poor good Rawdon, and what a great piece of luck it was that he had left his horses behind.

In the course of this day too, Mrs. Crawley, who saw not without anger the Bareacres party drive off, bethought her of the precaution which the countess had taken, and did a little needlework for her own advantage; she stitched away the major part of her trinkets, bills, and bank-notes about her person, and so prepared, was ready for any event—to fly if she thought fit, or to stay and welcome the conqueror, were he Englishman or Frenchman. And I am not sure that she did not dream that night of becoming a duchess and Madame la Maréchale, while Rawdon wrapped in his cloak, and making his bivouac under the rain at Mount Saint John, was thinking, with all the force of his heart, about the little wife whom he had left behind him.

The next day was a Sunday. And Mrs. Major O'Dowd had the satisfaction of seeing both her patients refreshed in health and spirits by some rest which they had taken during the night. She herself had slept on a great chair in Amelia's room, ready to wait upon her poor friend or the ensign, should either need her nursing. When morning came, this robust woman went back to the house where she and her Major had their billet; and here performed an elaborate and splendid toilette, befitting the day. And it is very possible that whilst alone in that chamber, which her husband had inhabited, and where his cap still lay on the pillow, and his cane stood in the corner, one prayer at least was sent up to Heaven for the welfare of the brave soldier, Michael O'Dowd.

When she returned she brought her prayer-book with her, and her uncle the Dean's famous book of

办。她一面想，一面庆幸他的马没有带去。

克劳莱太太看着贝亚爱格思一家坐车走掉，老大气不忿。就在当天，她想起伯爵夫人预防万一的手段，自己便也做了些缝纫工作，把大多数的首饰、钞票、支票，都缝在自己随身衣裳里面。这么准备好之后，什么都不怕了，到必要时可以逃难，再不然，就留下欢迎打胜的军队——不管是英国人还是法国人。说不定当晚她梦见自己做了公爵夫人，或是法国元帅的妻子。就在那一晚上，罗登在圣·约翰山上[①]守夜，裹着大衣站在雨里，一心一念惦记着撇在后方的妻子。

第二天是星期日。奥多少佐太太照看的两个病人晚上睡了一会儿，身体和精神都有了进步，她看了很满意。她自己睡在爱米丽亚房里的大椅子上，这样如果那旗手和她可怜的朋友需要她伺候，她随时能够起来。到早上，这位身子结实的太太回到她和少佐同住的公寓里去。因为是星期日，她细细地打扮了一下，把自己修饰得十分华丽。这间卧房是她丈夫住过的，他的帽子还在枕头上，他的手杖仍旧搁在屋角，当奥多太太独自在房里的时候，至少为那勇敢的兵士麦格尔·奥多念了一遍经。

她回来的时候，带了一本祈祷文和她叔叔副主教的有名的训戒——也就是她每逢安息日必读的书。书里的话大

① 滑铁卢大战之前，英国军队在这一带列阵准备和法国人交手。

sermons, out of which she never failed to read every Sabbath; not understanding all, haply, not pronouncing many of the words aright, which were long and abstruse—for the Dean was a learned man, and loved long Latin words—but with great gravity, vast emphasis, and with tolerable correctness in the main. How often has my Mick listened to these sermons, she thought, and me reading in the cabin of a calm! She proposed to resume this exercise on the present day, with Amelia and the wounded ensign for a congregation. The same service was read on that day in twenty thousand churches at the same hour; and millions of British men and women, on their knees, implored protection of the Father of all.

They did not hear the noise which disturbed our little congregation at Brussels. Much louder than that which had, interrupted them two days previously, as Mrs. O'Dowd was reading the service in her best voice, the cannon of Waterloo began to roar.

When Jos heard that dreadful sound, he made up his mind that he would bear this perpetual recurrence of terrors no longer, and would fly at once. He rushed into the sick man's room where our three friends had paused in their prayers, and further interrupted them by a passionate appeal to Amelia.

"I can't stand it any more, Emmy," he said; "I won't stand it; and you must come with me. I have bought a horse for you—never mind at what price—and you must dress and come with me, and ride behind Isidor."

"God forgive me, Mr. Sedley, but you are no better than a coward," Mrs. O'Dowd said, laying down the book.

"I say come, Amelia," the civilian went on; "never

概她并不全懂,字也有好些不认识。副主教是个有学问的人,爱用拉丁文,因此书里又长又深奥的字多得很。她读书的时候一本正经,不时用力地加重语气,大体说来,读别的字还不算多。她想:“海上没有风浪的时候,我在船舱里常常读它,我的密克也不知道听了多少回了。”那天她提议仍旧由她朗读训戒,爱米丽亚和受伤的旗手便算正在礼拜的会众。在同一个钟点,两万教堂里都在进行同样的宗教仪式。几百万英国人,男的女的,都跪着恳求主宰一切的天父保佑他们。

布鲁塞尔做礼拜的这几个人所听见的声音却是在英国的人所听不见的。当奥多太太用她最优美的声音领导宗教仪式的当儿,炮声又起了,并且比两天前的响得多。滑铁卢大战开始了。

乔斯听得这可怕的声音,觉得这样不断地担惊受怕实在不行,立定主意要逃命。

我们那三位朋友的祷告本来已给炮声打断,忽见乔斯又冲进病房来搅和他们。他恳切地向爱米丽亚哀求道:“爱米,我受不住了,我也不愿意再受罪了。你跟我来吧。我给你买了一匹马,——别管我出了多少钱买来的。快穿好衣服跟我来。你可以骑在伊息多后面。”

奥多太太放下书本说道:“请老天爷原谅我说话不留情!赛特笠先生,你简直是个没胆量的小子。”

印度官儿接着说道:“爱米丽亚,来吧!别理她。咱们

mind what she says; why are we to stop here and be butchered by the French men?"

"You forget the —th, my boy," said the little Stubble, the wounded hero, from his bed—"and—and you won't leave me, will you, Mrs. O'Dowd?"

"No, my dear fellow," said she, going up and kissing the boy. "No harm shall come to you while *I* stand by. I don't budge till I get the word from Mick. A pretty figure I'd be, wouldn't I, stuck behind that chap on a pillion?"

This image caused the young patient to burst out laughing in his bed, and even made Amelia smile. "I don't ask her," Jos shouted out—"I don't ask that—that Irishwoman, but you, Amelia; once for all, will you come?"

"Without my husband, Joseph?" Amelia said, with a look of wonder, and gave her hand to the Major's wife. Jos's patience was exhausted.

"Good—bye, then," he said, shaking his fist in a rage, and slamming the door by which he retreated. And this time he really gave his order for march: and mounted in the court-yard. Mrs. O'Dowd heard the clattering hoofs of the horses as they issued from the gate; and looking on, made many scornful remarks on poor Joseph as he rode down the street with Isidor after him in the laced cap. The horses, which had not been exercised for some days, were lively, and sprang about the street. Jos, a clumsy and timid horseman, did not look to advantage in the saddle. "Look at him, Amelia dear, driving into the parlour window. Such a bull in a china-shop *I* never saw." And presently the pair of riders disappeared at a canter down the street leading in the direction of the Ghent

何必等法国人来了挨刀呢。”

受伤的小英雄斯德博尔睡在床上说：“我的孩子，你忘了第×联队啦。奥多太太，你——你不会离开我吧？”

奥多太太上前吻着孩子道：“亲爱的，我不会走的。只要我在这里，绝不让你受苦。密克不叫我走，我无论如何不走。你想，我坐在那家伙的马屁股上像个什么样子！”

小病人想起这样子，在床上哈哈大笑，爱米丽亚也忍不住微笑起来。乔斯嚷道：“我又没有请她一起走。我又没请那个——那个爱尔兰婆子，我请的是你，爱米丽亚。一句话，你究竟来不来？”

爱米丽亚诧异道：“丢了丈夫跟你走吗，乔瑟夫？”说着，她拉了少佐太太的手。乔斯实在耐不住了，说道：“既然如此，再会了！”他怒不可遏的伸伸拳头，走出去砰的一声关了门。这一回他当真发出开步的命令，在院子里上了马。奥多太太听得他们马蹄嘚嘚的出门，便把头伸出去看，只见可怜的乔瑟夫骑在马上沿着街道跑，伊息多戴了金边帽子在后面跟，便说了许多挖苦的话。那两匹马已经好几天没有遛过脚力，不免在街上跳跳蹦蹦，乔斯胆子小，骑术又拙，骑在鞍上老大不像样。奥多太太道：“爱米丽亚亲爱的，快看，他骑到人家客厅的窗子上去啦。我一辈子没见过这样儿，真正是大公牛到了瓷器店里去了。”这两个人骑着马，向甘

road. Mrs. O'Dowd pursuing them with a fire of sarcasm so long as they were in sight.

All that day from morning until past sunset, the cannon never ceased to roar. It was dark when the cannonading stopped all of a sudden.

All of us have read of what occurred during that interval. The tale is in every Englishman's mouth; and you and I, who were children when the great battle was won and lost, are never tired of hearing and recounting the history of that famous action. It's remembrance rankles still in the bosoms of millions of the countrymen of those brave men who lost the day. They pant for an opportunity of revenging that humiliation; and if a contest, ending in a victory on their part, should ensue, elating them in their turn, and leaving its cursed legacy of hatred and rage behind to us, there is no end to the so-called glory and shame, and to the alternations of successful and unsuccessful murder, in which two high-spirited nations might engage. Centuries hence, we Frenchmen and Englishmen might be boasting and killing each other still, carrying out bravely the Devil's code of honour.

All our friends took their share and fought like men in the great field. All day long, whilst the women were praying ten miles away, the lines of the dauntless English infantry were receiving and repelling the furious charges of the French horsemen. Guns which were heard at Brussels were ploughing up their ranks, and comrades falling, and the resolute survivors closing in. Towards evening, the attack of the French, repeated and resisted so bravely, slackened in its fury. They had other foes besides the British to engage, or were preparing for a final onset. It came at last: the columns of the Imperial Guard marched

德的公路奔跑，奥多太太在后头大声嘲笑挖苦，直到看不见他们才罢。

那天从早晨到日落，炮声隆隆，没有停过。可是天黑之后，忽然没有声响了。

大家都曾经读过关于那时的记载。每个英国人都爱讲这篇故事。大战决定胜负的时候，我和你还都是小孩子，对于有名的战役，听了又听，讲了又讲，再也不觉得厌倦。几百万和当时战败的勇士们同国的人，至今想起这事便觉得懊丧，恨不得有机会赶快报仇雪耻。倘若战事再起，他们那边得胜，气焰大张，仇恨和愤怒这可恨的遗产由我们承受，那么两个不甘屈服的国家，只好无休无歇地拼个你死我活，世路上所说的光荣和羞耻，也互相消长，总没个了局了。几世纪之后，我们英国人和法国人也许仍在勇敢地维护着魔鬼的荣誉法典，继续夸耀武力，继续互相残杀。

在伟大的战斗中，我们所有的朋友都尽了责任，拿出大丈夫的气概奋勇杀敌。整整一天，女人们在十英里以外祷告的当儿，无畏的英国步兵队伍努力击退猛烈进攻的法国骑兵。布鲁塞尔居民所听见的炮火，打破了他们的阵势，弟兄们死伤倒地，活着的又坚决地冲上去。法军连续不断地向前进攻，攻得勇，守得也勇。傍晚，法军的攻势逐渐松懈，或许因为他们还有别的敌人，或许在准备最后再来一次总攻击。末了，两边终究又交起手来。法国皇家卫军的纵队

up the hill of St. Jean, at length and at once to sweep the English from the height which they had maintained all day, and spite of all: unscared by the thunder of the artillery, which hurled death from the English line—the dark rolling column pressed on and up the hill. It seemed almost to crest the eminence, when it began to wave and falter. Then it stopped, still facing the shot. Then at last the English troops rushed from the post from which no enemy had been able to dislodge them, and the Guard turned and fled.

No more firing was heard at Brussels—the pursuit rolled miles away. Darkness came down on the field and city: and Amelia was praying for George, who was lying on his face, dead, with a bullet through his heart.

冲上圣·约翰山，企图一下子把英国兵从他们占据了一天的山头上赶下去。英国队伍中发出震天的炮火，碰着的只有死。可是法国人不怕，黑魆魆的队伍蜂拥上前，一步步的上山。他们差不多已经到了顶点，可是渐渐的动摇犹豫。他们面对着炮火，停住了。然后英国队伍从据点上冲下来（任何敌人不能把他们从据点上赶走），法国兵只能回过身去逃走。

布鲁塞尔的居民听不见枪炮了，英军一直向前追逐了好几英里。黑暗笼罩着城市和战场；爱米丽亚正在为乔治祈祷；他呢，却扑倒在战场上，心口中了一颗子弹，死了。

How to Live Well on Nothing a Year

I suppose there is no man in this Vanity Fair of ours so little observant as not to think sometimes about the worldly affairs of his acquaintances, or so extremely charitable as not to wonder how his neighbour Jones, or his neighbour Smith, can make both ends meet at the end of the year. With the utmost regard for the family, for instance (for I dine with them twice or thrice in the season), I cannot but own that the appearance of the Jenkinses in the Park, in the large barouche with the grenadier-footmen, will surprise and mystify me to my dying day: for though I know the equipage is only jobbed, and all the Jenkins people are on boardwages, yet those three men and the carriage must represent an expense of six hundred a-year at the very least—and then there are the splendid dinners, the two boys at Eton, the prize governess and masters for the girls, the trip abroad, or to Eastbourne or Worthing in the autumn, the annual ball with a supper from Gunter's (who, by the way, supplies most of the first-rate dinners which J. gives, as I know very well, having been invited to one of them to fill a vacant place, when I saw at once that these repasts are very superior to the common run of entertainments for which the humbler sort of J.'s acquaintances get cards)—who, I say, with the most good-natured feelings in the world, can help wondering how the Jenkinses make out matters? What is Jenkins? We all know—Commissioner of the Tape and Sealing Wax Office, with £1,200 a-year for a sala-

全无收入的人怎么才能过好日子

我想，在我们这名利场上的人，总不至于糊涂得对于自己朋友们的生活情况全不关心，凭他心胸怎么宽大，想到邻居里面像琼斯和斯密士这样的人一年下来居然能够收支相抵，总忍不住觉得诧异。譬如说，我对于琴根士一家非常的尊敬，因为在伦敦请客应酬最热闹的时候，我总在他家吃两三顿饭，可是我不得不承认，每当我在公园里看见他们坐着大马车，跟班的打扮得像穿特别制服的大兵，就免不了觉得纳闷，这个谜是一辈子也猜不透的了。我知道他们的马车是租来的，他们的用人全是拿了工钱自理膳食的，可是这三个男用人和马车一年至少也得六百镑才维持得起呢。他们又时常请客，酒菜是丰盛极了；两个儿子都在伊顿公学①读书，家里另外给女儿们请着第一流的保姆和家庭教师。他们每到秋天便上国外游览，不到伊斯脱波恩便到窝丁；一年还要开一次跳舞会，酒席都是根脱饭馆预备的。我得补充一句，琴根士请客用的上等酒席大都叫他们包办。我怎么会知道的呢？原来有一回临时给他们拉去凑数，吃喝得真讲究，一看就知道比他们款待第二三流客人的普通酒菜精致许多。这么说来，凭你怎么马虎不管事，也免不了觉得疑惑，不知道琴根士他们到底是怎么一回事。琴根士本人是干哪一行的呢？我们都知道，他是照例行文局的委员，每年有一千二百镑的收入。他的妻子有钱吗？呸！她姓弗灵

① 英国最贵族化的公立学校。

ry. Had his wife a private fortune? Pooh!—Miss Flint—one of eleven children of a small squire in Buckinghamshire. All she ever gets from her family is a turkey at Christmas, in exchange for which she has to board two or three of her sisters in the off season; and lodge and feed her brothers when they come to town. How does Jenkins balance his income? I say, as every friend of his must say, How is it that he has not been outlawed long since; and that he ever came back (as he did to the surprise of everybody) last year from Boulogne?

"I" is here introduced to personify the world in general—the Mrs. Grundy of each respected reader's private circle—every one of whom can point to some families of his acquaintance who live nobody knows how. Many a glass of wine have we all of us drunk, I have very little doubt, hob-and-nobbing with the hospitable giver, and wondering how the deuce he paid for it.

Some three or four years after his stay in Paris, when Rawdon Crawley and his wife were established in a very small comfortable house in Curzon Street, Mayfair, there were scarcely one of the numerous friends whom they entertained at dinner, that did not ask the above question regarding them. The novelist, it has been said before, knows everything, and as I am in a situation to be able to tell the public how Crawley and his wife lived without any income, may I entreat the public newspapers which are in the habit of extracting portions of the various periodical works now published, not to reprint the following exact narrative and calculations—of which I ought, as the discoverer (and at some expense, too), to have the benefit. My son, I would say, were I blessed with a child—you may by deep inquiry and constant inter-

脱，父亲是白金汉郡的小地主，姊妹兄弟一共有十一个人。家里统共在圣诞节送她一只火鸡，她倒得在伦敦没有大应酬的时候供给两三个姊妹食宿，并且兄弟们到伦敦来的时候也得由她招待。琴根士究竟怎么能够撑得起这场面的呢？我真想问问："他至今能够逍遥法外，究竟是怎么回事呀？去年他怎么还会从波浪涅回来呢？"他所有别的朋友一定也在那么猜测。去年他从波浪涅回来，大家都奇怪极了。

这里所说的"我"，代表世界上一般的人，也可以说代表可敬的读者亲友里面的葛伦地太太[①]。这种莫名其妙靠不知什么过活下去的人，谁没有见过？无疑的，我们都曾和这些好客的主人一起吃喝作乐，一面喝他们的酒，一面心下揣摩，不知道他是哪里弄来的钱。

罗登·克劳莱夫妇在巴黎住了三四年后便回到英国，在梅飞厄的克生街上一所极舒服的小屋里住下来。在他们家里做客的许许多多朋友之中，差不多没有一个肚子里不在琢磨他们家用的来源。前面已经表过，写小说的人是无所不知的，因此我倒能够把克劳莱夫妇不花钱过日子的秘诀告诉大家。不幸现在的报纸常常随意把分期发表的小说摘录转载，所以我觉得担心，要请求各报的编辑先生不要抄袭我这篇情报和数字都绝对准确的文章。既然发现内中情节的是我，出钱调查的是我，所得的利润当然也应该归我才对。如果我有个儿子，我一定对他说，孩子啊，倘若你要知

---

① 莫登(T. Morton，1764—1838)的《快快耕田》(Speed the Plough)一剧，在1798年出版，剧中有一个从未露面的角色叫葛伦地太太(Mrs. Grundy)，现在已经成为拘泥礼法的英国人的象征。

course with him, learn how a man lives comfortably on nothing a-year. But it is best not to be intimate with gentlemen of this profession, and to take the calculations at secondhand, as you do logarithms, for to work them yourself, depend upon it, will cost you something considerable.

On nothing per annum then, and during a course of some two or three years, of which we can afford to give but a very brief history, Crawley and his wife lived very happily and comfortably at Paris. It was in this period that he quitted the Guards, and sold out of the army. When we find him again, his mustachios and the title of Colonel on his card are the only relics of his military profession.

It has been mentioned that Rebecca, soon after her arrival in Paris, took a very smart and leading position in the society of that capital, and was welcomed at some of the most distinguished houses of the restored French nobility. The English men of fashion in Paris courted her, too, to the disgust of the ladies their wives, who could not bear the parvenue. For some months the salons of the Faubourg St. Germain, in which her place was secured, and the splendours of the new Court, where she was received with much distinction, delighted, and perhaps a little intoxicated Mrs. Crawley, who may have been disposed during this period of elation to slight the people—honest young military men mostly—who formed her husband's chief society.

But the colonel yawned sadly among the duchesses and great ladies of the Court. The old women who played *écarté* made such a noise about a five-franc piece, that it was not worth Colonel Crawley's while to sit down at a

道有些毫无收入的人怎么能过得那么舒服，只要常常跟他们来往和不断寻根究底地追问他们。不过我劝你少和靠这一行吃饭的家伙来往，你需要资料的话，尽不妨间接打听，就像你运用现成的对数表似的就行了。信我的话，倘若自己调查的话，得花不少钱呢。

克劳莱夫妇两手空空地在巴黎住了两三年，过得又快乐又舒服，可惜这段历史，我只能简单叙述一下。就在那时，克劳莱把军官的职位出卖，离开了禁卫队。我们和他重逢的时候，唯有他的胡子和名片上上校的名衔还沾着点军官的气息。

我曾经说过，利蓓加到达法国首都巴黎不久之后，便在上流社会出入，又时髦，又出风头，连好些光复后的王亲国戚都和她来往。许多住在巴黎的英国时髦人也去奉承她，可是他们的妻子很不高兴，瞧着这个暴发户老大不入眼。在圣叶孟郊外一带的贵人家里，她的地位十分稳固，在灿烂豪华的新宫廷里，她也算得上有身份的贵客。克劳莱太太这么过了好几个月，乐得简直有些飘飘然。在这一段春风得意的日子里，大概她对于丈夫日常相与的一群老实的年轻军官很有些瞧不起。

上校混在公爵夫人和宫廷贵妇们中间，闷得直打哈欠。那些老太婆玩埃加脱①，输了五法郎便大惊小怪，因此克劳莱上校觉得根本不值得斗牌。他又不懂法文，对于他们的

① 原文为法文，纸牌的一种玩法。

card-table. The wit of their conversation he could not appreciate, being ignorant of their language. And what good could his wife get, he urged, by making curtsies every night to a whole circle of Princesses? He left Rebecca presently to frequent these parties alone; resuming his own simple pursuits and amusements amongst the amiable friends of his own choice.

The truth is, when we say of a gentleman that he lives elegantly on nothing a year, we use the word "nothing" to signify something unknown; meaning, simply, that we don't know how the gentleman in question defrays the expenses of his establishment. Now, our friend the Colonel had a great aptitude for all games of chance: and exercising himself, as he continually did, with the cards, the dice-box, or the cue, it is natural to suppose that he attained a much greater skill in the use of these articles than men can possess who only occasionally handle them. To use a cue at billiards well is like using a pencil, or a German flute, or a small-sword—you cannot master any one of these implements at first, and it is only by repeated study and perseverance, joined to a natural taste, that a man can excel in the handling of either. Now Crawley, from being only a brilliant amateur had grown to be a consummate master of billiards. Like a great general, his genius used to rise with the danger, and when the luck had been unfavourable to him for a whole game, and the bets were consequently against him, he would, with consummate skill and boldness, make some prodigious hits which would restore the battle, and come in a victor at the end, to the astonishment of everybody—of everybody, that is, who was a stranger to his play. Those who were accustomed to see it were cautious how

俏皮话一句也不懂。他的妻子天天晚上对着一大群公主屈膝行礼,这里面究竟有什么好处,他也看不出来。不久他让利蓓加独自出去做客,自己仍旧回到和他气味相投的朋友堆里来混,他是宁可过简单些的生活,找简单些的消遣的。

我们形容某某先生全无收入而过得舒服,事实上"全无收入"的意思就是"来路不明的收入",也就是说这位先生居然能够开销这么一个家庭,简直使我们莫名其妙。我们的朋友克劳莱上校对于各种赌博,像玩纸牌,掷骰子,打弹子,没一样不擅长,而且他经过长期练习,自然比偶然赌一两场的人厉害得多。打弹子也和写字、击轻剑、吹德国笛子一般,不但需要天赋的才能,而且应该有不懈的研究和练习,才能专精。克劳莱对于打弹子一道,本来是客串性质,不过玩得非常出色,到后来却成了技术高明的专家。他好像了不起的军事家,面临的危险愈大,他就愈有办法,往往一盘赌博下来,他手运一点也不好,所有的赌注都输了,然后忽然来几下子灵敏矫捷得出神入化的手法,把局势挽回过来,竟成了赢家。凡是对他赌博的本领不熟悉的人,看了没有

they staked their money against a man of such sudden resources, and brilliant and overpowering skill.

At games of cards he was equally skillful; for though he would constantly lose money at the commencement of an evening, playing so carelessly and making such blunders, that new comers were often inclined to think meanly of his talent; yet when roused to action, and awakened to caution by repeated small losses, it was remarked that Crawley's play became quite different, and that he was pretty sure of beating his enemy thoroughly before the night was over. Indeed, very few men could say that they ever had the better of him.

His successes were so repeated that no wonder the envious and the vanquished spoke sometimes with bitterness regarding them. And as the French say of the Duke of Wellington, who never suffered a defeat, that only an astonishing series of lucky accidents enabled him to be an invariable winner; yet even they allow that he cheated at Waterloo, and was enabled to win the last great trick:—so it was hinted at head-quarters in England, that some foul play must have taken place in order to account for the continuous successes of Colonel Crawley.

Though Frascati's and the Salon were open at that time in Paris, the mania for play was so widely spread, that the public gambling-rooms did not suffice for the general ardour, and gambling went on in private houses as much as if there had been no public means for gratifying the passion. At Crawley's charming little *réunions* of an evening this fatal amusement commonly was practised—much to good-natured little Mrs. Crawley's annoyance. She spoke about her husband's passion for dice with the deepest grief; she bewailed it to everybody who came

不惊奇的。知道他有这么一手的人,和他赌输赢时便小心一些,因为他有急智,脑子又快,手又巧,别人再也赌不赢他。

斗牌的时候他也照样有本事。到黄昏初上场的时候他老是输钱,新和他交手的人见他随随便便,错误百出,都不怎么瞧得起他。可是接连几次小输之后,他生了戒心,抖擞起精神大战,大家看得出他的牌风和本来完全两样了,一黄昏下来,总能够把对手打得服服帖帖。说真的,在他手里赢过钱的人实在少得可怜。

他赢钱的次数那么多,无怪乎眼红的人,赌输的人,有时说起这事便要发牢骚。法国人曾经批评常胜将军威灵顿公爵,说他所以能常胜的缘故,无非是意外的运气,可是他们不得不承认他在滑铁卢之战的确要过一些骗人的把戏,要不然那最后的一场比赛是赢不了的。同样的,在英国司令部,有好些人风里言风里语,总说克劳莱上校用了不老实的手段,才能保赢不输。

当时巴黎的赌风极盛,虽然弗拉斯加蒂和沙龙赌场都正式开放,可是一般人正在兴头上,觉得公共赌场还不过瘾,私人家里也公开聚赌,竟好像公共赌场从来就不存在,这股子赌劲没处发泄似的。在克劳莱家里,到黄昏往往有有趣的小聚会,也少不了这种有危险性的娱乐。克劳莱太太的心地忠厚,为这件事心上很烦恼。她一谈起丈夫好赌的脾气就伤心得不得了,每逢家里有客,她总是唉声叹气的

to her house. She besought the young fellows never, never to touch a box; and when young Green, of the Rifles, lost a very considerable sum of money, Rebecca passed a whole night in tears, as the servant told the unfortunate young gentleman, and actually went on her knees to her husband to beseech him to remit the debt, and burn the acknowledgment. How could he? He had lost just as much himself to Blackstone of the Hussars, and Count Punter of the Hanoverian Cavalry. Green might have any decent time; but pay? —of course he must pay; to talk of burning IOU's was child's-play.

Other officers, chiefly young—for the young fellows gathered round Mrs. Crawley—came from her parties with long faces, having dropped more or less money at her fatal card-tables. Her house began to have an unfortunate reputation. The old hands warned the less experienced of their danger. Colonel O'Dowd, of the —th regiment, one of those occupying in Paris, warned Lieutenant Spooney of that corps. A loud and violent fracas took place between the infantry-colonel and his lady, who were dining at the Café de Paris, and Colonel and Mrs. Crawley, who were also taking their meal there. The ladies engaged on both sides. Mrs. O'Dowd snapped her fingers in Mrs. Crawley's face, and called her husband "no better than a black-leg." Colonel Crawley challenged Colonel O'Dowd, C. B. The Commander-in-Chief hearing of the dispute sent for Colonel Crawley, who was getting ready the same pistols "which he shot Captain Marker," and had such a conversation with him that no duel took place. If Rebecca had not gone on her knees to General Tufto, Crawley would have been sent back to England; and he did not play, except with civilians, for some weeks

抱怨。她哀求所有的小伙子总不要挨近骰子匣。有一次来福枪联队里的葛里恩输了不少钱,害得利蓓加陪了一夜眼泪。这是她的用人后来告诉那倒霉的输家的。据说她还向丈夫下跪,求他烧了债票,不要再去讨债。她丈夫不肯。那怎么行呢?匈牙利轻骑兵联队的勃拉克斯顿和德国汉诺伐骑兵联队里的本脱伯爵也赢了他那么多钱呢!葛里恩当然不必马上付钱,不妨过一个适当的时期再说,至于赌债,那是非还不可的。谁听说过烧毁债票呢?简直是孩子气!

到他们家去的军官多数年纪很轻,因为这些小伙子都爱追随在克劳莱太太身边。他们去拜访一次,多少总得在他们的牌桌上留下些钱,所以告别的时候都垂头丧气地拉长了脸。渐渐的克劳莱太太一家的声名便不大好听了。老手们时常警告没经验的人,说这里头的危险太大。当时驻扎在巴黎的第×联队的奥多上校就曾对联队里的斯卜内中尉下过劝告。有一次,步兵上校夫妇和克劳莱上校夫妇碰巧都在巴黎饭馆吃饭,两边就气势汹汹地大声吵闹起来了。两位太太都开了口。奥多太太冲着克劳莱太太的脸打响指,说她的丈夫“简直是个骗子”。克劳莱上校向奥多上校挑战,要跟他决斗。到他把“打死马克上尉”的手枪收拾停当,总司令已经风闻这次争辩,把克劳莱上校传去结结实实地训斥了一顿,结果也就没有决斗。倘若利蓓加不向德夫托将军下跪,克劳莱准会给调回英国去。此后几个星期里

after.

But in spite of Rawdon's undoubted skill and constant successes, it became evident to Rebecca, considering these things, that their position was but a precarious one, and that, even although they paid scarcely anybody, their little capital would end one day by dwindling into zero. "Gambling," she would say, "dear, is good to help your income, but not as an income itself. Some day people may be tired of play, and then where are we?" Rawdon acquiesced in the justice of her opinion; and in truth he had remarked that after a few nights of his little suppers, gentlemen were tired of play with him, and, in spite of Rebecca's charms, did not present themselves very eagerly.

Easy and pleasant as their life at Paris was, it was after all only an idle dalliance and amiable trifling; and Rebecca saw that she must push Rawdon's fortune in their own country. She must get him a place or appointment at home or in the colonies; and she determined to make a move upon England as soon as the way could be cleared for her. As a first step she had made Crawley sell out of the Guards, and go on half-pay. His function as aide-de-camp to General Tufto had ceased previously. Rebecca laughed in all companies at that officer, at his toupee (which he mounted on coming to Paris), at his waistband, at his false teeth, at his pretensions to be a lady-killer above all, and his absurd vanity in fancying every woman whom he came near was in love with him. It was to Mrs. Brent, the beetle-browed wife of Mr. Commissary Brent, to whom the General transferred his attentions now—his bouquets, his dinners at the restaurateurs, his opera-boxes, and his knick-knacks. Poor Mrs.

面，他不敢赌了，最多找老百姓玩一下。

虽然罗登赌起来手法高明，百战百胜，利蓓加经过了这些挫折之后，觉得他们的地位并不稳。他们差不多什么账都不付，可是照这样下去，手头的一点儿款子总有一天会一文不剩。她常说："亲爱的，赌博只能贴补不足，不能算正经的收入。总有一天那些人赌厌了，咱们怎么办呢?"罗登觉得她的话不错；说实话，他发现先生们在他家里吃过几餐小晚饭之后，就不高兴再赌钱了，虽然利蓓加会迷人，他们还是不大愿意来。

他们在巴黎生活得又舒服又有趣，可是终究不过在偷安嬉耍，不是个久远之计。利蓓加明白她必须在本国替罗登打天下；或是在英国谋个出身，或是在殖民地上找个差使。她打定主意，一到有路可走的时候，就回英国。第一步，她先叫罗登把军官的职位出卖，只支半薪。他早已不当德夫托将军的副官了。利蓓加在不论什么应酬场上都讥笑那军官。她讥笑他的马(他进占巴黎时骑的就是它)，还讥笑他的绑腰带，他的假牙齿。她尤其爱形容他怎么荒谬可笑，自以为是风月场上的老手，只当凡是和他接近的女人个个受用。如今德夫托将军另有所欢，又去向军需处白瑞恩脱先生的凸脑门的妻子献殷勤儿了。花球，零星首饰，饭店里的酒席，歌剧院的包厢，都归这位太太受用。可怜的德夫

Tufto was no more happy than before, and had still to pass long evenings alone with her daughters, knowing that her General was gone off scented and curled to stand behind Mrs. Brent's chair at the play. Becky had a dozen admirers in his place to be sure; and could cut her rival to pieces with her wit. But as we have said, she was growing tired of this idle social life: opera-boxes and restaurateur-dinners palled upon her: nosegays could not be laid by as a provision for future years: and she could not live upon knick-knacks, laced handkerchiefs, and kid gloves. She felt the frivolity of pleasure, and longed for more substantial benefits.

At this juncture news arrived which was spread among the many creditors of the Colonel at Paris, and which caused them great satisfaction. Miss Crawley, the rich aunt from whom he expected his immense inheritance, was dying; the Colonel must haste to her bedside. Mrs. Crawley and her child would remain behind until he came to reclaim them. He departed for Calais, and having reached that place in safety, it might have been supposed that he went to Dover; but instead he took the diligence to Dunkirk, and thence travelled to Brussels, for which place he had a former predilection. The fact is, he owed more money at London than at Paris; and he preferred the quiet little Belgian city to either of the more noisy capitals.

Her aunt was dead. Mrs. Crawley ordered the most intense mourning for herself and little Rawdon. The Colonel was busy arranging the affairs of the inheritance. They could take the premier now, instead of the little entresol of the hotel which they occupied Mrs. Crawley and the landlord had a consultation about the new

托太太并没有比以前快乐；她明知丈夫洒了香水，卷了头发和胡子，在戏院里站在白瑞恩脱太太椅子背后讨好她，自己只能一黄昏一黄昏陪着女儿们闷在家里。蓓基身边有十来个拜倒在她裙下的人来顶替将军的位置，而且她谈吐俏皮，一开口就能把对手讥刺得体无完肤。可是我已经说过，她对于懒散的应酬生活已经厌倦了，坐包厢听戏和上馆子吃饭使她腻烦；花球不能作为日后衣食之计；她虽然有许多镂空手帕，羊皮手套，也不能靠着这些过日子。她觉得老是寻欢作乐空洞得很，渴望要些靠得住的资产。

正在紧要关头，上校在巴黎的债主们得到一个差强人意的消息，立刻传开了。他的有钱姑母克劳莱小姐病得很重，偌大的遗产快要传到他手里，因此他非得急忙赶回去送终。克劳莱太太和她的孩子留在法国等他来接。他先动身到加莱；别人以为他平安到达那里之后，一定再向杜弗出发。不料他乘了邮车，由邓克刻转到布鲁塞尔去了。对于布鲁塞尔，他一向特别爱好。原来他在伦敦欠下的账比在巴黎的更多，嫌这两大首都太吵闹，宁可住在比利时的小城里，可以安逸些。

她姑妈死了，克劳莱太太给自己和儿子定做了全套的丧服。上校正忙着办理承继遗产的手续。如今他们住得起二楼的正房了，不必再住底层和二楼之间的那几间小屋子。克劳莱太太和旅馆主人商量该挂什么帘子，该铺什么地毯，

hangings, an amicable wrangle about the carpets, and a final adjustment of everything except the bill. She went off in one of his carriages; her French *bonne* with her; the child by her side; the admirable landlord and landlady smiling farewell to her from the gate. General Tufto was furious when he heard she was gone, and Mrs. Brent furious with him for being furious; Lieutenant Spooney was cut to the heart; and the landlord got ready his best apartments previous to the return of the fascinating little woman and her husband. He *serré'd* the trunks which she left in his charge with the greatest care. They had been especially recommended to him by Madame Crawley. They were not, however, found to be particularly valuable when opened some time after.

But before she went to join her husband in the Belgic capital, Mrs. Crawley made an expedition into England, leaving behind her little son upon the continent, under the care of her French maid.

The parting between Rebecca and the little Rawdon did not cause either party much pain. She had not, to say truth, seen much of the young gentleman since his birth. After the amiable fashion of French mothers, she had placed him out at nurse in a village in the neighbourhood of Paris, where little Rawdon passed the first months of his life, not unhappily, with a numerous family of foster-brothers in wooden shoes. His father would ride over many a time to see him here, and the elder Rawdon's paternal heart glowed to see him rosy and dirty, shouting lustily, and happy in the making of mud-pies under the superintendence of the gardener's wife, his nurse.

Rebecca did not care much to go and see the son and heir. Once he spoiled a new dove-coloured pelisse of

为这事争得高兴。最后，什么都安排好了，只有账没有付。她动身的时候借用了他一辆马车，孩子和法国女用人坐在她的身边一齐出发，旅馆主人夫妇，那两个好人，站在门口笑眯眯地给她送行。德夫托将军听说她已经离开法国，气得不得了，白瑞恩脱太太因为他生气，也就生他的气。斯卜内中尉难受得要命。旅馆主人准备那妩媚动人的太太和她丈夫不久就会回来，把他最好的房间都收拾整齐，又把她留下的箱子细细心心地锁好，因为克劳莱太太特别嘱咐他留心照看的。可惜不久以后他们把箱子打开的时候，并没有发现什么值钱的东西。

克劳莱太太到比利时首都去找丈夫以前，先到英国去走了一趟，叫那法国女用人带着儿子留在欧洲大陆。

利蓓加和小罗登分手的时候两边都不觉得割舍不下。说句实话，从这小孩子出世以来，她根本不大和他在一起。她学习法国妈妈们的好榜样，把他寄养在巴黎近郊的村子里。小罗登出世以后住在奶妈家里，和一大群穿木屐的奶哥哥在一起，日子过得相当快乐。他的爸爸常常骑了马去看望他。罗登看见儿子脸色红润，浑身肮脏，跟在他奶妈旁边（就是那花匠的妻子）做泥饼子，快乐得大呼小叫，心里不由得感到一阵做父亲的得意。

利蓓加不大高兴去看她的儿子。有一回孩子把她一件

hers. He preferred his nurse's caresses to his mamma's, and when finally he quitted that jolly nurse and almost parent, he cried loudly for hours. He was only consoled by his mother's promise that he should return to his nurse the next day; indeed the nurse herself, who probably would have been pained at the parting too, was told that the child would immediately be restored to her, and for some time awaited quite anxiously his return.

In fact, our friends may be said to have been among the first of that brood of hardy English adventurers who have subsequently invaded the continent, and swindled in all the capitals of Europe. The respect in those happy days of 1817 – 18 was very great for the wealth and honour of Britons. They had not then learned, as I am told, to haggle for bargains with the pertinacity which now distinguishes them. The great cities of Europe had not been as yet open to the enterprise of our rascals. And whereas there is now hardly a town of France or Italy in which you shall not see some noble countryman of our own, with that happy swagger and insolence of demeanour which we carry everywhere, swindling inn-landlords, passing fictitious cheques upon credulous bankers, robbing coach-makers of their carriages, goldsmiths of their trinkets, easy travellers of their money at cards, even public libraries of their books—thirty years ago you needed but to be a Milor Anglais, travelling in a private carriage, and credit was at your hand wherever you chose to seek it, and gentlemen, instead of cheating, were cheated. It was not for some weeks after the Crawleys' departure that the landlord of the hotel which they occupied during their residence at Paris, found out the losses which he had sustained: not until Madame Marabou, the milli-

浅灰色的新外套给弄脏了。小罗登也宁可要奶妈,不要妈妈。他的奶妈老是兴高采烈,像生身母亲似的疼他,因此他离开她的时候扯起嗓子哭了好几个钟头。后来他母亲哄他说第二天就让他回奶妈那儿去,他这才不哭了。奶妈也以为孩子就会送回去,痴心等待了好些日子,倘若她知道从此分手,告别的时候一定也觉得伤心。

自从那时候起,就有一帮胆大妄为的英国流氓混进欧洲各个大都市去招摇撞骗,我们的这两位朋友,可以算是第一批骗子里面的脚色。从一八一七年到一八一八年,英国人的日子过得实在富裕,大陆上的人对于他们的财富和道德非常尊敬。现在大家知道英国人有名的会斤斤计较和人讲价钱,据说当时他们还没有学会这套本领,欧洲的大城市也还没有给英国的流氓所盘踞。到如今差不多无论在法国和意大利哪个城市都有我们高贵的本国人,一看就是英国来的;他们态度骄横,走起路来那点架子摆得恰到好处。这些人欺骗旅馆老板,拿了假支票到老实的银行家那儿去诳钱,定了马车买了首饰不付账,和不懂事的过路客人斗牌,做了圈套赢他们的钱,甚至于还偷公共图书馆的书。三十年前,只要你是英国来的大爷,坐着自备马车到处游览,爱欠多少账都由你;那时的英国先生们不会哄人,只会上当。克劳莱一家离开法国好几个星期以后,那一向供他们食宿的旅馆老板才发现自己损失多么大。起初他还不知道,后

ner, made repeated visits with her little bill for articles supplied to Madame Crawley; not until Monsieur Didelot from Boule d'Or in the Palais Royal had asked half-a-dozen times whether cette charmante Miladi who had bought watches and bracelets of him was de retour. It is a fact that even the poor gardener's wife, who had nursed Madame's child, was never paid after the first six months for that supply of the milk of human kindness with which she had furnished the lusty and healthy little Rawdon. No, not even the nurse was paid—the Crawleys were in too great a hurry to remember their trifling debt to her. As for the landlord of the hotel, his curses against the English nation were violent for the rest of his natural life. He asked all travellers whether they knew a certain Colonel Lor Crawley—avec sa femme—une petite dame, très spirituelle. "*Ah, Monsieur!*" he would add—"*ils m'ont affreusement volé.*" It was melancholy to hear his accents as he spoke of that catastrophe.

Rebecca's object in her journey to London was to effect a kind of compromise with her husband's numerous creditors, and by offering them a dividend of ninepence or a shilling in the pound, to secure a return for him into his own country. It does not become us to trace the steps which she took in the conduct of this most difficult negotiation; but, having shown them to their satisfaction, that the sum which she was empowered to offer was all her husband's available capital, and having convinced them that Colonel Crawley would prefer a perpetual retirement on the continent to a residence in this country with his debts unsettled; having proved to them that there was no possibility of money accruing to him from other quarters, and no earthly chance of their

来衣装铺子里的莫拉布太太拿着克劳莱太太的衣服账来找了她好几次，还有皇宫街金球珠宝店里的蒂拉洛先生也来跑了六七回，打听那位问他买手表镯子的漂亮太太究竟什么时候回来，他才恍然大悟。可怜的花匠老婆给太太当奶妈，把结实的小罗登抚养了一场，并且对他十分疼爱，也只拿到在最初六个月的工钱。克劳莱一家临行匆忙，哪里还记得这种没要紧的账目，所以奶妈的工钱也欠着。旅馆老板从此痛恨英国，一直到死，提起它便狠狠毒毒地咒骂。凡是有过往的客人住到他旅馆里来，他就问他们认识不认识一个克劳莱上校老爷——他的太太个子矮小，样子非常文雅。他总是说："唉，先生，他欠了我多少钱，害得我好苦！"他讲到那次倒霉的事件，声音真凄惨，叫人听着也觉得难受。

利蓓加回到伦敦，目的在和丈夫的一大群债主开谈判。她情愿把丈夫所欠的债每镑中偿还九便士到一先令，作为他们让他回国的条件。至于她采取什么方法来进行这棘手的交涉，这里也不便细说。第一，她使债主们明白了她丈夫名下只有这些钱，能够提出来还债的数目再也多不出了。第二，她向债主们解释，如果债务不能了结的话，克劳莱上校宁可一辈子住在欧洲大陆，永远不回国。第三，她向债主

getting a larger dividend than that which she was empowered to offer, she brought the Colonel's creditors unanimously to accept her proposals, and purchased with fifteen hundred pounds of ready money, more than ten times that amount of debts.

Mrs. Crawley employed no lawyer in the transaction. The matter was so simple, to have or to leave, as she justly observed, that she made the lawyers of the creditors themselves do the business. And Mr. Lewis representing Mr. Davids, of Red Lion Square, and Mr. Moss acting for Mr. Manasseh of Cursitor Street (chief creditors of the Colonel's), complimented his lady upon the brilliant way in which she did business, and declared that there was no professional man who could beat her.

Rebecca received their congratulations with perfect modesty; ordered a bottle of sherry and a bread cake to the little dingy lodgings where she dwelt, while conducting the business, to treat the enemy's lawyers: shook hands with them at parting, in excellent good humour, and returned straightway to the continent, to rejoin her husband and son, and acquaint the former with the glad news of his entire liberation. As for the latter, he had been considerably neglected during his mother's absence by Mademoiselle Genevieve, her French maid; for that young woman, contracting an attachment for a soldier in the garrison of Calais, forgot her charge in the society of this *militaire*, and little Rawdon very narrowly escaped drowning on Calais sands at this period, where the absent Genevieve had left and lost him.

And so, Colonel and Mrs. Crawley came to London: and it is at their house in Curzon Street, May Fair, that

们证明克劳莱上校的确没有弄钱的去处，他们所能得到的款子绝没有希望超过她所建议的数目。那么一来，上校的债主们一致同意接受建议；她用了一千五百镑现款把债务完全偿清，实际上只还了全数的十分之一。

克劳莱太太办事不用律师。她说的很对，这件事简单得很，愿意不愿意随他们的便，因此她只让代表债主的几个律师自己去做交易。红狮广场台维滋先生的代表路易斯律师和可息多街马那息先生的代表莫斯律师（这两处是上校的主要债主）都恭维上校太太办事聪明能干，吃法律饭的人都比不过她。

利蓓加受了这样的奉承，全无骄色。她买了一瓶雪利酒和一个面包布丁，在她那间又脏又小的屋子里（她办事的时候住这样的屋子）款待对手的两个律师，分手的时候还跟他们拉手，客气得了不得。然后她马上回到大陆去找丈夫和儿子，向罗登报告他重获自由的好消息。至于小罗登呢，母亲不在的时候给她的法国女用人叶尼薇爱芙丢来丢去的不当一回事。那年轻女人看中了一个加莱军营里的兵士，老是和他混在一起，哪里还想得着小罗登呢？有一回她把孩子丢在加莱海滩上自己走掉了，小罗登差点儿没淹死。

这样，克劳莱上校夫妇回到伦敦，在梅飞厄的克生街上

they really showed the skill which must be possessed by those who would live on the resources above named.

住下来。在那里,他们才真正施展出本领来;上面所谓没有收入而能过活的人,非要有这种能耐不可。

The Subject Continued

In the first place, and as a matter of the greatest necessity, we are bound to describe how a house may be got for nothing a year. These mansions are to be had either unfurnished, where, if you have credit with Messrs. Gillows or Bantings, you can get them splendidly *morntées* and decorated entirely according to your own fancy; or they are to be let furnished; a less troublesome and complicated arrangement to most parties. It was so that Crawley and his wife preferred to hire their house.

Before Mr. Bowls came to preside over Miss Crawley's house and cellar in Park Lane, that lady had had for a butler a Mr. Raggles, who was born on the family estate of Queen's Crawley, and indeed was a younger son of a gardener there. By good conduct, a handsome person and calves, and a grave demeanour, Raggles rose from the knife-board to the foot-board of the carriage; from the foot-board to the butler's pantry. When he had been a certain number of years at the head of Miss Crawley's establishment, where he had had good wages, fat perquisites, and plenty of opportunities of saving, he announced that he was about to contract a matrimonial alliance with a late cook of Miss Crawley's, who had subsisted in an honourable manner by the exercise of a mangle, and the keeping of a small green-grocer's shop in the neighbourhood. The truth is, that the ceremony had been clandestinely performed some years back; although the news of Mr. Raggles' marriage was first brought to Miss Crawley by a little boy and girl of seven and eight years

还是本来的题目

最要紧的，我们先得描写怎么能够不出钱租房子。出租的房屋分两种：一种是不连家具的，只要吉洛士的铺子或是班丁的铺子肯让你赊账，你就能完全依照自己的意思把屋子富丽堂皇地装潢陈设起来；第二种是连家具出租的，租这种房子，为大家都省事省麻烦。克劳莱夫妇愿意租的就是这一种。

鲍尔斯在派克街管酒窖当听差头脑之前，克劳莱小姐曾经雇过一个拉哥尔斯先生。他生长在女王的克劳莱庄地上，原是本家花匠的小儿子。他品行端方，举止庄重，相貌长得整齐，小腿生得匀称，因此渐渐从洗刀叉的打杂做到站在马车背后的跟班，一直升到掌管酒窖和伙食房的总管。他在克劳莱小姐府上做了几年管事，工钱又大，外快又多，攒钱的机会也不少，便公开说要和克劳莱小姐以前的厨娘结婚。这厨娘相当体面；她有一架轧布机，附近还开了一家小小的菜蔬铺子，靠着过活。事实上他们好几年前就秘密结了婚，不过克劳莱小姐直到看见了一男一女两个孩子才知道拉哥尔斯先生成亲的事。这两个孩子一个八岁一个七

of age, whose continual presence in the kitchen had attracted the attention of Miss Briggs.

Mr. Raggles then retired and personally undertook the superintendence of the small shop and the greens. He added milk and cream, eggs and country-fed pork to his stores, contenting himself, whilst other retired butlers were vending spirits in public-houses, by dealing in the simplest country produce. And having a good connection amongst the butlers in the neighbourhood, and a snug back parlour where he and Mrs. Raggles received them, his milk, cream, and eggs got to be adopted by many of the fraternity, and his profits increased every year. Year after year he quietly and modestly amassed money, and when at length that snug and complete bachelor's residence at No. 201, Curzon Street, May Fair, lately the residence of the Honourable Frederick Deuceace, gone abroad, with its rich and appropriate furniture by the first makers, was brought to the hammer, who should go in and purchase the lease and furniture of the house but Charles Raggles? A part of the money he borrowed, it is true, and at rather a high interest, from a brother butler, but the chief part he paid down, and it was with no small pride that Mrs. Raggles found herself sleeping in a bed of carved mahogany, with silk curtains, with a prodigious cheval glass opposite to her, and a wardrobe which would contain her, and Raggles, and all the family.

Of course, they did not intend to occupy permanently an apartment so splendid. It was in order to let the house again that Raggles purchased it. As soon as a tenant was found, he subsided into the green-grocer's shop once more; but a happy thing it was for him to walk out of that tenement and into Curzon Street, and there

岁，老在他们厨房里，引起了布立葛丝小姐的注意。

此后拉哥尔斯便退休了，亲自掌管着那菜蔬铺子。除掉蔬菜以外，他又卖牛奶、奶油、鸡子儿和乡下运来的猪肉。大多数退休的管事都开酒店卖酒，他却只卖乡下的土产。附近一带的管事们都和他相熟，而且他又有个舒服的后客厅，夫妇俩常常招待他们，所以他的同僚中人替他捎去不少牛奶、奶油和鸡子儿；他的进益也就一年比一年多。他不声不响一点儿一点儿的攒钱，年年一样。梅飞厄的克生街二百零一号本来是一位弗莱特立克·杜西斯先生的公馆。这屋子很舒服，陈设也齐备，为单身汉子住家最合适。这位杜西斯先生出国去了；他这屋子的永久租赁权，连屋子里高手匠人特制的富丽合用的家具，都公开拍卖。你道出钱的是谁？竟是却尔斯·拉哥尔斯！当然，其中一部分的钱是他出了高利钱从另外一个总管那里借来的，可是大部分的钱都是自己拿出来。拉哥尔斯太太一旦睡上了镂花桃心木的床，眼看床上挂着丝绸的帐子，对面摆着大穿衣镜，衣橱大得可以把他们夫妻儿女一股脑儿都装进去，那得意就不用说了。

当然他们不准备永远住在这么讲究的房子里。拉哥尔斯买了房子是预备出租的。找着房客之后，他又搬回菜蔬铺子里去住。他从铺子里踱出来，到克生街上望望他的房子——他自己的房子——看见窗口摆着石榴红，门上装着

survey his house—his own house—with geraniums in the window and a carved bronze knocker. The footman occasionally lounging at the area railing, treated him with respect; the cook took her green stuff at his house and called him Mr. Landlord; and there was not one thing the tenants did, or one dish which they had for dinner, that Raggles might not know of, if he liked.

He was a good man; good and happy. The house brought him in so handsome a yearly income, that he was determined to send his children to good schools, and accordingly, regardless of expense, Charles was sent to boarding at Dr. Swishtail's, Sugar-cane Lodge, and little Matilda to Miss Peckover's, Laurentinum House, Clapham.

Raggles loved and adored the Crawley family as the author of all his prosperity in life. He had a silhouette of his mistress in his back shop, and a drawing of the Porter's Lodge at Queen's Crawley, done by that spinster herself in India ink—and the only addition he made to the decorations of the Curzon Street house was a print of Queen's Crawley in Hampshire, the seat of Sir Walpole Crawley, Baronet, who was represented in a gilded car drawn by six white horses, and passing by a lake covered with swans, and barges containing ladies in hoops, and musicians with flags and periwigs. Indeed Raggles thought there was no such palace in all the world, and no such august family.

As luck would have it, Raggles' house in Curzon Street was to let when Rawdon and his wife returned to London. The Colonel knew it and its owner quite well; the latter's connexion with the Crawley family had been kept up constantly, for Raggles helped Mr. Bowls when-

镂花的铜门环，在他也是一件乐事。房客的听差有时懒洋洋地在栅栏旁闲逛，碰见他总对他非常尊敬。房客的厨娘在他店里买菜蔬，称他为房东先生。只要拉哥尔斯高兴打听，房客做什么事，吃什么菜，他都能知道。

他是个好人，也是个快乐的人。房子每年的租金非常可观，因此他决计把儿女送到像样的学校里去受教育。他不惜工本，让却尔斯到甘蔗庐斯威希退尔博士那里去上学。小玛蒂尔达呢，便进了克拉本区里劳伦铁纳姆大厦佩格渥佛小姐开的女学堂。

克劳莱一家使他致富，因此他爱他们敬他们。店铺的后客厅里挂着他女主人的侧影，还有一幅钢笔画，上面是女王的克劳莱大厦的门房，还是老小姐自己的手笔。在克生街的房子里他只添了一件摆设，就是从男爵华尔泊尔·克劳莱爵士在汉泊郡女王的克劳莱庄地上的行乐图。这是一幅石印画，从男爵本人坐在一辆镀金的马车里，驾着六匹白马经过湖边；湖上满是天鹅和小船；船里的太太小姐穿着大裙子，里面还撑着鲸骨圈，音乐家们戴着假头发，打着旗子。说实话，在拉哥尔斯看来，全世界最华美的宫殿和最高贵的世家都在这里。

事有凑巧，罗登夫妇回伦敦时，克生街上拉哥尔斯的屋子恰好空着。上校对于房子和房东都很熟悉，因为拉哥尔斯一向不断地在克劳莱家里走动，每逢克劳莱小姐请客，他就来帮忙鲍尔斯伺候客人。老头儿不但把房子租给上校，

ever Miss Crawley received friends. And the old man not only let his house to the Colonel, but officiated as his butler whenever he had company; Mrs. Raggles operating in the kitchen below, and sending up dinners of which old Miss Crawley herself might have approved. This was the way, then, Crawley got his house for nothing; for though Raggles had to pay taxes and rates, and the interest of the mortgage to the brother butler; and the insurance of his life; and the charges for his children at school; and the value of the meat and drink which his own family—and for a time that of Colonel Crawley too—consumed; and though the poor wretch was utterly ruined by the transaction, his children being flung on the streets, and himself driven into the Fleet Prison: yet somebody must pay even for gentlemen who live for nothing a year—and so it was this unlucky Raggles was made the representative of Colonel Crawley's defective capital.

I wonder how many families are driven to roguery and to ruin by great practitioners in Crawley's way? —how many great noblemen rob their petty tradesmen, condescend to swindle their poor retainers out of wretched little sums, and cheat for a few shillings? When we read that a noble nobleman has left for the continent, or that another noble nobleman has an execution in his house—and that one or other owes six or seven millions, the defeat seems glorious even, and we respect the victim in the vastness of his ruin. But who pities a poor barber who can't get his money for powdering the footmen's heads; or a poor carpenter who has ruined himself by fixing up ornaments and pavilions for my lady's *dejeûner*; or the poor devil of a tailor whom the steward patronizes,

而且每逢上校请客就去替他当差；拉哥尔斯太太在底下厨房里做饭，送上去的菜肴连克劳莱老小姐都会赞赏的。这样，克劳莱一文不花地租得了房子。拉哥尔斯不但得付各种赋税和他同行总管抵押单上的利息，他自己的人寿保险费，孩子们的学杂费，一家老小的食用，而且有一段时期连克劳莱上校一家的食用也由他负担。因为这次交易，这可怜虫后来竟倾了家，他的两个孩子弄得流离失所，他自己也给关在弗利脱监狱里吃官司。原来悬空过日子的绅士也得别人代他开销家用；克劳莱上校背了债，倒霉的拉哥尔斯倒得代他受苦。

我常想不知有多少人家给克劳莱一类有本事的家伙害得倾家荡产，甚至于渐渐堕落，干坏事——不知有多少名门贵胄欺负小商人，不惜降低了身份去哄骗穷苦的厮养，诈他们几个小钱，为几个先令也肯要不老实的把戏。当我们在报上看见某某贵人到欧洲大陆去了，某某勋爵的房屋充公了，其中一人甚至于欠了六七百万镑的债等等，往往觉得他们亏空得有光彩，因为能够欠这么一大笔钱，也是令人佩服的事。至于可怜的理发司务给他们家的听差梳头洒粉，结果白辛苦一场；可怜的木匠因为太太请早饭需要大篷帐和特别的陈设，把自己弄得精穷；还有那给总管当差的裁缝，

and who has pledged all he is worth, and more, to get the liveries ready which my lord has done him the honour to bespeak? —When the great house tumbles down, these miserable wretches fall under it unnoticed: as they say in the old legends, before a man goes to the devil himself, he sends plenty of other souls thither.

Rawdon and his wife generously gave their patronage to all such of Miss Crawley's tradesmen and purveyors as chose to serve them. Some were willing enough, especially the poor ones. It was wonderful to see the pertinacity with which the washerwoman from Tooting brought the cart every Saturday, and her bills week after week. Mr. Raggles himself had to supply the green-groceries. The bill for servants' porter at the Fortune of War public-house is a curiosity in the chronicles of beer. Every servant also was owed the greater part of his wages, and thus kept up perforce an interest in the house. Nobody in fact was paid. Not the blacksmith who opened the lock; nor the glazier who mended the pane; nor the jobber who let the carriage; nor the groom who drove it; nor the butcher who provided the leg of mutton; nor the coals which roasted it; nor the cook who basted it; nor the servants who ate it: and this I am given to understand is not unfrequently the way in which people live elegantly on nothing a year.

In a little town such things cannot be done without remark. We know there the quantity of milk our neighbour takes, and espy the joint or the fowls which are going in for his dinner. So, probably, 200 and 202 in Curzon Street might know what was going on in the house between them, the servants communicating through the area-railings; but Crawley and his wife and his friends

那倒霉鬼，受了勋爵的嘱托，倾其所有，甚至于还借了债，给他们家的用人做号衣——这些做买卖的有谁同情呢？显赫的世家一旦倒坍下来，这些可怜虫倒霉鬼就给压在下面，死了也没人看见。从前有个传说里面打的譬喻很对：将要掉在魔鬼手掌心里的人，惯常总要送些别的灵魂先去遭殃。

罗登夫妇十分慷慨，凡是以前和克劳莱小姐交易的商人和买办有愿意给他们效劳的，统统答应照顾。好些买卖人家，尤其是比较穷苦的，巴不得接这注生意。有个洗衣的女人每星期六赶着车子从都丁来，账单也是每星期带着，那坚忍不拔的精神真可佩服。他们家吃的菜蔬是拉哥尔斯先生自己供给的。下人喝的麦酒经常到运道酒店去赊，那账单在麦酒史上简直算得上是件希罕物儿。用人的工钱也大半欠着，这样他们当然不肯走了。说实话，克劳莱家一样账都不付。开锁的铁匠，修窗子的玻璃匠，出租马车的车行主人，赶车的车夫，供给他们羊腿的屠户，卖煤给他们烤羊腿的煤店老板，在羊腿上洒粉铺盐滴油的厨子，吃羊腿的用人，谁都拿不到钱。据说没有收入的人往往用这种方法过好日子。

在小市镇上，这类事情少不得引起别人的注意。邻居喝了多少牛奶，我们知道，他晚饭吃肉还是吃鸡吃鸭，我们也看见。克生街二百号和二百零二号的住户，有家里的用人隔着栅栏传信，大概对于他们隔壁屋子里的情形知道得很清楚。好在克劳莱夫妇和他们的朋友并不认得这两家。

did not know 200 and 202. When you came to 201 there was a hearty welcome, a kind smile, a good dinner, and a jolly shake of the hand from the host and hostess there, just for all the world, as if they had been undisputed masters of three or four thousand a year —and so they were, not in money, but in produce and labour—if they did not pay for the mutton, they had it: if they did not give bullion in exchange for their wine, how should we know? Never was better claret at any man's table than at honest Rawdon's; dinners more gay and neatly served. His drawing-rooms were the prettiest, little, modest salons conceivable: they were decorated with the greatest taste, and a thousand knick-knacks from Paris, by Rebecca: and when she sate at her piano trilling songs with a lightsome heart, the stranger voted himself in a little paradise of domestic comfort, and agreed that if the husband was rather stupid, the wife was charming, and the dinners the pleasantest in the world.

Rebecca's wit, cleverness, and flippancy, made her speedily the vogue in London among a certain class. You saw demure chariots at her door, out of which stepped very great people. You beheld her carriage in the Park, surrounded by dandies of note. The little box in the third tier of the Opera was crowded with heads constantly changing; but it must be confessed that the ladies held aloof from her, and that their doors were shut to our little adventurer.

With regard to the world of female fashion and its customs, the present writer of course can only speak at second hand. A man can no more penetrate or understand those mysteries than he can know what the ladies talk about when they go up-stairs after dinner. It is only

你到二百零一号里去，主人和主妇脸上总挂着笑，诚诚恳恳地欢迎你，怪亲热的跟你拉手，还请你享用丰盛的酒菜。他们对所有的人都是这样，仿佛他们一年稳稳的有三四千镑进款。事实上他们虽然没有这么多现钱，享用的人力物力也确实抵得过这个数目。羊肉虽没有出钱去买，反正总有得吃；好酒虽然没有用金银去换，外面人也不会知道。老实的罗登家里请客，喝的红酒是最上等的，菜肴上得整齐，空气也融洽，谁家比得过他呢？他的客厅并不富丽，却是小巧精致，说不出有多好看。利蓓加把里面布置得非常文雅，搁了好些巴黎带回来的小摆设。陌生人看见她无忧无虑地坐在钢琴旁边唱歌，总觉得这是美满家庭，人间乐园，做丈夫的虽然蠢些，那妻子却实在可爱，而且每逢请客，都是宾主尽欢的。

利蓓加人又聪明，口角又俏皮，喜欢油嘴滑舌地说笑话，在伦敦自有一等人捧她，立刻就成了这些人里面的尖儿。她门前常常停着一辆辆马车，行止十分掩密，里面走出来的全是大阔人。她常常在公园兜风，马车旁边挤满了有名的花花公子。她在歌剧院三层楼有个小包厢，里面总有一大堆人，而且每次不同。可是说句实话，所有的太太看她不是正经货，从来不和她打交道。

关于太太小姐堆里的风气和习惯，写书的当然只能间接听见一些。这里面的奥妙，男人不能领会理解，譬如她们晚饭以后在楼上说些什么话，先生们就无从知道，这道理是

by inquiry and perseverance, that one sometimes gets hints of those secrets; and by a similar diligence every person who treads the Pall Mall pavement and frequents the clubs of this metropolis, knows, either through his own experience or through some acquaintance with whom he plays at billiards or shares the joint, something about the genteel world of London, and how, as there are men (such as Rawdon Crawley, whose position we mentioned before) who cut a good figure to the eyes of the ignorant world and to the apprentices in the Park, who behold them consorting with the most notorious dandies there, so there are ladies, who may be called men's women, being welcomed entirely by all the gentlemen, and cut or slighted by all their wives. Mrs. Firebrace is of this sort; the lady with the beautiful fair ringlets whom you see every day in Hyde Park, surrounded by the greatest and most famous dandies of this empire. Mrs. Rockwood is another, whose parties are announced laboriously in the fashionable newspapers, and with whom you see that all sorts of ambassadors and great noblemen dine; and many more might be mentioned had they to do with the history at present in hand. But while simple folks who are out of the world, or country people with a taste for the genteel, behold these ladies in their seeming glory in public places, or envy them from afar off, persons who are better instructed could inform them that these envied ladies have no more chance of establishing themselves in "Society," than the benighted squire's wife in Somersetshire, who reads of their doings in the *Morning post*. Men living about London are aware of these awful truths. You hear how pitilessly many ladies of seeming rank and wealth are excluded from this "Society". The frantic ef-

一样的。你只有不断地细心打听，才能偶然长些见识。同样的，常在帕尔莫尔街上走动，在伦敦各个俱乐部里出入的人，只要肯下功夫，对于时髦场上的情形自然也会熟悉起来。有时是亲身的经验，有时是和人打弹子或吃饭听见的闲话，都能供给你不少资料。譬如说，天下有一种像罗登·克劳莱一类的家伙（他的身份上文已经表过），在一般局外人和那些呆在公园学时髦的新手看起来，真是非常了不起，因为他竟能和最出风头的花花公子混在一起。又有一种女人，先生们都欢迎，他们的太太却瞧不起，甚至于不理睬。法爱白蕾丝太太就属于这种人，你在海德公园每天都能看见她，一头美丽的金头发梳成一卷一卷，到东到西有国内最闻名的豪华公子们簇拥着。另外还有一个洛克乌德太太，每逢她请客，时髦的报纸上便细细地登载着宴会花絮，王公大使都是她的座上客。此外还有好些别的人，可是和本文无关，不必说了。好些不知世务的老实人，喜欢学时髦的乡下佬，看见她们摆的虚场面，远远地瞧着只觉得眼红，明白底细的人，却知道这些给人羡慕的太太原来在“上流社会”是一无地位的。在涩默赛脱郡的不见世面的地主老婆，当然只能在《晨报》上读读她们请客作乐的消息，可是两下里比较起来，她们踏进“上流社会”的机会并不能比乡下女人多些。这些可怕的事实，住在伦敦的人都知道。原来这类表面上尊荣富贵的夫人们毫不留情地给圈在“上流社会”之

forts which they make to enter this circle, the meannesses to which they submit, the insults which they undergo, are matters of wonder to those who take human or womankind for a study; and the pursuit of fashion under difficulties would be a fine theme for any very great person who had the wit, the leisure, and the knowledge of the English language necessary for the compiling of such a history.

Now the few female acquaintances whom Mrs. Crawley had known abroad, not only declined to visit her when she came to this side of the channel, but cut her severely when they met in public places. It was curious to see how the great ladies forgot her, and no doubt not altogether a pleasant study to Rebecca. When Lady Bareacres met her in the waiting-room at the Opera, she gathered her daughters about her as if they would be contaminated by a touch of Becky, and retreating a step or two, placed herself in front of them, and stared at her little enemy. To stare Becky out of countenance required a severer glance than even the frigid old Bareacres could shoot out of her dismal eyes. When Lady de la Mole, who had ridden a score of times by Becky's side at Brussels, met Mrs. Crawley's open carriage in Hyde Park, her Ladyship was quite blind, and could not in the least recognise her former friend. Even Mrs. Blenkinsop, the banker's wife, cut her at church. Becky went regularly to church now; it was edifying to see her enter there with Rawdon by her side, carrying a couple of large gilt prayer-books, and afterwards going through the ceremony with the gravest resignation.

Rawdon at first felt very acutely the slights which were passed upon his wife, and was inclined to be gloomy

外。凡是研究心理学——尤其是女人的心理学——的人，看见她们千方百计地想挤进去，使尽多少下流的伎俩，受尽多少侮辱委屈，准会觉得奇怪。她们不怕艰难追求虚荣的故事，倒是写书的好题目。凡是笔下流利，文章写得俏皮，又有闲空，能够当得下这重任的大作家，不妨把这些事迹编录下来。

克劳莱太太在外国结交的几个朋友，一过了英吉利海峡，不但不来拜访她，而且在公共场所对她不瞅不睬。真奇怪，贵夫人们都不记得她了。利蓓加见她们把自己忘得这么快，自然很不高兴。有一回贝亚爱格思夫人在歌剧院的休息室里看见蓓基，立刻把女儿们叫拢来，仿佛一碰着蓓基便会玷污了她们。她退后一两步，站在女儿们前面，对她的冤家瞪着眼瞧。可惜连贝亚爱格思老太婆冷冰冰的态度和恶狠狠的眼光也还不能叫蓓基脸上下不来。特拉莫尔夫人在布鲁塞尔常常和蓓基一起坐着马车出去兜风，总有二十来次，不想到了海德公园，她明明碰见蓓基坐在敞篷车里，却像瞎了眼睛似的不认得老朋友了。连银行家的妻子白兰金索泊太太在教堂里遇见她也不打个招呼。如今蓓基按时上教堂，罗登手里拿着两大本金边圣书，跟在旁边。她态度端庄，一副逆来顺受的样子，叫人看着感动。

起初的时候，罗登见别人瞧不起他的妻子，心里又气又

and savage. He talked of calling out the husbands or brothers of every one of the insolent women who did not pay a proper respect to his wife; and it was only by the strongest commands and entreaties on her part, that he was brought into keeping a decent behaviour. "you can't shoot me into society," she said, good-naturedly. "Remember, my dear, that I was but a governess, and you, you poor silly old man, have the worst reputation for debt, and dice, and all sorts of wickedness. We shall get quite as many friends as we want by and by, and in the meanwhile you must be a good boy, and obey your schoolmistress in everything she tells you to do. When we heard that your aunt had left almost everything to Pitt and his wife, do you remember what a rage you were in? You would have told all Paris, if I had not made you keep your temper, and where would you have been now? —in prison at Ste. Pélagie for debt, and not established in London in a handsome house, with every comfort about you—you were in such a fury you were ready to murder your brother, you wicked Cain you, and what good would have come of remaining angry? All the rage in the world won't get us your aunt's money; and it is much better that we should be friends with your brother's family than enemies, as those foolish Butes are. When your father dies, Queen's Crawley will be a pleasant house for you and me to pass the winter in. If we are ruined, you can carve and take charge of the stable, and I can be a governess to Lady Jane's children. Ruined! fiddlededee! I will get you a good place before that; or Pitt and his little boy will die, and we will be Sir Rawdon and my lady. While there is life, there is hope, my dear, and I intend to make a man of you yet. Who sold your horses

闷，十分难受。他说这些混账的女人既然不尊敬他的妻子，他打算和她们的丈夫或是兄弟一个个决斗。还算蓓基软骗硬吓，才没有让他惹出祸来。她脾气真好，说道："你不能靠放枪把我放进上流社会里去。亲爱的，别忘了我不过是个女教师，你这可怜的傻东西名誉又不好，人家都知道你爱赌，爱欠账，还有许多说不完的毛病。将来咱们爱交多少朋友都行，可是眼前呢，你得乖乖地听着老师的话，她叫你怎么着你就怎么着。你还记得吗？一起头的时候，咱们听说你姑妈把财产差不多一股脑儿都传给了毕脱夫妻俩，你多生气呀！若不是我叫你管着你那性子，整个巴黎都会知道这件事情了。然后怎么样？你准会给关进圣·贝拉齐监牢里去，因为你付不出账。到那时你还能回到伦敦来住好房子，过好日子吗？你，你这可恶的该隐①！气得恨不得把你哥哥马上杀死。生气有什么用？你生了天大的气也不能把姑妈的钱拿过来。跟你哥哥作对没有好处，还是交个朋友有用。咱们可不能像别德一家子那么糊涂。你父亲死了以后，我跟你可以上女王的克劳莱过冬，那房子舒服得很呢。倘或咱们弄得两手空空，你还能替他们切切鸡鸭，管管马房，我就做吉恩夫人孩子们的女教师。两手空空！哼哼！我总会给你找个好饭碗，再不，毕脱和他儿子也许会死掉，咱们就做罗登爵士和爵士夫人。亲爱的，一个人活着就有希望，我还打算叫你干一番事业呢。是谁替你卖了马，谁给

① 《圣经》中杀弟的恶人。

for you? Who paid your debts for you?" Rawdon was obliged to confess that he owed all these benefits to his wife, and to trust himself to her guidance for the future.

Indeed, when Miss Crawley quitted the world, and that money for which all her relatives had been fighting so eagerly was finally left to Pitt, Bute Crawley, who found that only five thousand pounds had been left to him instead of the twenty upon which he calculated, was in such a fury at his disappointment, that he vented it in savage abuse upon his nephew; and the quarrel always rankling between them ended in an utter breach of intercourse. Rawdon Crawley's conduct, on the other hand, who got but a hundred pounds, was such as to astonish his brother and delight his sister-in-law, who was disposed to look kindly upon all the members of her husband's family. He wrote to his brother a very frank, manly, good-humoured letter from Paris. He was aware, he said, that by his own marriage he had forfeited his aunt's favour; and though he did not disguise his disappointment that she should have been so entirely relentless towards him, he was glad that the money was still kept in their branch of the family, and heartily congratulated his brother on his good fortune. He sent his affectionate remembrances to his sister, and hoped to have her good-will for Mrs. Rawdon; and the letter concluded with a postscript to Pitt in the latter lady's own handwriting. She, too, begged to join in her husband's congratulations. She should ever remember Mr. Crawley's kindness to her in early days when she was a friendless orphan, the instructress of his little sisters, in whose welfare she still took the tenderest interest. She wished him every happiness in his married life, and, asking his permission to

你还了账的?”罗登只得承认这些都是妻子赏给他的恩惠,答应将来永远依照她的指示做人。

克劳莱小姐去世之后,亲戚们气势汹汹争夺的财产到了毕脱手里,别德·克劳莱原来预料可以得二万镑,结果只到手五千镑,失望气恼得发昏,只好把大侄儿毒骂一顿出气。他们两房本来一向心里不和,到那时便断绝来往了。罗登·克劳莱只拿到一百镑,而他的态度却大方得叫他哥哥诧异。他嫂子本来就对婆家的人很有好意,所以更觉得喜欢。罗登从巴黎寄给哥哥的信口气诚恳直爽,并没有表示半点不乐意。他说他早已知道由于婚姻问题失了姑妈的欢心;姑妈的狠心虽然使他失望,不过财产仍旧传给自己一支的近亲,总是好的。他诚诚心心地向哥哥道喜,又很亲热地问候嫂子,希望她将来提携自己的太太。信尾附着蓓基自己写给毕脱的几句话。她也跟他道喜;她说克劳莱先生从前十分照顾她那样一个无依无靠的孤儿,是她永远不会忘记的。她做女教师管教了毕脱的妹妹们一场,至今关心

offer her remembrances to Lady Jane (of whose goodness all the world informed her), she hoped that one day she might be allowed to present her little boy to his uncle and aunt, and begged to bespeak for him their good-will and protection.

Pitt Crawley received this communication very graciously—more graciously than Miss Crawley had received some of Rebecca's previous compositions in Rawdon's hand-writing; and as for Lady Jane, she was so charmed with the letter that she expected her husband would instantly divide her aunt's legacy into two equal portions, and send off one-half to his brother at Paris.

To her ladyship's surprise, however, Pitt declined to accommodate his brother with a cheque for thirty thousand pounds. But he made Rawdon a handsome offer of his hand whenever the latter should come to England and choose to take it; and, thanking Mrs. Crawley for her good opinion of himself and Lady Jane, he graciously pronounced his willingness to take any opportunity to serve her little boy.

Thus an almost reconciliation was brought about between the brothers. When Rebecca came to town Pitt and his wife were not in London. Many a time she drove by the old door in Park Lane to see whether they had taken possession of Miss Crawley's house there. But the new family did not make its appearance; it was only through Raggles that she heard of their movements—how Miss Crawley's domestics had been dismissed with decent gratuities, and how Mr. Pitt had only once made his appearance in London, when he stopped for a few days at the house, did business with his lawyers there, and sold off all Miss Crawley's French novels to a bookseller out of Bond

她们的前途。她希望他婚后快乐，请他代自己向吉恩夫人致意，说是到处听见别人称扬她的好处。她希望有一天能够带着儿子去拜望大伯和伯母，还恳求他们对于那孩子多多照应。

毕脱·克劳莱收到这封信，对弟弟弟妇这番好意很赞赏。从前克劳莱小姐也曾经收过好几封这样的信，全是利蓓加起了稿子叫罗登抄的，她可没有这样宽大。吉恩夫人看完了信，十分欢喜，以为她丈夫马上就会把姑母的遗产平分为二，送一半到巴黎给弟弟去花。

后来吉恩夫人很诧异，原来毕脱并不愿意送一张三万镑的支票给他弟弟，可是他很大方地回信说如果罗登回国以后需要他帮忙的话，他很愿意出力。他又向克劳莱太太表示感激她对自己和吉恩夫人的好意，侄儿将来需要照料，他当然肯尽力的。

这么一来，两兄弟差不多算是言归于好。利蓓加到伦敦的时候，毕脱夫妇不在城里。她时常特地赶着车走过派克街克劳莱小姐的房子，看他们有没有住进去，可是他们一家总不露脸，她只能在拉哥尔斯那里打听他们的动静。据说克劳莱小姐的用人都得到丰厚的赏钱给打发掉了；毕脱先生只到伦敦来过一回，在公馆里耽搁了几天，和他律师办了些事情，把克劳莱小姐的法文小说统统都卖给邦德街上

Street. Becky had reasons of her own which caused her to long for the arrival of her new relation. "When Lady Jane comes," thought she, "she shall be my sponsor in London society; and as for the women! bah! the women will ask me when they find the men want to see me."

An article as necessary to a lady in this position as her brougham or her bouquet, is her companion. I have always admired the way in which the tender creatures, who cannot exist without sympathy, hire an exceedingly plain friend of their own sex from whom they are almost inseparable. The sight of that inevitable woman in her faded gown seated behind her dear friend in the opera-box, or occupying the back seat of the barouche, is always a wholesome and moral one to me, as jolly a reminder as that of the Death's-head which figured in the repasts of Egyptian *bon-vivants*, a strange sardonic memorial of Vanity Fair. What? —even battered, brazen, beautiful, conscienceless, heartless Mrs. Firebrace, whose father died of her shame: even lovely, daring Mrs. Mantrap, who will ride at any fence which any man in England will take, and who drives her greys in the Park, while her mother keeps a huxter's stall in Bath still;—even those who are so bold, one might fancy they could face anything, dare not face the world without a female friend. They must have somebody to cling to, the affectionate creatures! And you will hardly see them in any public place without a shabby companion in a dyed silk, sitting somewhere in the shade close behind them.

"Rawdon," said Becky, very late one night, as a party of gentlemen were seated round her crackling drawing-room fire (for the men came to her house to finish the night; and she had ice and coffee for them, the best

一家书铺子。蓓基急着要认新亲是有道理的。她想:“吉恩夫人来了之后,就能替我在伦敦上流社会里撑腰。哼!那些太太们发现男人爱跟我周旋,还能不请我吗?”

在她地位上的女人,除了马车和花球之外,到处跟着伺候的女伴也是必不可少的。那些温柔的小东西往往雇着相貌丑陋的女伴,形影不离地在一起,好像她们没有同情就不能活下去,我看了非常赞赏。做伴儿的穿着褪色的旧衣裳,老是跟着好朋友坐在戏院包厢的后排或是马车的倒座上,我认为真是能够整顿风气的好榜样,譬如爱享福的埃及人一面吃喝,一面还叫当差的托着个骷髅出来兜一圈。这女伴跟骷髅一样,使人记得在名利场上混了一世不过是这样下场,倒是对于人生的一个讽刺。真奇怪,拿着漂亮的法爱白雷丝太太来说,真可以说是个钝皮老脸、久经风霜、全没心肝的女人,她的父亲甚至于为她活活气死;还有那风流放荡的孟脱拉浦太太,骑马跳栏的本领比得过英国任何男人,她在公园里亲自赶着灰色马儿兜风,她的母亲仍旧在温泉摆个小摊子过活——你总以为这么大胆的人物,该是天不怕地不怕的了,不想连她们都得由女伴陪着才敢露脸。原来这些热心肠的小东西没有朋友依傍着是不行的。她们在公共场所出入的时候,差不多总有女伴陪着。这些人样子寒酸,穿着染过色的绸衣服,坐在离她们不远、人家不着眼的地方。

有一晚,夜已深了,一群男人坐在蓓基客厅里的壁炉旁边烤火,炉里的火毕剥毕剥的响。男人们都喜欢到她家里度黄昏,她就请他们享用全伦敦最讲究的冰淇淋和咖啡。

in London):"I must have a sheep-dog."

"A what?"said Rawdon, looking up from an *écarté* table.

"A sheep-dog!" said young Lord Southdown. "My dear Mrs. Crawley, what a fancy! Why not have a Danish dog? I know of one as big as a camel-leopard, by Jove. It would almost pull your brougham. Or a Persian greyhound, eh? (I propose, if you please); or a little pug that would go into one of Lord Steyne's snuff-boxes? There's a man at Bayswater got one with such a nose that you might—I mark the king and play—that you might hang your hat on it."

"I mark the trick,"Rawdon gravely said. He attended to his game commonly, and didn't much meddle with the conversation except when it was about horses and betting.

"What *can* you want with a shepherd's dog?" the lively little Southdown continued.

"I mean a *moral* shepherd's dog,"said Becky, laughing, and looking up at Lord Steyne.

"What the devil's that?"said his Lordship.

"A dog to keep the wolves off me,"Rebecca continued. "A companion."

"Dear little innocent lamb, you want one,"said the Marquis; and his jaw thrust out, and he began to grin hideously, his little eyes leering towards Rebecca.

The great Lord of Steyne was standing by the fire sipping coffee. The fire crackled and blazed pleasantly. There were a score of candles sparkling round the mantelpiece, in all sorts of quaint sconces, of gilt and bronze and porcelain. They lighted up Rebecca's figure to admiration, as she sat on a sofa covered with a pattern of

蓓基说道:“罗登,我要一只看羊狗。”

罗登正在牌桌上玩埃加脱,抬头问道:“一只什么?”

莎吴塞唐勋爵也道:“看羊狗!亲爱的克劳莱太太,你这心思好古怪。为什么不养丹麦狗呢?我看见过一条丹麦狗大得像一只长颈鹿,喝!差一点儿就能拉你的马车了。要不,就找一只波斯猎狗也好,你看怎么样?(对不起,这次该我开牌。)还有一种小哈巴狗,小得可以搁在斯丹恩勋爵的鼻烟壶里。在贝思活脱有一个人,他有一只小狗,那鼻子——我记点了,是皇帝——那鼻子上可以挂帽子。”

罗登一本正经说道:“这一圈的牌都由我记点儿罢。”往常他只注意斗牌,除非大家谈到马和赌博,他对于别人说的话全不留心。

活泼的莎吴塞唐接下去说道:“你要看羊狗做什么?”

“我所说的看羊狗不过是比喻。”蓓基一面说,一面笑着抬头望望斯丹恩勋爵。

勋爵道:“见鬼!你是什么意思?”

利蓓加道:“有了狗,豺狼就不能近身了。我要个女伴。”

勋爵道:“亲爱的小羔羊,你多么纯洁,真需要一只看羊狗来保护你。”他伸出下巴涎着脸儿笑起来,也斜着一双小眼睛对她一溜,那样子难看极了。

了不起的斯丹恩侯爵站在火旁边喝咖啡。炉里的火烧得正旺,毕剥毕剥的响,越显得屋子里舒服。壁炉周围亮着二十来支蜡烛;墙上的蜡台各个不同,式样别致,有铜的,有瓷的,有镀金的。利蓓加坐在一张花色鲜艳的安乐椅上,蜡烛光照着她,把她的身材越发衬得好看。她穿一件娇嫩得

gaudy flowers. She was in a pink dress, that looked as fresh as a rose; her dazzling white arms and shoulders were half covered with a thin hazy scarf through which they sparkled; her hair hung in curls round her neck; one of her little feet peeped out from the fresh crisp folds of the silk: the prettiest little foot in the prettiest little sandal in the finest silk stocking in the world.

The candles lighted up Lord Steyne's shining bald head, which was fringed with red hair. He had thick bushy eyebrows, with little twinkling bloodshot eyes, surrounded by a thousand wrinkles. His jaw was underhung, and when he laughed, two white buck-teeth protruded themselves and glistened savagely in the midst of the grin. He had been dining with royal personages, and wore his garter and ribbon. A short man was his Lordship, broad-chested, and bow-legged, but proud of the fineness of his foot and ankle, and always caressing his garter-knee.

"And so the Shepherd is not enough," said he, "to defend his lambkin?"

"The Shepherd is too fond of playing at cards and going to his clubs," answered Becky, laughing.

"Gad, what a debauched Corydon!" said my lord—"what a mouth for a pipe!"

"I take your three to two," here said Rawdon, at the card-table.

"Hark at Meliboeus," snarled the noble Marquis; "he's pastorally occupied too: he's shearing a Southdown. What an innocent mutton, hey? Damme, what a snowy fleecce!"

Rebecca's eyes shot out gleams of scornful humour. "My lord," she said, "you are a knight of the Order." He

像玫瑰花一般的粉红袍子；肩膀和胳膊白得耀眼，上面半披着一条云雾似的透明纱巾，白皮肤在下面隐隐发亮。她的头发卷成圈儿挂在颈边；一层层又松又挺的新绸裙子底下露出一只美丽的小脚，脚上穿的是最细的丝袜和最漂亮的镂空鞋。

蜡烛光把斯丹恩勋爵的秃脑袋照得发亮，脑袋上还留着一圈红头发。他的眉毛又浓又粗，底下两只的溜骨碌的小眼睛，上面布满红丝，眼睛周围千缕万条的皱纹。他的下半张脸往外突出，张开口就看见两只雪白的暴牙。每逢他对人嬉皮扯脸一笑，那两个暴牙就直发亮，看上去很可怕。那天他刚在宫中领过宴，身上戴着勋章挂着绶带。他大人是个矮个子，宽宽的胸脯，一双罗圈腿。他对于自己的细脚踝和小脚板非常得意，又不住地抚摩自己左膝盖底下的勋章。[①]

他说："原来有了放羊的还不够照顾他的小羔羊？"

蓓基笑着答道："放羊的太爱打牌，又老是上俱乐部去。"

勋爵道："天哪！好个腐败的考里同！[②] 他的嘴就配衔烟斗。"

罗登在牌桌上说道："我跟你二对三。"

高贵的侯爵喝道："听听这梅里勃斯[③]，他倒的确在尽他看羊人的本分，正在剪莎吴塞唐的羊毛呢[④]。喝！这头羊倒容易上当得很。你瞧他好一身雪白的羊毛！"

利蓓加对他瞅了一眼，那表情很幽默，却又有些嘲笑的

---

① 英国的嘉德勋章是箍在左腿上的。

② 维吉尔及底渥克立斯等拉丁诗人诗里的牧羊人，现在成为牧羊人的通称。

③ 维吉尔《牧歌》中牧羊人的名字。

④ 骗别人的钱就说"剪某某的羊毛"。

had the collar round his neck, indeed—a gift of the restored Princes of Spain.

Lord Steyne in early life had been notorious for his daring and his success at play. He had sat up two days and two nights with Mr. Fox at hazard. He had won money of the most august personages of the realm: he had won his marquisate, it was said, at the gaming-table; but he did not like an allusion to those by-gone *fredaines*. Rebecca saw the scowl gathering over his heavy brow.

She rose up from her sofa, and went and took his coffee-cup out of his hand with a little curtsey. "Yes," she said, "I must get a watchdog. But he won't bark at *you*." And, going into the other drawing-room, she sat down to the piano, and began to sing little French songs in such a charming, thrilling voice, that the mollified nobleman speedily followed her into that chamber, and might be seen nodding his head and bowing time over her.

Rawdon and his friend meanwhile played *écarté* until they had enough. The Colonel won; but, say that he won ever so much and often, nights like these, which occurred many times in the week—his wife having all the talk and all the admiration, and he sitting silent without the circle, not comprehending a word of the jokes, the allusions, the mystical language within, must have been rather wearisome to the ex-dragoon.

"How is Mrs. Crawley's husband?" Lord Steyne used to say to him by way of a good-day when they met: and indeed that was now his avocation in life. He was Colonel Crawley no more. He was Mrs. Crawley's husband.

意味,说道:“勋爵,您还不是得了金羊毛勋章吗”这话倒是真的,那时他脖子上还套着勋章,是复辟的西班牙亲王们送给他的礼物。

原来斯丹恩勋爵早年出名的胆大,赌钱的本领是了不起的。他和福克斯先生曾经连赌两天两夜。国内最尊贵的大人物都输过钱给他。据说他的爵位也是牌桌上赢来的。可是别人说起他年轻时候捣鬼淘气的事情,他却不爱听。利蓓加看见他的浓眉毛皱在一起,一脸不高兴的样子。

她从椅子上站起来,走过去接了他的咖啡杯子,稍微屈了一屈膝道:“说真话,我非找一只看羊狗不可,不过它不会对你咬。”她走到另外一间客厅里,坐在琴旁边唱起法文歌来,那声音婉转动人,听得那爵爷心都软了,立刻跟过来。他一面听唱歌,一面和着拍子点头弯腰。

罗登和他的朋友两个人玩埃加脱,一直玩到兴尽为止。上校是赢家,可是虽然他赢的次数又多,数目又大,而且像这样的请客每星期总有好几回,这前任的骑兵一定觉得很气闷;因为所有的谈话和客人的赞叹都给他太太一个人占了去,他只能悄悄默默地坐在圈子外面,这些人说的笑话,援引的典故,用的希奇古怪的字眼,他一点儿也不懂。

斯丹恩勋爵碰见他和他招呼的时候,总是说:“克劳莱太太的丈夫好哇?”说真的,这就是他的职业——他不再是克劳莱上校,只是克劳莱太太的丈夫。

About the little Rawdon, if nothing has been said all this while, it is because he is hidden up-stairs in a garret somewhere, or has crawled below into the kitchen for companionship. His mother scarcely ever took notice of him. He passed the days with his French *bonne* as long as that domestic remained in Mr. Crawley's family, and when the Frenchwoman went away, the little fellow, howling in the loneliness of the night, had compassion taken on him by a housemaid, who took him out of his solitary nursery into her bed in the garret hard by, and comforted him.

Rebecca, my Lord Steyne, and one or two more were in the drawing-room taking tea after the Opera, when this shouting was heard overhead. "It's my cherub crying for his nurse," she said. She did not offer to move to go and see the child. "Don't agitate your feelings by going to look for him," said Lord Steyne sardonically. "Bah!" replied the other, with a sort of blush, "he'll cry himself to sleep"; and they fell to talking about the Opera.

Rawdon had stolen off, though, to look after his son and heir; and came back to the company when he found that honest Dolly was consoling the child. The Colonel's dressing-room was in those upper regions. He used to see the boy there in private. They had interviews together every morning when he shaved; Rawdon minor sitting on a box by his father's side and watching the operation with never-ceasing pleasure. He and the sire were great friends. The father would bring him sweetmeats from the dessert, and hide them in a certain old epaulet box, where the child went to seek them, and laughed with joy on discovering the treasure: laughed, but not too loud: for mamma was below asleep and must not be disturbed. She

我们为什么好久没有提起小罗登呢，只为他不是躲在阁楼上，便是钻到楼下厨房里找伴儿去了。他的母亲差不多从来不理会他。他的法国女用人在克劳莱家里的一阵子，他便跟着她。后来那法国女人走了，这孩子夜里没有人陪伴，哇哇地啼哭。总算家里的一个女用人可怜他，把他从冷清清的育儿室抱出来，带到近旁的阁楼里，哄着他睡在自己的床上。

他在楼上啼哭的当儿，利蓓加，斯丹恩勋爵，还有两三个别的客人，恰巧看了歌剧回来，在楼底下喝茶。利蓓加道："这是我的小宝贝要他的用人，在那儿哭呢。"嘴里这么说，却不动身上去看看。斯丹恩勋爵带着冷笑的口气说道："你不必去看他了，省得叫你自己心神不安。"蓓基脸上讪讪的答道："得了，他哭哭就会睡着的。"接下去大家就议论起刚才看的歌剧来。

只有罗登偷偷地溜上去看他的儿子，他见忠厚的桃立在安慰孩子，才又回到客人堆里来。上校的梳妆室在最高一层，他时常私底下和孩子见面。每天早晨他刮胡子，父子俩便在一起。小罗登坐在父亲身旁一只箱子上看父亲刮胡子，再也看不厌。他和父亲两个非常好，做父亲的时常把甜点心留下一点儿藏在一只从前搁肩饰的匣子里，孩子总到那里去找吃的，找着以后便乐得直笑。他虽然快乐，却不敢放声大笑，因为妈妈在楼下睡觉，不能吵醒她。她睡得很

did not go to rest till very late, and seldom rose till after noon.

Rawdon bought the boy plenty of picture-books, and crammed his nursery with toys. Its walls were covered with pictures pasted up by the father's own hand, and purchased by him for ready money. When he was off duty with Mrs. Rawdon in the Park, he would sit up here, passing hours with the boy; who rode on his chest, who pulled his great mustachios as if they were driving-reins, and spent days with him in indefatigable gambols. The room was a low room, and once, when the child was not five years old, his father, who was tossing him wildly up in his arms, hit the poor little chap's skull so violently against the ceiling that he almost dropped the child, so terrified was he at the disaster.

Rawdon minor had made up his face for a tremendous howl—the severity of the blow indeed authorised that indulgence: but just as he was going to begin, the father interposed.

"For God's sake, Rawdy, don't wake mamma," he cried. And the child, looking in a very hard and piteous way at his father, bit his lips, clenched his hands, and didn't cry a bit. Rawdon told that story at the clubs, at the mess, to everybody in town. "By Gad, sir," he explained to the public in general, "what a good-plucked one that boy of mine is—what a trump he is! I half sent his head through the ceiling, by Gad, and he wouldn't cry for fear of disturbing his mother."

Sometimes—once or twice in a week—that lady visited the upper regions in which the child lived. She came in like a vivified figure out of the *Magasin des Modes*—blandly smiling in the most beautiful new clothes and

晚，难得在中午之前起床。

罗登买了许多图画书给儿子，又在育儿室塞满了各种玩具。墙上满是画儿，都是他出现钱买来，亲手粘上的。有时罗登太太在公园兜风，用不着他在旁边伺候，他就上楼陪着孩子一玩几个钟头。孩子骑在他身上，把他的大胡子拉着当马缰，连日跟他两个揪呀，滚呀，永远不觉得累。那间屋子很低；有一年，孩子还不到五岁，父亲把他抱起来抛上抛下闹着玩，把小可怜儿的头顶砰的一声撞在天花板上。罗登吓得要命，差点儿又把他掉在地上。

小罗登皱起脸儿准备大哭——那一下撞得实在厉害，怪不得他要哭。他刚要开口的时候，他父亲急得叫道："老天哪，罗迪，别吵醒了妈妈。"孩子怪可怜的紧紧瞅着父亲；他咬着嘴唇，握着拳头，一声儿都没有哼出来。罗登把这事讲给俱乐部的人听，讲给军营食堂里的人听，逢人便告诉说："喝！我的儿子真有胆子，真了不起。天哪，我把他半个脑袋都插进天花板里去了，可是他怕吵醒妈妈，一点儿也不哭。"

有的时候——一星期里有那么一两回——那位太太也上楼到孩子房里来看看他。她简直像时装画报里的美人变活了，总是穿着漂亮的新衣服、新靴子，戴着新手套，很温和

little gloves and boots. Wonderful scarfs, laces, and jewels glittered about her. She had always a new bonnet on: and flowers bloomed perpetually in it: or else magnificent curling ostrich feathers, soft and snowy as camellias. She nodded twice or thrice patronizingly to the little boy, who looked up from his dinner or from the pictures of soldiers he was painting. When she left the room, an odour of rose, or some other magical fragrance, lingered about the nursery. She was an unearthly being in his eyes, superior to his father—to all the world: to be worshipped and admired at a distance. To drive with that lady in the carriage was an awful rite: he sat up in the back seat, and did not dare to speak: he gazed with all his eyes at the beautifully dressed princess opposite to him. Gentlemen on splendid prancing horses came up, and smiled and talked with her. How her eyes beamed upon all of them! Her hand used to quiver and wave gracefully as they passed. When he went out with her he had his new red dress on. His old brown holland was good enough when he stayed at home. Sometimes, when she was away, and Dolly his maid was making his bed, he came into his mother's room. It was as the abode of a fairy to him—a mystic chamber of splendour and delights. There in the wardrobe hung those wonderful robes—pink and blue, and many-tinted. There was the jewel-case, silver-clasped: and the wondrous bronze hand on the dressing-table, glistening all over with a hundred rings. There was the cheval-glass, that miracle of art, in which he could just see his own wondering head, and the reflection of Dolly (queerly distorted, and as if up in the ceiling), plumping and patting the pillows of the bed. O thou poor lonely little benighted boy! Mother is the name for God

地微笑着。她身上有美丽的披肩和花边，还有晶晶发亮的珠宝首饰。她每次上楼，总戴着新帽子，帽子上老是簪着花朵儿，不然就挂着弯弯的鸵鸟毛，又白又软，像一簇茶花，看上去真是富丽堂皇。她公主娘娘似的向孩子点点头，孩子有时在吃饭，有时在画大兵，抬起头来对她望着。她走开之后，屋里总留了一股子玫瑰香味，或是别的迷人的味儿。在他看来，她像个天上的神仙，比他父亲，比所有的别人都高出多多少少，凡人只好远远地望着她顶礼膜拜。跟这位太太一起坐马车兜风是个大典，他坐在倒座上，一声儿不敢言语，只瞪着大眼向对面装点得花团锦簇的公主出神地看。先生们骑着神气十足的骏马，笑吟吟的上前跟她说话。她也是满面春风，对大家眯着眼笑。先生们走开的时候，妈妈挥着手和他们告别，那风度真是优雅。孩子跟她出门总换上新的红衣服，在家却只穿一身棕色的旧麻布衣。有时她不在家，照管他的桃立替他铺床，他就走到母亲的房里去东张西望，觉得这屋子真是神仙洞府，又好看，又有趣，耀得人眼都花了。衣橱里挂着漂亮的衣服，淡红的，浅蓝的，花花绿绿的。梳妆台上摆着一只美丽的铜手，挂满了闪亮闪亮的戒指，旁边还有镶银扣的珠宝盒子。屋里又有一架穿衣镜，真是神妙的艺术品。他刚好能在镜子里照见自己的头脸，看了那么多希罕物儿，脸上都傻了。他在镜子里看见桃立正在拍打床上的枕头，把它们弄松；她的影子歪歪扭扭的，又好像高高吊在天花板上。唉！你这没见世面，没人理，没人管的小可怜儿！在别的孩子们心里口里，妈妈便是

in the lips and hearts of little children;and here was one who was worshipping a stone!

Now Rawdon Crawley, rascal as the Colonel was, had certain manly tendencies of affection in his heart, and could love a child and a woman still. For Rawdon minor he had a great secret tenderness then, which did not escape Rebecca, though she did not talk about it to her husband. It did not annoy her: she was too good-natured. It only increased her scorn for him. He felt somehow ashamed of this paternal softness, and hid it from his wife—only indulging in it when alone with the boy.

He used to take him out of mornings, when they would go to the stables together and to the Park. Little Lord Southdown, the best-natured of men, who would make you a present of the hat from his head, and whose main occupation in life was to buy knick-knacks that he might give them away afterwards, bought the little chap a pony not much bigger than a large rat, the donor said, and on this little black Shetland pygmy young Rawdon's great father was pleased to mount the boy, and to walk by his side in the Park. It pleased him to see his old quarters, and his old fellow-guardsmen at Knights-bridge: he had begun to think of his bachelorhood with something like regret. The old troopers were glad to recognise their ancient officer, and dandle the little Colonel. Colonel Crawley found dining at mess and with his brother-officers very pleasant. "Hang it. I ain't clever enough for her—I know it. She won't miss me," he used to say: and he was right: his wife did not miss him.

Rebecca was fond of her husband. She was always perfectly good-humoured and kind to him. She did not even show her scorn much for him; perhaps she liked him

上帝的别名,你崇拜的却不过是一块冥顽不灵的石头。

罗登·克劳莱上校虽然是个流氓,心地倒还厚道,有些丈夫气概,能够爱女人,爱孩子。他心底里非常疼爱小罗登,利蓓加虽然不说穿他的秘密,心里却明白。她性子好,所以并不生气,只不过对于丈夫更加看不起。罗登那么喜欢儿子,自己也觉得不好意思,在妻子面前不肯露出来,只有跟孩子两个人在一起的时候才尽情疼他一下子。

他时常在早上带儿子出门,看看马房,逛逛公园。莎吴塞唐伯爵性情最随和,要他把头上的帽子脱下来送人,他也肯。他的人生大事就是不断地买了各色各样的小东西放着,闲常好送人。他买给小罗登一只小马,照送礼的人自己的话,这马儿简直和大老鼠差不多大小。小罗登的高大的爸爸时常喜欢叫儿子骑在这匹喜脱伦小黑马背上在公园里溜达,自己在旁边跟着。他喜欢重游当兵时的旧地,常到武士桥去看望禁卫队里的老同事,想起当年的光棍生涯,很有些恋恋不舍。军队里的老兵看见从前的上司来了,也很高兴,都来摩弄小上校。克劳莱上校和军官们在食堂里吃饭,觉得十分有趣。他常说:“唉,我不够聪明,配不上她,这个我也明白。她不会记挂我的。”他这话一点不错,他妻子并不记挂他。

利蓓加很喜欢丈夫,对他总是非常和顺疼爱,甚至于不大明白表示自己瞧不起他。说不定她宁可丈夫颟顸些。他

the better for being a fool. He was her upper servant and *maître-d'hôtel*. He went on her errands: obeyed her orders without question: drove in the carriage in the ring with her without repining; took her to the opera-box; solaced himself at his club during the performance, and came punctually back to fetch her when due. He would have liked her to be a little fonder of the boy: but even to that he reconciled himself. "Hang it, you know, she's so clever," he said, "and I'm not literary and that, you know." For, as we have said before, it requires no great wisdom to be able to win at cards and billiards, and Rawdon made no pretensions to any other sort of skill.

When the companion came, his domestic duties became very light. His wife encouraged him to dine abroad: she would let him off duty at the Opera. "Don't stay and stupefy yourself at home to-night, my dear," she would say. "Some men are coming who will only bore you. I would not ask them, but you know it's for your good, and now I have a sheep-dog, I need not be afraid to be alone."

"A sheep-dog—a companion! Becky Sharp with a companion! Isn't it good fun?" thought Mrs. Crawley to herself. The notion tickled hugely her sense of humour.

One Sunday morning, as Rawdon Crawley, his little son, and the pony were taking their accustomed walk in the Park, they passed by an old acquaintance of the Colonel's. Corporal Clink, of the regiment, who was in conversation with a friend, an old gentleman, who held a boy in his arms about the age of little Rawdon. This other youngster had seized hold of the Waterloo medal which the Corporal wore, and was examining it with de-

是她的上等用人和总管。他受她的使唤，绝对地服从。他陪她坐了马车在公园的圆场兜风，从来不出怨言。他送她上歌剧院坐进包厢，然后一个人到俱乐部里去解闷，散场时又准时回去接她。他只希望妻子能够多疼些儿子，可是连这一点他也原谅她。他说："唉，你知道的，她真能干，而我又不是文绉绉的人。"前面已经说过，靠打弹子和玩纸牌赢人家的钱并不需要多少聪明，除此之外，罗登又没有别的本事。

女伴一来之后，他在家里的责任就轻松了。他的妻子怂恿他到外面去吃饭，而且上歌剧院也不要他接送。她总是说："亲爱的，别留在家里发傻，今儿晚上有几个人要来，你见了他们准觉得讨厌。若不是为你的好处，我也不高兴请他们到家里来。现在我有了一条看羊狗，没有你也不怕了。"

"看羊狗——女伴！蓓基·夏泼有个女伴！多滑稽！"克劳莱太太想着这一点，觉得有趣得不得了。

有一天，正是星期日，罗登·克劳莱按例和他儿子骑着小马在公园里散步，碰见上校的一个熟人，是联队里的克林克下士。下士正在和一个老先生谈天，老先生手里抱着一个男孩子，年龄和小罗登相仿。那孩子抓着下士身上挂的滑铁卢勋章，看得高兴。

light.

"Good-morning, your honour," said Clink, in reply to the "How do, Clink?" of the Colonel. "This'ere young gentleman is about the little Colonel's age, sir," continued the Corporal.

"His father was a Waterloo man, too," said the old gentleman, who carried the boy. "Wasn't he, Georgy?"

"Yes," said Georgy. He and the little chap on the pony were looking at each other with all their might—solemnly scanning each other as children do.

"In a line regiment," Clink said, with a patronizing air.

"He was a Captain in the —th regiment," said the old gentleman rather pompously. "Captain George Osborne, sir—perhaps you knew him. He died the death of a hero, sir, fighting against the Corsican tyrant."

Colonel Crawley blushed quite red. "I knew him very well, sir," he said, "and his wife, his dear little wife, sir—how is she?"

"She is my daughter, sir," said the old gentleman, putting down the boy, and taking out a card with great solemnity, which he handed to the Colonel. On it was written—

"Mr. Sedley, Sole Agent for the Black Diamond and Anti-Cinder Coal Association, Bunker's Wharf, Thames Street, and Anna-Maria Cottages, Fulham Road West."

Little Georgy went up and looked at the Shetland pony.

"Should you like to have a ride?" said Rawdon minor from the saddle.

"Yes," said Georgy. The Colonel, who had been looking at him with some interest, took up the child and put

上校说:“好啊,克林克?”克林克答道:“早上好,大爷,这位小先生跟小上校差不多大。”

抱孩子的老先生说道:“他父亲也在滑铁卢打仗的。对不对,乔杰?”

乔杰道:“对。”他和小马上的孩子正颜厉色一眼不眨地对看半天,正是小孩子普通的样子。

克林克老腔老调地说道:“常备军里的。”

老人神气活现地说:“他是第×联队里的上尉,乔治·奥斯本上尉,也许您还认识他。他死得像个英雄,和科西嘉的恶霸拼命到底。”

克劳莱上校涨红了脸道:“我跟他很熟的。他的妻子,他的亲爱的妻子,怎么样了?”

“她是我的女儿,”老人家说着,放下孩子,一本正经地从口袋里掏出一张纸牌子交给上校,上面写着:“赛特笠先生,泰晤士街白伦格码头无灰黑金刚钻煤公司经理。住址:福兰西路安娜·玛丽亚小屋。”

小乔杰走过去望着那喜脱伦小马。

小罗登从鞍子上问他道:“你要骑马吗?”

乔杰答道:“我要。”上校瞧瞧他,似乎对他很感兴趣,把他抱起来坐在小罗登后面。

him on the pony behind Rawdon minor.

"Take hold of him, Georgy," he said—"take my little boy round the waist—his name is Rawdon." And both the children began to laugh.

"You won't see a prettier pair, I think, *this* summer's day, sir," said the good-natured Corporal; and the Colonel, the Corporal, and old Mr. Sedley with his umbrella, walked by the side of the children.

他说："拉着他，乔杰。抱着我孩子的腰——他叫罗登。"两个孩子都笑起来了。

好性情的下士说："你上哪儿也找不着这么两个漂亮的孩子。"上校、下士、赛特笠老先生拿着伞，都跟在孩子们旁边散步。

Our Friend the Major

Our Major had rendered himself so popular on board the Ramchunder, that when he and Mr. Sedley descended into the welcome shore-boat which was to take them from the ship, the whole crew, men and officers, the great Captain Bragg himself leading off, gave three cheers for Major Dobbin, who blushed very much, and ducked his head in token of thanks. Jos, who very likely thought the cheers were for himself, took off his gold-laced cap and waved it majestically to his friends, and they were pulled to shore and landed with great dignity at the pier, whence they proceeded to the Royal George Hotel.

Although the sight of that magnificent round of beef, and the silver tankard suggestive of real British home-brewed ale and porter, which perennially greet the eyes of the traveller returning from foreign parts, who enters the coffee-room of the George, are so invigorating and delightful, that a man entering such a comfortable snug homely English inn, might well like to stop some days there, yet Dobbin began to talk about a post-chaise instantly, and was no sooner at Southampton than he wished to be on the road to London. Jos, however, would not hear of moving that evening. Why was he to pass the night in a post-chaise instead of a great large undulating downy featherbed which was there ready to replace the horrid little narrow crib in which the portly Bengal gentleman had been confined during the voyage? He could not think of moving till his baggage was cleared, or of

我们的朋友都宾少佐

少佐在拉姆轻特船上的人缘真好。那天他和赛特笠先生欢欢喜喜地下了摆渡船准备上岸，全船的职员和水手，由了不起的白拉格船长带头，欢呼三声给都宾少佐送行。少佐满面通红，点着头表示给他们道谢。乔斯大约以为他们是为他欢呼，脱下金箍帽子神气活现地向朋友们摇晃着。他们给摆渡到岸边，很威风地上了码头，出发到皇家乔治旅馆去。

乔治旅馆的咖啡室里一年到头摆着大块肥美的牛腿肉，还有银子打的大酒杯，使人联想到真正英国家乡酿造的浓麦酒和淡麦酒。从国外回来的旅客一进门来看见这两样东西，自会兴致蓬勃、精神抖擞。如此说来，不论是谁，进了这样一个舒服愉快的英国旅馆，总愿意盘桓几天再走，哪知道都宾一到沙乌撒泼顿就想上路到伦敦去，立刻打算雇马车。乔斯呢，那天晚上是随便怎么也不肯动身的了。这位肥胖的孟加拉绅士一路只能睡在又窄小又不舒服的铺位上，如今刚有了宽敞的大床，上面铺着鸭绒被褥，软绵绵的一睡一个窝儿，他又何必在马车里过夜呢？他说行李没有整理好以前他不愿意动身；没有水烟袋，他是不高兴出门

travelling until he could do so with his chillum. So the Major was forced to wait over that night, and despatched a letter to his family announcing his arrival; entreating from Jos a promise to write to his own friends Jos promised, but didn't keep his promise. The Captain, the surgeon, and one or two passengers came and dined with our two gentlemen at the inn; Jos exerting himself in a sumptuous way in ordering the dinner, and promising to go to town the next day with the Major. The landlord said it did his eyes good to see Mr. Sedley take off his first pint of porter. If I had time and dared to enter into digressions, I would write a chapter about that first pint of porter drunk upon English ground. Ah, how good it is! It is worth while to leave home for a year, just to enjoy that one draught.

Major Dobbin made his appearance the next morning very neatly shaved and dressed, according to his wont. Indeed, it was so early in the morning, that nobody was up in the house except that wonderful Boots of an inn who never seems to want sleep: and the Major could hear the snores of the various inmates of the house roaring through the corridors as he creaked about in those dim passages. Then the sleepless Boots went shirking round from door to door, gathering up at each the Bluchers, Wellingtons, Oxonians, which stood outside. Then Jos's native servant arose and began to get ready his master's ponderous dressing apparatus, and prepare his hookah: then the maid-servants got up, and meeting the dark man in the passages, shrieked, and mistook him for the devil. He and Dobbin stumbled over their pails in the passages as they were scouring the decks of the Royal George. When the first unshorn waiter appeared and un-

的。少佐没法，只能等过了那一夜再说。他写了一封信到家里，报告上岸的消息，又恳求乔斯也写封信通知他家里的人。乔斯嘴里答应，可并没有照做。船长、医生，还有一两个旅客，都从船上下来和我们这两位先生一同吃晚饭，乔斯非常卖力，点了许多好菜，并且答应第二天和少佐一起到伦敦去。旅馆主人说赛特笠先生喝第一派因脱浓麦酒的时候，他瞧着就觉得痛快。如果我有时间说闲话，准会另写一章，形容刚回英国时喝第一派因脱浓麦酒的滋味。嗬，那滋味多好呀！单为受用这一次痛饮，特地离家一年也值得。

第二天早上，都宾少佐起来，照他平时的习惯，把胡子剃光，穿得整整齐齐。那时天色很早，旅馆里除了那擦鞋工人之外，都没有起身——这些擦鞋的仿佛从来不需要睡觉，真是了不起。少佐在朦朦胧胧的走廊里踱来踱去，皮鞋吱吱的响，到处听得客人们打呼噜的声音。那不睡觉的擦鞋工人躲躲藏藏地顺着各个房门走过去，把门前的长统靴、半统靴、浅口鞋都收集起来。然后乔斯的印度用人起身给主人把笨重的梳妆家伙拿出来，又给他收拾水烟袋。再过一会儿，女用人们也起身了，她们在过道里碰见这么个黑不溜秋的人，以为是魔鬼出现，都尖叫起来。她们打水擦洗旅馆的地板，印度人和都宾两个便失脚绊在她们的水桶上。等到第一个茶房带着隔夜的胡子去开大门的时候，少佐觉得

barred the door of the inn, the Major thought that the time for departure was arrived, and ordered a post-chaise to be fetched instantly, that they might set off.

He then directed his steps to Mr. Sedley's room, and opened the curtains of the great large family bed wherein Mr. Jos was snoring. "Come, up! Sedley," the Major said; "it's time to be off; the chaise will be at the door in half an hour."

Jos growled from under the counterpane to know what the time was; but when he at last extorted from the blushing Major (who never told fibs, however much they might be to his advantage) what was the real hour of the morning, he broke out into a volley of bad language, which we will not repeat here, but by which he gave Dobbin to understand that he would jeopardy his soul if he got up at that moment, that the Major might go and be hanged, that he would not travel with Dobbin, and that it was most unkind and ungentlemanlike to disturb a man out of his sleep in that way; on which the discomfited Major was obliged to retreat, leaving Jos to resume his interrupted slumbers.

The chaise came up presently, and the Major would wait no longer.

If he had been an English nobleman travelling on a pleasure tour, or a newspaper courier bearing despatches (government messages are generally carried much more quietly), he could not have travelled more quickly. The post-boys wondered at the fees he flung amongst them. How happy and green the country looked as the chaise whirled rapidly from mile-stone to mile-stone, through neat country towns where landlords came out to welcome him with smiles and bows; by pretty road-side inns,

可以动身了,吩咐下人立刻去雇一辆车来,打算上路。

他走到赛特笠先生的卧房里,只见乔斯睡在一张又宽又大的双人床上,正在打呼噜。他把帐子拉开,叫道:“赛特笠,起来吧,可以动身了。马车再隔半个钟头就来。”

乔斯在被窝里发怒,咕噜着问他几点钟了。少佐是老实人,不管扯谎可以帮他多大的忙,他也扯不来,所以给乔斯一逼,只好红了脸把实话告诉他。乔斯一听,立刻破口大骂。骂人的话这里不必再说,总之他让都宾明白:第一,倘若他那么早起来,简直有危险给打入地狱;第二,都宾少佐是个该死的东西;第三,他不高兴和都宾一路走;第四,这样把人叫醒,真是没心肝,不像个上等人。少佐没法,只好退出来,让乔斯重新再睡觉。

不久,马车来了,少佐不肯再等了。

英国贵族出门游览,或是报馆里送信的快差带着急信赶路,也不能比他更着急,政府里传递公文的专差更要慢得多。车夫们见他大手大脚地花钱,都觉得希罕。马车飞快地跑过一块块的里程碑,穿过整齐的乡镇,那儿的客店主人堆着笑,哈着腰来迎接他。路旁有美丽的小客店,招牌就挂

where the signs hung on the elms, and horses and waggoners were drinking under the chequered shadow of the trees; by old halls and parks; rustic hamlets clustered round ancient grey churches—and through the charming friendly English landscape. Is there any in the world like it? To a traveller returning home it looks so kind —it seems to shake hands with you as you pass through it. Well, Major Dobbin passed through all this from Southampton to London, and without noting much beyond the milestones along the road. You see he was so eager to see his parents at Camberwell.

He grudged the time lost between Piccadilly and his old haunt at the Slaughters', whither he drove faithfully. Long years had passed since he saw it last, since he and George, as young men, had enjoyed many a feast, and held many a revel there. He had now passed into the stage of old-fellow-hood. His hair was grizzled, and many a passion and feeling of his youth had grown grey in that interval. There, however, stood the old waiter at the door, in the same greasy black suit, with the same double chin and flaccid face, with the same huge bunch of seals at his fob, rattling his money in his pockets as before, and receiving the Major as if he had gone away only a week ago. "Put the Major's things in twenty-three, that's his room," John said, exhibiting not the least surprise. "Roast-fowl for your dinner, I suppose? You ain't got married? They said you was married—the Scotch surgeon of yours was here. No, it was Captain Humby of the thirty-third, as was quartered with the —th in Injee. Like any warm water? What do you come in a chay for—ain't the coach good enough?" And with this, the faithful waiter, who knew and remembered every officer who used

在榆树枝上，赶货车的人马都在浓淡不一的树荫里喝水；还有古色古香的大宅子、大花园，灰色的教堂，旁边成窝儿的小村屋。一路都是眼熟的英国风景，非常可爱，田野里绿油油的一派欢乐的气象。世界上哪里有这样的好地方？在新回国的人看来，家乡真是和蔼可亲，仿佛一路在跟他拉手。可惜都宾少佐从沙乌撒泼顿到伦敦，除了路旁的里程碑之外什么都没有看见。那当然是因为他急着要回坎勃威尔去看望父母的缘故。

他诚诚心心地坐车回到以前常去的斯洛德咖啡馆，只恨毕加迪莱到咖啡馆的一段路上太费时间。他和乔治年轻的时候常在那里吃喝作乐。那已经是多年前的旧事，如今他也算得上是个"老家伙"了。他的头发已经灰白，少年时的好些痴情，好些感触，也渐渐的淡忘了。那老茶房倒还站在门口，仍旧穿着那套油腻腻的黑衣服，双叠的下巴颏儿，腮帮子又松又软，表链上一大嘟噜印戳子，像从前一样把口袋里的钱摇得哗啷啷的响。约翰迎接少佐的样子，竟好像他离开那儿不过一个星期。他脸上没半点儿惊奇的表情，说道："把少佐的东西搁在二十三号他自己房间里。今儿您大概吃烤鸡吧？您没有结婚？他们说您已经娶了太太了——你们那苏格兰军医到这儿来过的。不对！是三十三联队的亨倍上尉说的，他从前跟着第×联队驻扎在西印度。您要热水吗？您今儿怎么另外雇车呢？坐邮车不是挺好吗？"凡是在那里住过的军官，忠心的茶房都认识，也都记

the house, and with whom ten years were but as yesterday, led the way up to Dobbin's old room, where stood the great moreen bed, and the shabby carpet, a thought more dingy, and all the old black furniture covered with faded chintz, just as the Major recollected them in his youth.

He remembered George pacing up and down the room, and biting his nails, and swearing that the Governor must come round, and that if he didn't, he didn't care a straw, on the day before he was married. He could fancy him walking in, banging the door of Dobbin's room, and his own hard by —

"You ain't got young," John said, calmly surveying his friend of former days.

Dobbin laughed. "Ten years and a fever don't make a man young, John," he said. "It is you that are always young: —No, you are always old."

"What became of Captain Osborne's widow?" John said. "Fine young fellow that. Lord, how he used to spend his money. He never came back after that day he was married from here. He owes me three pound at this minute. Look here, I have it in my book. 'April 10, 1815, Captain Osborne: 3*l*.' I wonder whether his father would pay me," and so saying, John of the Slaughters' pulled out the very morocco pocket-book in which he had noted his loan to the Captain, upon a greasy faded page still extant, with many other scrawled memoranda regarding the bygone frequenters of the house.

Having inducted his customer into the room, John retired with perfect calmness; and Major Dobbin, not without a blush and a grin at his own absurdity, chose out of his kit the very smartest and most becoming civil cos-

得。在他,十年好比一天。他说完了话,领着路走到都宾从前常住的屋子里。里面有一张大床,周围挂着粗呢的幔子;旧地毯比从前更旧了一些,那套黑木的旧家具也还在,椅子上印花布的面子都褪了色。一切和他年轻的时候没有两样。

他还记得乔治结婚的前一天在房里走来走去,咬着指甲,赌神发誓地说他老子总会回心转意,就是他不肯回心,他也不在乎。都宾还想象得出他跑进来的样子,把都宾的房门和他自己的房门碰得山响。当年他的房间就在都宾的房间近旁。

约翰不慌不忙地把老朋友打量了一番,说道:"您没有变得怎么年轻。"

都宾笑道:"过了十年,害了一场热病,还能叫人年轻不成?你才是个不老公公。或者可以说你根本没有做过年轻人。"

约翰问道:"奥斯本上尉的太太怎么了?那小伙子长得很不错。天哪,他可真会花钱!结婚以后他一直没有回来,到今天还欠我三镑钱呢。瞧这儿,我的本子上还记着呢:'一八一五年四月十日,奥斯本上尉,三镑。'不知道他爸爸肯不肯把钱还给我。"斯洛德咖啡馆的约翰说着,从口袋里掏出一本皮面的记事本子,上面油腻腻字迹模糊的一页上还记着这笔旧账,旁边另外有好些歪歪斜斜的字,全是关于当年别的老主顾的事情。

约翰把客人送进了房间,又从从容容地走了。都宾少佐从小箱子里挑了一身最漂亮最好看的随常服装,一面笑

tume he possessed, and laughed at his own tanned face and grey hair, as he surveyed them in the dreary little toilet-glass on the dressing-table.

"I'm glad old John didn't forget me," he thought. "She'll know me, too, I hope." And he sallied out of the inn, bending his steps once more in the direction of Brompton.

Every minute incident of his last meeting with Amelia was present to the constant man's mind as he walked towards her house. The arch and the Achilles statue were up since he had last been in Piccadilly; a hundred changes had occurred which his eye and mind vaguely noted. He began to tremble as he walked up the lane from Brompton, that well-remembered lane leading to the street where she lived. Was she going to be married or not? If he were to meet her with the little boy—good God, what should he do? He saw a woman coming to him with a child of five years old—was that she? He began to shake at the mere possibility. When he came up to the row of houses, at last, where she lived, and to the gate, he caught hold of it and paused. He might have heard the thumping of his own heart. "May God Almighty bless her, whatever has happened," he thought to himself. "Psha! she may be gone from here," he said, and went in through the gate.

The window of the parlour which she used to occupy was open, and there were no inmates in the room. The Major thought he recognised the piano, though, with the picture over it, as it used to be in former days, and his perturbations were renewed. Mr. Clapp's brass plate was still on the door, at the knocker of which Dobbin performed a summons.

嘻嘻的红了脸，觉得自己实在荒谬。他对着梳妆台上一面昏暗的小镜子端详自己灰白的头发和黧黑的皮肤，不由得好笑起来。他想："约翰老头儿居然没把我忘掉，倒不错。希望她也还记得我。"他从客店里出发，往白朗浦顿那边走去。

这忠实的好人一路行来，细细地回想他最后一次跟爱米丽亚见面时的每一件小事情。他末了一回在毕加迪莱的时候，拱门和亚基里斯的像还没有造起来。他恍惚觉得视线所及随处都有变动。过了白朗浦顿，就有一条小路直通到她街上，他走上从前走熟的小路，身上已经在打哆嗦。她究竟是不是打算结婚呢？倘若这时候她和她孩子对面走来——天啊，那怎么办呢？他看见一个女人带着一个五岁的孩子，心里想："是不是她呀？"他一想到有这样的可能，激动得浑身发抖。总算走到她住的屋子一带了。他走近栅栏门的时候，手握着栅栏顿了一顿，几乎听得见自己的心在扑通扑通地跳。他想道："不管出了什么事，总求老天保佑她。"接着他又说："呸，没准她早就搬走了，"说着，走进门去。

她以前住的会客室的窗户开着，里面并没有人。少佐恍惚看见那钢琴和上面的图画还是从前的老样子，心里又慌张起来。大门上仍旧安着克拉浦先生的铜牌子；都宾拉起门环敲了一下。

A buxom-looking lass of sixteen, with bright eyes and purple cheeks, came to answer the knock, and looked hard at the Major as he leant back against the little porch.

He was as pale as a ghost, and could hardly falter out the words—"Does Mrs. Osborne live here?"

She looked him hard in the face for a moment—and then turning white too—said, "Lord bless me—it's Major Dobbin." She held out both her hands shaking—"Don't you remember me?" she said. "I used to call you Major Sugarplums." On which, and I believe it was for the first time that he ever so conducted himself in his life, the Major took the girl in his arms and kissed her. She began to laugh and cry hysterically, and calling out "Ma, Pa!" with all her voice, brought up those worthy people, who had already been surveying the Major from the casement of the ornamental kitchen, and were astonished to find their daughter in the little passage in the embrace of a greattall man in a blue frock-coat and white duck trousers.

"I'm an old friend," he said—not without blushing though. "Don't you remember me, Mrs. Clapp, and those good cakes you used to make for tea? —Don't you recollect me, Clapp? I'm George's godfather, and just come back from India?" A great shaking of hands ensued—Mrs. Clapp was greatly affected and delighted; she called upon heaven to interpose a vast many times in that passage.

The landlord and landlady of the house led the worthy Major into the Sedley's room (whereof he remembered every single article of furniture, from the old brass ornamented piano, once a natty little instrument, Sto-

一个肥硕的小姑娘，大约十六岁，一双眼睛亮晶晶的，脸蛋儿红里带紫，出来开了门，对少佐紧紧地瞅着。

少佐站在那窄小的过道里，靠着墙，脸色白得像个鬼，支支吾吾的挣出一句："奥斯本太太住在这儿吗？"

她瞪眼看了他半晌，然后脸上也泛白了，说道："天老爷，是都宾少佐呀！"她抖巍巍的伸出两手说道："您不记得我啦？我从前常叫您糖子儿少佐的。"少佐一听这话，抱住女孩儿吻了她一下，我看他这辈子还是第一遭这么大胆呢。她歇斯底里似的又哭又笑，使劲大叫"爹，妈！"把这两个好人儿给叫出来了。夫妻俩本来在他们那装饰得挺漂亮的厨房窗口往外端详他。他们看见一个大高个儿的男人，穿着钉长方扣子的蓝色外套，底下是白色细布裤子，站在门口抱着女孩儿，心上老大诧异。

少佐忍不住红了脸说道："我是你们的老朋友。克拉浦太太，不记得我了吗？你从前不是还做许多好吃的糕饼给我当点心吗？克拉浦，你忘了吗？我是乔治的干爹，刚从印度回来。"接着大家忙着拉手；克拉浦太太又喜欢，又感动，在过道里不住口地叫天老爷。

房东夫妇把好少佐让到赛特笠的房里——房里每一件家具陈设他都记得：用黄铜装潢的小小的旧钢琴（斯多泰牌

thard maker, to the screens and the alabaster miniature tombstone, in the midst of which ticked Mr. Sedley's gold watch), and there as he sat down in the lodger's vacant arm-chair, the father, the mother, and the daughter, with a thousand ejaculatory breaks in the narrative, informed Major Dobbin of what we know already, but of particulars in Amelia's history of which he was not aware-namely of Mrs. Sedley's death, of George's reconcilement with his grandfather Osborne, of the way in which the widow took on at leaving him, and of other particulars of her life. Twice or thrice he was going to ask about the marriage question, but his heart failed him. He did not care to lay it bare to these people. Finally, he was informed that Mrs. O. was gone to walk with her Pa in Kensington Gardens, whither she always went with the old gentleman (who was very weak and peevish now, and led her a sad life, though she behaved to him like an angel, to be sure,) of a fine afternoon after dinner.

"I'm very much pressed for time," the Major said, "and have business to-night of importance. I should like to see Mrs. Osborne tho'. Suppose Miss Polly would come with me and show me the way."

Miss Polly was charmed and astonished at this proposal. She knew the way. She would show Major Dobbin. She had often been with Mr. Sedley when Mrs. O. was gone—was gone Russell Square way: and knew the bench where he liked to sit. She bounced away to her apartment, and appeared presently in her best bonnet and her mamma's yellow shawl and large pebble brooch, of which she assumed the loan in order to make herself a worthy companion for the Major.

That officer, then, in his blue frock-coat and buck-

子的货色，本来很讲究的），还有屏风，还有大理石的小墓碑，当中嵌着赛特笠先生的金表，正在滴答滴答地响。他坐在房客的圈椅里面，那父母女三人就把爱米丽亚的遭遇一样样地说给他听，讲到赛特笠太太怎么死，乔治怎么给他祖父奥斯本先生领去，寡妇离了儿子怎么伤心等等，一面说，一面唉啊唷地叹息个不完。这些事情我们早已听过，少佐却还不知道。有两三回，他很想扯到她的婚姻上去，可是总鼓不起勇气来，而且他也不愿意把心事向这些人吐露。后来他们告诉他说奥太太陪着她爹到坎新登花园去散步了。老先生身体不好，脾气也坏，把她折磨得难过日子，不过她倒真是和顺得像个天使。如今每逢饭后天气好，她总带他出去。

少佐道："我没有多少时候，今天晚上还有要紧的事情得办。不过我很想见见奥斯本太太。最好请玛丽小姐陪我去，给我领领路。"

玛丽小姐听了这话觉得出乎意外，可是也很高兴。她说她认得这条路，可以领都宾少佐去；有的时候奥太太到——到勒塞尔广场去，就由她陪着赛特笠先生，所以知道他最喜欢的座位在什么地方。她跳跳蹦蹦地走到卧房里，一会儿戴上自己最好的帽子回来。她还借了她妈妈的黄披肩跟大石子儿别针，为的是要配得上少佐的势派。

少佐穿上方扣子蓝外套，戴上黄皮手套，伸出胳膊给小

skin gloves, gave the young lady his arm, and they walked away very gaily. He was glad to have a friend at hand for the scene which he dreaded somehow. He asked a thousand more questions from his companion about Amelia: his kind heart grieved to think that she should have had to part with her son. How did she bear it? Did she see him often? Was Mr. Sedley pretty comfortable now in a worldly point of view? Polly answered all these questions of Major Sugarplums to the very best of her power.

And in the midst of their walk an incident occurred which, though very simple in its nature, was productive of the greatest delight to Major Dobbin. A pale young man with feeble whiskers and a stiff white neckcloth, came walking down the lane, *en sandwich*:—having a lady, that is, on each arm. One was a tall and commanding middleaged female, with features and a complexion similar to those of the clergyman of the Church of England by whose side she marched, and the other a stunted little woman with a dark face, ornamented by a fine new bonnet and white ribbons, and in a smart pelisse with a rich gold watch in the midst of her person. The gentleman, pinioned as he was by these two ladies, carried further a parasol, shawl, and basket, so that his arms were entirely engaged, and of course he was unable to touch his hat in acknowledgment of the curtsey with which Miss Mary Clapp greeted him.

He merely bowed his head in reply to her salutation, which the two ladies returned in a patronizing air, and at the same time looking severely at the individual in the blue coat and bamboo cane, who accompanied Miss Polly.

"Who's that?" asked the Major, amused by the

姑娘勾着，两个人快快乐乐地一起出门。他想起要跟爱米丽亚见面，心里慌张，很愿意旁边有个朋友。他又问玛丽许许多多关于爱米丽亚的问题。他这人是忠厚不过的，听到她被逼和儿子分手，不由得扎心的难受。她受得了吗？她常跟他见面吗？在物质生活方面，赛特笠先生舒服吗？玛丽尽她所知回答糖子儿少佐的问题。

半路上发生了一件事，虽然没什么要紧，却把都宾少佐乐坏了。小路那一头来了一个脸皮苍白的后生，他一嘴稀稀拉拉的胡子，戴着又硬又白的领巾，一手勾着一个女的，自己给挤在当中。两个女人里头有一个已经中年，高高的身材，样子很威武，五官和脸色和身旁的英国国教牧师很像，走起路来迈着大步。另外一个是个小矮个子，黑皮肤，头上戴一顶漂亮的新帽子，上面配着白缎带，身上穿一件时髦的外套，挂一只漂亮的金表，恰恰在她身子中央。这位先生的两只胳膊已经给两位女士扣住，还得捧一把阳伞，一条披肩，一只篮子。他手里这么满满的，克拉浦小姐对他屈膝招呼的时候他当然不能举起手来碰帽子边还礼。

他只点了一点头，两位女士倚老卖老的样子还了礼，虎起脸儿瞪着玛丽小姐旁边那个穿蓝外套、拿竹子拐棍儿的男人。

少佐瞧着他们觉得好笑，站在路旁边让他们过去。然

group, and after he had made way for the three to pass up the lane. Mary looked at him rather roguishly.

"That is our curate, the Reverend Mr. Binny" (a twitch from Major Dobbin), "and his sister Miss B. Lord bless us, how she did use to worret us at Sunday-school; and the other lady, the little one with a cast in her eye, and the handsome watch, is Mrs. Binny—Miss Grits that was; her Pa was a grocer, and kept the Little Original Gold Tea Pot in Kensington Gravel Pits. They were married last month, and are just come back from Margate. She's five thousand pound to her fortune; but her and Miss B., who made the match, have quarrelled already."

If the Major had twitched before he started now, and slapped the bamboo on the ground with an emphasis which made Miss Clapp cry, "Law," and laugh too. He stood for a moment silent with open mouth looking after the retreating young couple, while Miss Mary told their history; but he did not hear beyond the announcement of the reverend gentleman's marriage; his head was swimming with felicity. After this rencontre he began to walk double quick towards the place of his destination—and yet they were too soon (for he was in a great tremor at the idea of a meeting for which he had been longing any time these ten years)—through the Brompton lanes, and entering at the little old portal in Kensington Garden wall.

"There they are," said Miss Polly, and she felt him again start back on her arm. She was a confidante at once of the whole business. She knew the story as well as if she had read it in one of her favourite novel-books—"Fatherless Fanny," or the "Scottish Chiefs."

"Suppose you were to run on and tell her," the Ma-

后问道："他们是谁？"玛丽顽皮地瞧着他，说道：

"那是我们的副牧师平尼先生"（都宾少佐愣了一愣），"一个是他姐姐平尼小姐。天哪，在主日学校里她把我们折磨得好苦啊！另外那个斜眼的小女人，挂着漂亮的金表的，就是平尼太太。她娘家姓葛立滋。她爹开杂货铺子，在坎新登石子坑还有一家铺子叫小金茶壶老店。他们上个月才结婚，如今刚从玛该脱回来。她名下有五千镑财产。这头亲事虽然是平尼小姐一手拉拢的，可是姑嫂俩已经吵过架了。"

少佐刚才一愣，如今简直是托的一跳。他把竹子拐棍儿在地上重重的打了一下，克拉浦小姐见他这样，笑着叫起天老爷来。玛丽议论他们家历史的当儿，他一声不言语，张开口瞧着那一对小夫妻的后影。他喜欢得昏头昏脑，除了牧师结婚的消息之外，什么都没有听进去。经过这件事情，他加紧脚步，恨不得快快地赶到地头。一方面他又嫌自己走得太快，只觉得一忽儿的工夫已经穿过白朗浦顿的街道，从那又小又旧的园门走进坎新登花园了。十年来他时时刻刻希望和她见面，事到临头却又紧张起来。

玛丽小姐说："他们在那儿。"她说了这话，觉得身旁的少佐又是一愣，心里恍然大悟。故事里面的情节她全知道了。她最爱看《没爹的法尼》和《苏格兰领袖》这类小说，如今少佐的心事她已经一目了然，仿佛已经在书里看过一样。

少佐说："请你跑过去告诉她一声好不好？"玛丽拔脚就

jor said. Polly ran forward, her yellow shawl streaming in the breeze.

Old Sedley was seated on a bench, his handkerchief placed over his knees, prattling away according to his wont, with some old story about old times, to which Amelia had listened, and awarded a patient smile many a time before. She could of late think of her own affairs, and smile or make other marks of recognition of her father's stories, scarcely hearing a word of the old man's tales. As Mary came bouncing along, and Amelia caught sight of her, she started up from her bench. Her first thought was, that something had happened to Georgy; but the sight of the messenger's eager and happy face dissipated that fear in the timorous mother's bosom.

"News! News!" cried the emissary of Major Dobbin. "He's come! He's come!"

"Who is come?" said Emmy, still thinking of her son.

"Look there," answered Miss Clapp, turning round and pointing; in which direction Amelia looking, saw Dobbin's lean figure and long shadow stalking across the grass. Amelia started in her turn, blushed up, and, of course, began to cry. At all this simple little creature's fêtes, the *grandes eaux* were accustomed to play.

He looked at her—oh, how fondly—as she came running towards him, her hands before her, ready to give them to him. She wasn't changed. She was a little pale: a little stouter in figure. Her eyes were the same, the kind trustful eyes. There were scarce three lines of silver in her soft brown hair. She gave him both her hands as she looked up flushing and smiling through her tears into his honest homely face. He took the two little hands be-

跑，黄披肩在微风中飘荡着。

赛特笠老头儿坐在长凳上，膝盖上铺了一条手帕，像平常一般唠叨着从前的事情。这些话他说过不止一回，爱米丽亚总是很耐烦地微笑着让他说。近来她能够尽让父亲唠叨，一面想自己的心事，有时脸上挂着笑，有时用别的姿势来表示自己正在用心倾听，其实差不多一个字都没听见。爱米丽亚看见玛丽跳跳蹦蹦走上前来，急忙从长凳上站起来，第一个心思就是以为乔杰出了事情。可是传信的孩子脸上那么快乐高兴，胆小的母亲也就放心了。

都宾少佐的专差叫道："有新闻！有新闻！他来了！他来了！"

爱米仍旧惦记着儿子，问道："谁来了？"

克拉浦小姐道："瞧那儿！"她一面说，一面转过身去用手往回指着。爱米丽亚顺着她指点的方向一看，只见那瘦骨伶仃的都宾正在迈着大步穿过草坪向她这边走，长长的影子随着他。这回轮到爱米丽亚发愣了。她涨红了脸，眼泪当然也跟着流下来。这老实的小东西有了高兴的事是非哭不可的。

她张开两手向他跑过去，准备跟他拉手。他一往情深地瞧着她，觉得她没有变，只是脸色没有从前红润，身材也胖了一点。她的眼睛还是老样子，眼神很和蔼，仿佛对人十分信赖。她那软绵绵的栗色头发里只有两三根白头发。她把两只手都伸给他，脸红红的抬起头对他的忠厚老实的脸

tween his two, and held them there. He was speechless for a moment. Why did he not take her in his arms, and swear that he would never leave her? She must have yielded: she could not but have obeyed him.

"I—I've another arrival to announce," he said, after a pause.

"Mrs. Dobbin?" Amelia said, making a movement back —Why didn't he speak?

"No," he said, letting her hands go: "Who has told you those lies? —I mean, your brother Jos came in the same ship with me, and is come home to make you all happy."

"Papa, papa!" Emmy cried out, "here are news! My brother is in England. He is come to take care of you. Here is Major Dobbin."

Mr. Sedley started up, shaking a great deal, and gathering up his thoughts. Then he stepped forward and made an old-fashioned bow to the Major, whom he called Mr. Dobbin, and hoped his worthy father, Sir William, was quite well. He proposed to call upon Sir William, who had done him the honour of a visit a short time ago. Sir William had not called upon the old gentleman for eight years—it was that visit he was thinking of returning.

"He is very much shaken," Emmy whispered, as Dobbin went up and cordially shook hands with the old man.

Although he had such particular business in London that evening, the Major consented to forego it upon Mr. Sedley's invitation to him to come home and partake of tea. Amelia put her arm under that of her young friend with the yellow shawl, and headed the party on their re-

儿含着眼泪微笑。他双手捧着她的小手,拉着她不放,半晌说不出话。他为什么不搂住她,发誓永远不离开她呢?她准会让步;她没法不服从他。

顿了一顿,他说:“还有另外一个人也来了。”

爱米丽亚往后退了一步,问道:“都宾太太吗?”一面估量他为什么不回答。

他松了手,说道:“不是的。谁在造我的谣言?我要说的是,你哥哥乔斯跟我同船来的。他回家来叫你们大家过好日子了。”

爱米叫道:“爸爸!爸爸!有消息来了!哥哥回英国来了。他来照顾你了。都宾少佐在这儿呢。”

赛特笠先生霍地坐起来,浑身哆嗦,定了一定神。然后他走上前来,向少佐很老派地鞠了一躬,称他“都宾先生”,并且问候他的老太爷威廉爵士。他说承爵士看得起,不久以前来望过他,他自己正打算去回拜。威廉爵士已经八年没有来看过他,他说起的就是八年前的旧事。

爱米轻轻地说道:“他身子虚得很。”都宾迎着老头儿,亲亲热热地跟他拉手。

少佐本来说过那天晚上在伦敦还有要紧事,可是赛特笠先生请他回家吃茶点,他就把这件事情搁下来了。爱米丽亚和她那围黄披肩的小朋友勾着胳膊领头向回家的路上先走,让都宾去招呼赛特笠先生。老头儿慢慢地走着,说起

turn homewards, so that Mr. Sedley fell to Dobbin's share. The old man walked very slowly, and told a number of ancient histories about himself and his poor Bessy, his former prosperity, and his bankruptcy. His thoughts, as is usual with failing old men, were quite in former times. The present, with the exception of the one catastrophe which he felt, he knew little about. The Major was glad to let him talk on. His eyes were fixed upon the figure in front of him—the dear little figure always present to his imagination and in his prayers, and visiting his dreams wakeful or slumbering.

Amelia was very happy, smiling, and active all that evening; performing her duties as hostess of the little entertainment with the utmost grace and propriety, as Dobbin thought. His eyes followed her about as they sat in the twilight. How many a time had he longed for that moment, and thought of her far away under hot winds and in weary marches, gentle and happy, kindly ministering to the wants of old age, and decorating poverty with sweet submission—as he saw her now. I do not say that his taste was the highest, or that it is the duty of great intellects to be content with a bread-and-butter paradise, such as sufficed our simple old friend; but his desires were of this sort whether for good or bad; and, with Amelia to help him, he was as ready to drink as many cups of tea as Doctor Johnson.

Amelia seeing this propensity, laughingly encouraged it; and looked exceedingly roguish as she administered to him cup after cup. It is true she did not know that the Major had had no dinner, and that the cloth was laid for him at the Slaughters, and a plate laid thereon to mark that the table was retained, in that very box in

许多老话，有些是关于他自己的，有些是关于可怜的蓓茜的，又提到他从前怎么发达，后来怎么破产等等。他像一切气力衰退的老人一样，一心只想过去。关于眼前的遭遇，他只记得一件伤心事，其余都不在心上。少佐很愿意让他说话；他的眼睛只盯着前面那心爱的人儿。这多少年他老是想她，给她祷告，睡里梦里也惦记着她。

那天晚上爱米丽亚笑眯眯活泼泼的非常快乐。都宾认为她做主妇做得又得体，又大方。他们坐在朦胧的暮色里，他的眼睛只是跟着她。这个机会，他已经渴望了多少时候了。在他远离家乡的时候，不管是在印度的热风里，或是在辛苦的征途上，他老是惦着她，想起她正像现在这样，很温柔，很快乐，孝顺体贴的伺候年老的父母，甘心情愿过苦日子，把贫穷的生活点缀得非常美丽。我并不称赞他的见解怎么高明，也不主张有大才智的人都应该像我们这位忠厚的老朋友一样，只求能得到这样的家常乐趣。可是这就是他的愿望，究竟是好是坏就不去管它了。只要爱米丽亚在替他斟茶，他就很愿意和约翰逊博士那么一杯杯的尽喝下去。

爱米丽亚见他爱喝茶，笑着劝他多喝几杯。当她一杯一杯替他斟茶的时候，脸上的表情着实顽皮。原来她并不知道少佐还没吃晚饭，也不知道那餐晚饭还在斯洛德咖啡馆等着他。店里的人已经给他铺上桌布，摆好盘子，定了

which the Major and George had sat many a time carousing, when she was a child just come home from Miss Pinkerton's school.

The first thing Mrs. Osborne showed the Major was Georgy's miniature, for which she ran up-stairs on her arrival at home. It was not half handsome enough of course for the boy, but wasn't it noble of him to think of bringing it to his mother? Whilst her papa was awake she did not talk much about Georgy. To hear about Mr. Osborne and Russell Square was not agreeable to the old man, who very likely was unconscious that he had been living for some months past mainly on the bounty of his richer rival; and lost his temper if allusion was made to the other.

Dobbin told him all, and a little more perhaps than all, that had happened on board the Ramchunder; and exaggerated Jos's benevo-lent dispositions towards his father, and resolution to make him comfortable in his old days. The truth is that during the voyage the Major had impressed this duty most strongly upon his fellow-passenger and extorted promises from him that he would take charge of his sister and her child. He soothed Jos's irritation with regard to the bills which the old gentleman had drawn upon him, gave a laughing account of his own sufferings on the same score, and of the famous consignment of wine with which the old man had favoured him: and brought Mr. Jos, who was by no means an ill-natured person when well pleased and moderately flattered, to a very good state of feeling regarding his relatives in Europe.

And in fine I am ashamed to say that the Major stretched the truth so far as to tell old Mr. Sedley that it

座。从前他和乔治时常吃喝作乐,使的就是那座儿。那时候,爱米丽亚刚从平克顿女学校出来,还是个孩子呢。

奥斯本太太第一件事就是把乔治的肖像给他看。她一到家就忙忙地跑上楼去把它拿下来。这肖像当然及不到本人一半那么漂亮,可是孩子居然想得着送肖像给母亲,由此可见他心地高尚。爱米丽亚在父亲醒着的时候没有多谈乔杰。老头儿不喜欢人家谈起奥斯本先生和勒塞尔广场,恐怕根本不知道最后几个月来他就靠着有钱的仇人救济他。每逢有人提起奥斯本,他就发脾气。

都宾把拉姆轻特船上的经过都告诉他——说不定还编了些话,夸张乔斯对父亲怎么孝顺,怎么决意让他享几年老福。真情是这样的,少佐一路上结结实实地对同船的乔斯谈过话,使他明白自己对父亲的责任,而且逼他答应从此照料他的妹妹和外甥。关于那一回老头儿擅自开发票卖酒给他的事,乔斯很生气,都宾劝解了一番,并且笑着把他自己怎么问老头儿买酒,后来怎么吃亏的情形说了一遍。乔斯只要在高兴头上,再有人家奉承他几句,性子并不坏;都宾这么一调解,他对于欧洲的亲人就很有好心了。

总而言之,少佐不顾事实,甚至于对赛特笠先生说乔斯

was mainly a desire to see his parent which brought Jos once more to Europe.

At his accustomed hour Mr. Sedley began to doze in his chair, and then it was Amelia's opportunity to commence her conversation, which she did with great eagerness! —it related exclusively to Georgy. She did not talk at all about her own sufferings at breaking from him, for indeed this worthy woman, though she was half-killed by the separation from the child, yet thought it was very wicked in her to repine at losing him; but everything concerning him, his virtues, talents, and prospects, she poured out. She described his angelic beauty; narrated a hundred instances of his generosity and greatness of mind whilst living with her: how a Royal Duchess had stopped and admired him in Kensington Gardens; how splendidly he was cared for now, and how he had a groom and a pony; what quickness and cleverness he had, and what a prodigiously well-read and delightful person the Reverend Lawrence Veal was, George's master. "He knows *everything*," Amelia said. "He has the most delightful parties. You who are so learned yourself, and have read so much, and are so clever and accomplished—don't shake your head and say no—*He* always used to say you were—you will be charmed with Mr. Veal's parties. The last Tuesday in every month. He says there is no place in the bar or the senate that Georgy may not aspire to. Look here," and she went to the piano drawer and drew out a theme of Georgy's composition. This great effort of genius, which is still in the possession of George's mother, is as follows:

"On Selfishness—Of all the vices which degrade the

回欧洲主要的原因就是看望父亲，这话说出来连我也觉得不好意思。

到了一定的钟点，赛特笠先生坐在椅子里打盹儿，爱米丽亚才有机会开始说她的话。她满心急着要和他谈，说来说去都离不了乔杰。关于娘儿俩分离时的苦楚，她一句也不提。这个好人儿失掉了儿子虽然伤心得半死，可是总觉得自己罪孽深重，不该离了孩子就怨艾不平。她说的都是儿子的事，把他品行怎么好，才干怎么高，将来有什么前途，倾筐倒箧讲给少佐听。她描写孩子天使一样的相貌，举了多多少少的例子证明他为人慷慨，人格高超——这些都还是他和母亲同住的时候的事情。她说起有一次在坎新登花园，一位公爵夫人特地停下来夸赞他长得好看；又说起他现在的环境多么好，自己有小马，还有马夫。她形容他读书聪明，做事敏捷；他的老师劳伦斯·维尔牧师是个极有修养、很可爱的人物。爱米丽亚说："他什么都懂。他的聚会真有趣。你自己也是怪有学问的，书看得又多，人又聪明，又有才学——你别摇头不承认，他从前总那么说。我想你准喜欢参加维尔牧师的聚会。他每个月的末一个星期二开会。他说乔杰将来要做议员就做议员，要做律师就做律师，要做得多高就是多高呢。瞧这儿。"说着，她走过去在钢琴的抽屉里拿出乔杰的一篇作文。这篇天才的作品，乔治的妈妈至今还收着。内容是这样的：

自　　私

在一切使人格堕落的不道德的行为之中，自私是

human character, Selfishness is the most odious and contemptible. An undue love of Self leads to the most monstrous crimes; and occasions the greatest misfortunes both in States and Families. As a selfish man will impoverish his family and often bring them to ruin; so a selfish king brings ruin on his people and often plunges them into war.

"Example: The selfishness of Achilles, as remarked by the poet Homer, occasioned a thousand woes to the Greeks —μυρι" 'Αχαιοῖς "ἄλγε" εΘηκε—(Hom. I1. A. 2). The selfishness of the late Napoleon Bonaparte occasioned innumerable wars in Europe, and caused him to perish, himself, in a miserable island—that of St. Helena in the Atlantic Ocean.

"We see by these examples that we are not to consult our own interest and ambition, but that we are to consider the interests of others as well as our own.

"George S. Osborne.

"Athene House, 24 April, 1827."

"Think of him writing such a hand, and quoting Greek too, at his age," the delighted mother said. "O William," she added, holding out her hand to the Major—"what a treasure Heaven has given me in that boy! He is the comfort of my life—and he is the image of—of him that's gone!"

"Ought I to be angry with her for being faithful to him?" William thought. "Ought I to be jealous of my friend in the grave, or hurt that such a heart as Amelia's can love only once and for ever. Oh, George, George, how little you knew the prize you had, though." This sentiment passed rapidly through William's mind, as he was holding Amelia's hand, whilst the handkerchief was veiling her eyes.

最可恨最可耻的。过分的自爱使人走上犯大罪的道路，对于国家和家庭有极大的损害。自私的人使他家庭贫困，往往弄得一家人倾家荡产。自私的国王使他的人民受灾难，往往把他们卷入战争。

举例来说，亚基利斯的自私，使希腊人受到无数的痛苦，正像诗人荷马在他的《伊里亚特》第二卷中所说的："给希腊人带来了极大的灾祸。"已故的拿破仑·波拿巴，也因为他的自私，在欧洲引起许多次的战争，结果自己也只能死在大西洋中的圣海里娜荒岛上。

由此可见我们不能只顾到自己的野心和利益，也要为别人着想才对。

乔治·奥斯本于雅典学院一八二七，四，二四。

做母亲的得意地说："你想想看，他小小年纪就写得这么一笔好字，还会引用希腊文。"她伸出手来说道："唉，威廉，这孩子真是天赏给我的宝贝。他是我的安慰，而且跟——跟死了的人长得真像。"

威廉想道："她对他忠诚到底，难道我反倒生气吗？像爱米丽亚这样的心只能爱一次，她是永远不变的，难道我还能因此觉得不高兴，反而跟我死去的朋友吃醋不成？唉，乔治，乔治，你真不知道自己的福气。"爱米丽亚正在拿着手帕擦眼泪，威廉拉着她的手，这个心思就很快地在他心上掠过。

"Dear friend," she said, pressing the hand which held hers, "how good, how kind you always have been to me! See! Papa is stirring. You will go and see Georgy to-morrow, won't you?"

"Not to-morrow," said poor old Dobbin. "I have business." He did not like to own that he had not as yet been to his parents' and his dear sister Ann—a remissness for which I am sure every well-regulated person will blame the Major. And presently he took his leave, leaving his address behind him for Jos, against the latter's arrival. And so the first day was over, and he had seen her.

When he got back to the Slaughters', the roast-fowl was of course cold, in which condition he ate it for supper. And knowing what early hours his family kept, and that it would be needless to disturb their slumbers at so late an hour, it is on record, that Major Dobbin treated himself to half-price at the Haymarket Theatre that evening, where, let us hope, he enjoyed himself.

她紧紧握着拉住她的手说："亲爱的朋友，你对我真好！瞧，爸爸在动了。你明天就去看乔杰，好吗？"

可怜的都宾答道："明天不行。我还有事呢。"他不愿意承认说他还没有回家去见过他父母和亲爱的安恩妹妹。他这样怠慢自己的亲人，想来凡是顾体统的人都要嗔怪他的。不久他和爱米丽亚父女俩告别，留下地址，等乔斯回家的时候给他。这样，第一天就算过去，他和她已经见过面了。

当他回到斯洛德咖啡馆的时候，烤鸡当然已经冷掉，他就吃了一餐冷饭。他知道家里安息得早，不必深更半夜打搅他们，便到海依市场戏院出半价去看了一出戏。这事在历史上有过记载。我希望他那晚过得快活。

The Old Piano

The Major's visit left old John Sedley in a great state of agitation and excitement. His daughter could not induce him to settle down to his customary occupations or amusements that night. He passed the evening fumbling amongst his boxes and desks, untying his papers with trembling hands, and sorting and arranging them against Jos's arrival. He had them in the greatest order—his tapes and his files, his receipts, and his letters with lawyers and correspondents; the documents relative to the Wine Project (which failed from a most unaccountable accident, after commencing with the most splendid prospects), the Coal Project (which only a want of capital prevented from becoming the most successful scheme ever put before the public), the Patent Sawmills and Sawdust Consolidation Project, All night, until a very late hour, he passed in the preparation of these documents, trembling about from one room to another, with a quivering candle and shaky hands.—Here's the wine papers, here's the sawdust, here's the coals; here's my letters to Calcutta and Madras, and replies from Major Dobbin. C. B., and Mr. Joseph Sedley to the same. "He shall find no irregularity about *me*, Emmy," the old gentleman said.

Emmy smiled. "I don't think Jos will care about seeing those papers, papa," she said.

"You don't know anything about business, my dear," answered the sire, shaking his head with an important air. And it must be confessed, that on this point Emmy was very ignorant, and that it is a pity, some people

旧 钢 琴

少佐来过之后，约翰·赛特笠老头儿兴奋得不得了。当晚他的女儿简直没法使他按老习惯行事，或是找往常的消遣。整个黄昏，他就在箱子桌子堆里摸索，手抖抖地解开许多文件，把它们收拾整齐，准备乔斯回家的时候给他看。他的带子、文件、收据，他和律师来往的信札，都拾掇得有条有理。此外还有关于卖酒计划的文件，卖煤计划的文件，木材木屑统一专卖计划的文件等等。那卖酒的计划起先希望大极了，不知怎么后来会失败；卖煤计划就因为缺少本钱，要不然准有空前的成功。他的准备工作直做到夜深。在摇曳不定的蜡烛光里，他抖巍巍地在几间房间里摸来摸去，两只手不停地打哆嗦。老先生说道："这是卖酒计划的文件，这是卖煤的，这是卖木屑的；这是我写到加尔各答和玛德拉斯的信，还有下级骑士都宾少佐和乔瑟夫·赛特笠先生的回信。爱米，我不愿意他回来看见我把事情办得乱七八糟。"

爱米笑了一笑，说道："爸爸，我想乔斯不会要看这些文件吧？"

父亲摇头摆脑的答道："亲爱的，正经事你是不懂的。"说实话，关于这一点爱米的确什么也不懂，我只觉得有些人

are so knowing. All these twopenny documents arranged on a side-table, old Sedley covered them carefully over with a clean bandanna handkerchief (one out of Major Dobbin's lot), and enjoined the maid and landlady of the house, in the most solemn way, not to disturb those papers, which were arranged for the arrival of Mr. Joseph Sedley the next morning. "Mr. Joseph Sedley of the Honourable East India Company's Bengal Civil Service."

Amelia found him up very early the next morning, more eager, more hectic, and more shaky than ever. "I didn't sleep much, Emmy my dear," he said. "I was thinking of my poor Bessy. I wish she was alive, to ride in Jos's carriage once again. She kept her own, and became it very well." And his eyes filled with tears, which trickled down his furrowed old face. Amelia wiped them away, and smilingly kissed him, and tied the old man's neckcloth in a smart bow, and put his brooch into his best shirt-frill, in which, in his Sunday suit of mourning, he sat from six o'clock in the morning awaiting the arrival of his son.

There are some splendid tailors' shops in the High Street of Southampton, in the fine plate-glass windows of which hang gorgeous waistcoats of all sorts, of silk and velvet, and gold and crimson, and pictures of the last new fashions, in which those wonderful gentlemen with quizzing-glasses, and holding on to little boys with the exceeding large eyes and curly hair, ogle ladies in riding habits prancing by the Statue of Achilles at Apsley House. Jos, although provided with some of the most splendid vests that Calcutta could furnish, thought he could not go to town until he was supplied with one or two of these gar-

懂得太多，反是件憾事。赛特笠老头儿把这些不值钱的文件整整齐齐搁在靠墙的一张桌子上，很小心地拿块干净的细布手帕盖好（手帕还是都宾少佐送的），郑重其事地吩咐女用人和房东太太不要把这些东西乱动，因为第二天早上乔瑟夫·赛特笠先生来了要查看的。他告诉她们说："乔瑟夫·赛特笠先生现在在东印度公司孟加拉民政部做事。"

第二天早晨，爱米丽亚发现他一早就起来了，比前一天更急切，更兴奋，也更虚瑟瑟的没力气。他说："爱米，亲爱的，我没有睡多少时候，夜里一直在想着可怜的蓓茜。可惜她不在了，不能再坐乔斯的马车了。从前她有自己的马车，她坐在里头也很像样。"说着，他满眼是泪，沿着打皱的腮帮子流下来。爱米丽亚替他擦眼泪，微笑着吻他，给他打了一个漂亮的领结，还在他最好的衬衫上别上别针。这样，他穿了最讲究的丧服，从早上六点钟起就坐着等儿子回家。

在沙乌撒泼顿的大街上有几家讲究的时装铺子，橱窗里摆着各种漂亮的背心，有绸缎的，有丝绒的，有金色的，有红色的。橱窗里还挂着时装画报，上面画着漂亮的先生，戴着单片眼镜，手里牵着大眼睛卷头发的小男孩儿，斜着眼在看太太小姐们；那些女的穿着骑马装，骑在跳跃的马上，在亚泼斯莱大厦的亚基里斯雕像旁边走过。乔斯已经在加尔各答买了几件背心，在当地算得上数一数二的漂亮，可是他觉得走进伦敦之前，非得再买一两件橱窗里摆着的新背心

ments, and selected a crimson satin, embroidered with gold butterflies, and a black and red velvet tartan with white stripes and a rolling collar, with which, and a rich blue satin stock and a gold pin, consisting of a five-barred gate with a horseman in pink enamel jumping over it, he thought he might make his entry into London with some dignity. For Jos's former shyness and blundering blushing timidity had given way to a more candid and courageous self-assertion of his worth. "I don't care about owning it," Waterloo Sedley would say to his friends, "I am a dressy man." and though rather uneasy if the ladies looked at him at the Government House balls, and though he blushed and turned away alarmed under their glances, it was chiefly from a dread lest they should make love to him, that he avoided them, being averse to marriage altogether. But there was no such swell in Calcutta as Waterloo Sedley, I have heard say: and he had the handsomest turn-out, gave the best bachelor dinners, and had the finest plate in the whole place.

To make these waistcoats for a man of his size and dignity took at least a day, part of which he employed in hiring a servant to wait upon him and his native; and in instructing the agent who cleared his baggage, his boxes, his books, which he never read; his chests of mangoes, chutney, and currie-powders; his shawls for presents to people whom he didn't know as yet; and the rest of his *Persicos apparatus*.

At length, he drove leisurely to London on the third day, and in the new waistcoat: the native, with chattering teeth, shuddering in a shawl on the box by the side of the new European servant; Jos puffing his pipe at intervals within, and looking so majestic, that the little boys cried

不可。他挑了一件绣着金色蝴蝶的红缎子背心，一件红黑方格上加白条子的丝绒背心，一个反卷的硬领，一条鲜艳的领带，还买了一只金别针，是一扇五根栅栏的小门，一个粉红色的珐琅人骑在马上正在跳过去。他认为在走进伦敦的时候非有这个排场不可。乔斯从前很怕羞，胆子又小，见了人就涨红了脸，做出事来脱枝失节。可是现在不同了，变得很喜欢逞能，总让人家知道他的重要。滑铁卢赛特笠对他的朋友们说："我是讲究穿衣服的，我也不怕人家知道。"有时总督府开跳舞会，碰上女人对他一端详，他还是免不了着急，吓得红了脸转身就逃。不过他慌张的原因多半是怕她们追求他，因为他根本不要结婚。据说在加尔各答就数滑铁卢赛特笠是头等的阔佬。他的排场最大，单身汉子里面，只有他请客最讲究，他的碗盏器皿也最精致。

要替他这样气派、这样大小的人物做背心，最少得一整天。在这一天里头，他雇了一个用人伺候他跟他的印度人。同时又吩咐代理人替他集叠行李、箱子、书籍（这些书他从来也不看）、一匣匣的芒果、腌渍的酸辣菜、咖喱粉，还有披肩和各种礼物，还不知该送给谁。此外还有许多东方带回来的奢侈品，也需要收拾。

到第三天，他穿了新背心很悠闲地坐了马车到伦敦来。他的印度用人裹着一条披肩，冷得牙齿格格的打战，挨着那个欧洲用人坐在马夫座位上发抖。乔斯坐在马车里面，不时抽抽烟斗，样子十分威风，引得路上的小孩儿大声欢呼，

Hooray, and many people thought he must be a Governor-General. *He*, I promise, did not decline the obsequious invitations of the landlords to alight and refresh himself in the neat country towns. Having partaken of a copious breakfast, with fish, and rice, and hard eggs, at Southampton, he had so far rallied at Winchester as to think a glass of sherry necessary. At Alton he stepped out of the carriage, at his servant's request, and imbibed some of the ale for which the place is famous. At Farnham he stopped to view the Bishop's Castle, and to partake of a light dinner of stewed eels, veal cutlets, and French beans, with a bottle of claret. He was cold over Bagshot Heath, where the native chattered more and more, and Jos Sahib took some brandy-and-water; in fact, when he drove into town, he was as full of wine, beer, meat, pickles, cherry-brandy, and tobacco, as the steward's cabin of a steam-packet. It was evening when his carriage thundered up to the little door in Brompton, whither the affectionate fellow drove first, and before hieing to the apartments secured for him by Mr. Dobbin at the Slaughters'.

All the faces in the street were in the windows; the little maidservant flew to the wicket-gate, the Mesdames Clapp looked out from the casement of the ornamented kitchen; Emmy, in a great flutter, was in the passage among the hats and coats, and old Sedley in the parlour inside, shaking all over. Jos descended from the post-chaise and down the creaking swaying steps in awful state, supported by the new valet from Southampton and the shuddering native, whose brown face was now livid with cold, and of the colour of a turkey's gizzard. He created an immense sensation in the passage presently,

有许多人以为他准是一个大总督。我可以肯定地说一句，当他路过干净的乡镇，有酒店主人出来奉迎他，请他下车吃东西，他从来不拒绝。他在沙乌撒泼顿吃过一顿丰盛的早饭，有鱼，有米饭，有煮老鸡蛋，哪知道到了温却斯特，他已经又觉得需要喝一杯雪利酒了。在亚尔顿，他听了用人的话，下车喝了些当地闻名的淡麦酒。在法纳姆，他去参观主教堡，又吃了一餐便饭，有焖鳝鱼、小牛肉片、法国豆子和一瓶红酒。到了巴格夏荒地，天气很冷，印度人越抖越凶，因此乔斯大爷又喝了些掺水的白兰地酒。总而言之，到达伦敦的时候，他的肚子活像汽船上总管的房间，装满了葡萄酒、啤酒、肉、酸辣菜、樱桃白兰地和香烟。直到傍晚时分，他的马车才轰隆轰隆来到白朗浦顿，在小门前面停下来。这家伙很重感情，都宾先生已经在斯洛德咖啡馆给他定了房间，他却先到家里来。

这条街上的人都从窗口探出头来张望；那小丫头飞奔到栅栏门口；克拉浦母女从兼做会客间的厨房窗口往外看；爱米心慌意乱，在过道里挂衣帽的地方等着；赛特笠老头儿在客室里浑身索索的抖。乔斯在马车里踩着那摇摇晃晃的踏步下来，脚底下吱吱的直响，真是威风十足。沙乌撒泼顿雇来的新用人和那印度听差一边一个扶着。印度人浑身发抖，棕黄的脸皮冻得泛青，活是火鸡肫的颜色。他在过道里轰动了一屋子的人；原来克拉浦太太和克拉浦小姐走上楼

where Mrs. and Miss Clapp, coming perhaps to listen at the parlour door, found Loll Jewab shaking upon the hall-bench under the coats, moaning in a strange piteous way, and showing his yellow eyeballs and white teeth.

For, you see, we have adroitly shut the door upon the meeting between Jos and the old father, and the poor little gentle sister inside. The old man was very much affected: so, of course, was his daughter: nor was Jos without feeling. In that long absence of ten years, the most selfish will think about home and early ties. Distance sanctifies both. Long brooding over those lost pleasures exaggerates their charm and sweetness. Jos was unaffectedly glad to see and shake the hands of his father, between whom and himself there had been a coolness—glad to see his little sister, whom he remembered so pretty and smiling, and pained at the alteration which time, grief, and misfortune had made in the shattered old man. Emmy had come out to the door in her black clothes and whispered to him of her mother's death, and not to speak of it to their father. There was no need of this caution, for the elder Sedley himself began immediately to speak of the event, and prattled about it, and wept over it plenteously. It shocked the Indian not a little, and made him think of himself less than the poor fellow was accustomed to do.

The result of the interview must have been very satisfactory, for when Jos had reascended his post-chaise, and had driven away to his hotel, Emmy embraced her father tenderly, appealing to him with an air of triumph, and asking the old man whether she did not always say that her brother had a good heart?

梯，大概想在客厅门外偷听里面的动静，不承望看见洛耳·奇活勃坐在大衣下面的一张板凳上发抖，露出一口白牙齿，眼睛倒插上去，只剩发黄的眼白，一面怪可怜的哼哼唧唧，那声音古怪极了。

我乖巧地关上了门，把里面乔斯和他年老的父亲和可怜的温柔的小妹妹怎么见面的情形，略过不谈了。老头儿非常感动；他的女儿当然也非常感动；乔斯呢，也不是无情的人。他离家十年，在这么长的一段时期之中，哪怕最自私的人也会想到老家和小时候的亲人。路程越隔得远，老家和亲人越显得神圣。过去的赏心乐事在长期的回忆当中更添了情趣，更令人向往。乔斯从前虽然对于父亲不满意，不过现在能够重新和他见面，和他拉手，倒是觉得出于衷心的喜欢。他记得小妹妹一向容貌俊俏，满面笑容，现在重逢，自然也是高兴的。瞧着父亲年纪大了，而且给伤心不幸的遭遇磨折得老态龙钟，他心里又觉得凄惨。一起头的时候，爱米穿了黑衣服先迎出来，在门口悄悄地告诉他说母亲已经不在了，叮嘱他不要在父亲面前提起这事。其实这个警告也是多余的，赛特笠老头儿立刻就谈到这件事，啰啰嗦嗦说了许多话，掉了许多眼泪。那印度人看了老大害怕；可怜的家伙平常只想自己，吃了这一惊，把自己的事情忘掉了好些。

看来重逢以后大家很满意。等到乔斯重新坐了马车上旅馆之后，爱米很温柔地搂着父亲，得意地说她早就夸过哥哥心肠好。

Indeed, Joseph Sedley, affected by the humble position in which he found his relations, and in the expansiveness and overflowing of heart occasioned by the first meeting, declared that they should never suffer want or discomfort any more, that he was at home for some time at any rate, during which his house and everything he had should be theirs: and that Amelia would look very pretty at the head of his table—until she would accept one of her own.

She shook her head sadly, and had, as usual, recourse to the waterworks. She knew what he meant. She and her young confidante, Miss Mary, had talked over the matter most fully, the very night of the Major's visit: beyond which time the impetuous Polly could not refrain from talking of the discovery which she had made, and describing the start and tremor of joy by which Major Dobbin betrayed himself when Mr. Binny passed with his bride, and the Major learned that he had no longer a rival to fear. "Didn't you see how he shook all over when you asked if he was married, and he said, 'Who told you those lies?' O Ma'am," Polly said, "he never kept his eyes off you; and I'm sure he's grown grey a-thinking of you."

But Amelia, looking up at her bed, over which hung the portraits of her husband and son, told her young *protégée*, never, never to speak on that subject again; that Major Dobbin had been her husband's dearest friend, and her own and George's most kind and affectionate guardian; that she loved him as a brother—but that a woman who had been married to such an angel as that, and she pointed to the wall, could never think of any other union. Poor Polly sighed: she thought what she should do if young Mr. Tomkins, at the surgery, who always looked

这话倒是真的。乔瑟夫·赛特笠看着家里的人生活这么清苦，心里很感动，再加初次会面时热情冲动，他在兴头上，便起誓说以后不让他们再过苦日子了。他说反正他预备在本国住一阵子，他的屋子和他的一切都给他们享用。他还说爱米丽亚在他请客的时候做起主妇来一定很得体，所以她尽不妨和他同住，到她愿意自立门户的时候再说。

她很伤心地摇摇头，又像平时一样掉下泪来。她懂得哥哥话里有因。少佐来过以后，当晚她就和她的心腹小朋友玛丽小姐细细地谈过这件事。玛丽是急性子，发现了秘密，到晚上再也忍不住，便对爱米描写都宾少佐看见平尼先生带着新娘走过的时候，起先怎么发怔，后来怎么乐得浑身打哆嗦，就因为他知道不必把平尼先生当做情敌的缘故。玛丽说："他问您说：'谁在造谣言？'一边说一边发抖，您难道没看见吗？嗳唷，太太啊，他两个眼睛一直瞧着您。我想他准是因为生相思病所以把头发都想白了。"

爱米丽亚抬头看看床面前丈夫和儿子的画像，一面告诉那受她照顾的小姑娘以后再也不准提起这件事。她说都宾少佐是她丈夫最好的朋友，又是乔杰和她自己最亲近最好心的保护人，她把他当做哥哥一样爱他，"可是，"她指指墙上说，"一个女人已经嫁过天使一般的好丈夫，绝不愿意再嫁第二回。"可怜的玛丽叹了一口气，心里想着外科医生诊所里那年轻的汤姆金先生。在教堂做礼拜的时候他老是

at her so at church, and who, by those mere aggressive glances, had put her timorous little heart into such a flutter that she was ready to surrender at once, —what she should do if he were to die? She knew he was consumptive, his cheeks were so red, and he was so uncommon thin in the waist.

Not that Emmy, being made aware of the honest Major's passion, rebuffed him in any way, or felt displeased with him. Such an attachment from so true and loyal a gentleman could make no woman angry. Desdemona was not angry with Cassio, though there is very little doubt she saw the Lieutenant's partiality for her (and I for my part believe that many more things took place in that sad affair than the worthy Moorish officer ever knew of); why, Miranda was even very kind to Caliban, and we may be pretty sure for the same reason. Not that she would encourage him in the least, —the poor uncouth monster—of course not. No more would Emmy by any means encourage her admirer, the Major. She would give him that friendly regard, which so much excellence and fidelity merited; she would treat him with perfect cordiality and frankness until he made his proposals; and *then* it would be time enough for her to speak, and to put an end to hopes which never could be realised.

She slept, therefore, very soundly that evening, after the conversation with Miss Polly, and was more than ordinarily happy, in spite of Jos's delaying. "I am glad he is not going to marry that Miss O'Dowd," she thought. "Colonel O'Dowd never could have a sister fit for such an accomplished man as Major William." Who was there amongst her little circle, who would make him a good wife? Not Miss Binny, she was too old and ill-tempered;

那么瞧着她；一看他挑逗的眼光，她那怯弱的心就跳个不停，准备把自己终身托付给他。如果他死了，那可怎么办呢？她知道他有痨病，他脸上时常上火，腰身比别人瘦小得多。

爱米知道忠厚的少佐热烈地爱她，可是并不嫌他，也不对他表示冷淡。男人肯这么死心塌地地一直爱到底，女人总不会因此生气。拿着苔丝迪梦娜[①]来说，她多半知道加西奥中尉喜欢她，可并没有生他的气。照我的看法，在那次悲剧里面还有好些事情都是那位贤明的摩尔军官不知道的。还有密兰达[②]，她对加立本还挺客气的呢，看来一定也是为这个原因。我当然并不是说她有意怂恿他来追求自己，那可怜东西不过是个又野又粗的怪物罢了。同样的，爱米也没有鼓励少佐来追求她。她只准备拿出又热和又尊敬的态度来对待他，因为他为人好，待朋友忠诚，值得人家尊重。在他开口求婚之前，她一定要努力让自己的态度坦白亲切。到他求婚的时候，她当然就叫他死了心，因为他这些希望是不可能实现的。

因为这样，当晚她和玛丽谈过话以后睡得很香，而且虽然乔斯没有准时回家，她却是异乎寻常地快乐。她想："他不娶奥多小姐我倒是很高兴。奥多上校决计不会有个妹妹配得上像威廉少佐那么多才多艺的人。"在她的小圈子里谁嫁给他最合适呢？平尼小姐不行，她太老了，脾气又不好。

---

① 莎士比亚悲剧《奥瑟罗》中的女主角，后来因为有人毁谤她和丈夫手下的军官加西奥私通，给丈夫杀死，摩尔军官就是指奥瑟罗本人。

② 莎士比亚喜剧《暴风雨》中的女主角，加立本不过是服她父亲指挥的一个怪物。萨克雷此地不过在开玩笑，他的说法是全无根据的。

Miss Osborne? —too old too. Little Polly was too young. Mrs. Osborne could not find anybody to suit the Major before she went to sleep.

However, when the postman made his appearance, the little party were put out of suspense by the receipt of a letter from Jos to his sister, who announced, that he felt a little fatigued after his voyage, and should not be able to move on that day, but that he would leave Southampton early the next morning, and be with his father and mother at evening. Amelia, as she read out the letter to her father, paused over the latter word; her brother, it was clear, did not know what had happened in the family. Nor could he: for the fact is, that though the Major rightly suspected that his travelling companion never would be got into motion in so short a space as twenty-four hours, and would find some excuse for delaying, yet Dobbin had not written to Jos to inform him of the calamity which had befallen the Sedley family: being occupied in talking with Amelia until long after post-hour.

The same morning brought Major Dobbin a letter to the Slaughters' Coffee House from his friend at Southampton; begging dear Dob to excuse Jos for being in a rage when awakened the day before (he had a confounded headache, and was just in his first sleep), and entreating Dob to engage comfortable rooms at the Slaughters' for Mr. Sedley and his servants. The Major had become necessary to Jos during the voyage. He was attached to him, and hung upon him. The other passengers were away to London. Young Ricketts and little Chaffers went away on the coach that day- Ricketts on the box, and taking the reins from Botley; the Doctor was off to his family at Portsea; Bragg gone to town to his copartners:

奥斯本小姐吗？也太老。小玛丽又太年轻。奥斯本太太睡觉以前想来想去也没找出一个配得上少佐的人。

第二天，邮差送来一封信，是乔斯写给妹妹的，信里说他刚下了船，觉得很疲倦，所以那天不能动身，必须等到第二天一早才能离开沙乌撒泼顿，傍晚时分便能和父母见面。有了信，家里的人也就不心焦了。爱米丽亚把信念给父亲听，念到"和父母见面"一句，顿了一顿。看上去她的哥哥还不知道家里的情形。这不能怪他；事情是这样的，都宾少佐虽然明知他的旅伴绝不会在二十四小时内动身回家，准会找推托随处流连，却没有写信把乔斯家里的坏消息先通知他，因为他隔夜和爱米丽亚谈得太久，来不及寄信了。

也就在那天早晨，都宾少佐在斯洛德咖啡馆里接到他朋友从沙乌撒泼顿寄来的信，信上提到他隔天早晨给吵醒以后发脾气的事情，求亲爱的都宾原谅，因为他那时刚刚睡着不久，头痛得厉害。同时他又委托都宾在斯洛德咖啡馆给他和他的两个用人定下几间舒服的房间。一路回国的时候，乔斯什么都依赖都宾。他离不开他，老是纠缠着他。那天，别的旅客都已经回到伦敦。年轻的里该滋和却弗斯是坐着邮车去的；里该滋坐在马车夫鲍脱莱旁边，把缰绳抢过来自己赶车子。医生回到包德西的老家去了；白拉格船长

and the first mate busy in the unloading of the Ramchunder. Mr. Jos was very lonely at Southampton, and got the landlord of the George to take a glass of wine with him that day; at the very hour at which Major Dobbin was seated at the table of his father, Sir William, where his sister found out (for it was impossible for the Major to tell fibs) that he had been to see Mrs. George Osborne.

Jos was so comfortably situated in Saint Martin's Lane, he could enjoy his hookah there with such perfect ease, and could swagger down to the theatres, when minded, so agreeably, that perhaps he would have remained altogether at the Slaughters' had not his friend, the Major, been at his elbow. That gentleman would not let the Bengalee rest until he had executed his promise of having a home for Amelia and his father. Jos was a soft fellow in anybody's hands; Dobbin most active in anybody's concerns but his own; the civilian was, therefore, an easy victim to the guileless arts of this good-natured diplomatist, and was ready to do, to purchase, hire, or relinquish whatever his friend thought fit. Loll Jewab, of whom the boys about Saint Martin's Lane used to make cruel fun whenever he showed his dusky countenance in the street, was sent back to Calcutta in the Lady Kicklebury East Indiaman, in which Sir William Dobbin had a share; having previously taught Jos's European the art of preparing curries, pilaus, and pipes. It was a matter of great delight and occupation to Jos to superintend the building of a smart chariot, which he and the Major ordered in the neighbouring Long Acre: and a pair of handsome horses were jobbed, with which Jos drove about in state in the Park, or to call upon his Indian friends. Amelia was not seldom by his side on these excursions, when

到伦敦去找其余的股东;船上的大副正忙着把货物从拉姆轻特船上卸下来。乔斯先生在沙乌撒泼顿冷静得很,只好请乔治旅馆的老板一块儿喝酒。就在那时候,都宾也在家里吃饭,跟父母和妹妹们坐在一桌。都宾少佐不会撒谎,他的妹妹把话一套,马上知道他回家之前已经先去拜访过奥斯本太太。

乔斯在圣马丁街住得很舒服。他不但能够静静儿地抽水烟,如果有兴致的话,也可以大摇大摆地上戏院看戏。他的生活那么安逸,倘若没有少佐在旁边催促着他,说不定他就会一直在斯洛德咖啡馆住下去。这位孟加拉客人曾经答应给他父亲和爱米丽亚布置一个家,因此少佐逼着他赶紧践约,要不然就不让他过安静日子。好在乔斯是肯听人调度的,都宾又是除了自己的事以外都肯出死力干的。这好性子的家伙手段着实圆滑,把那印度官儿笼络得言听计从,该买什么,该租什么,什么事该办,什么东西该脱手,全让他做主。洛耳·奇活勃不久就给送回加尔各答;他坐的是吉格尔白莱夫人号邮船,威廉·都宾爵士就是那家船公司的股东。印度人在圣马丁街的时候,每逢上街,顽童们瞧见了他的黑脸就来捉弄他。后来他把做咖喱、煮比劳、装水烟的法子教会了乔斯的欧洲用人,自己回家了。乔斯和少佐在附近朗爱格地方定做了一辆漂亮的马车;乔斯忙忙碌碌监看着工人打造马车,兴头得不得了。他又租了两匹好马,于是排场十足地在公园里兜风,或是去拜访在印度结交的朋友。爱米丽亚常常陪他出去,在这些时候,都宾便也来了,

also Major Dobbin would be seen in the back seat of the carriage. At other times old Sedley and his daughter took advantage of it: and Miss Clapp, who frequently accompanied her friend, had great pleasure in being recognised as she sate in the carriage, dressed in the famous yellow shawl, by the young gentleman at the surgery, whose face might commonly be seen over the window-blinds as she passed.

Shortly after Jos's first appearance at Brompton, a dismal scene indeed took place at that humble cottage, at which the Sedleys had passed the last ten years of their life. Jos's carriage (the temporary one, not the chariot under construction) arrived one day and carried off old Sedley and his daughter—to return no more. The tears that were shed by the landlady and the landlady's daughter at that event were as genuine tears of sorrow as any that have been outpoured in the course of this history. In their long acquaintanceship and intimacy they could not recall a harsh word that had been uttered by Amelia. She had been all sweetness and kindness, always thankful, always gentle, even when Mrs. Clapp lost her own temper, and pressed for the rent. When the kind creature was going away for good and all, the landlady reproached herself bitterly for ever having used a rough expression to her—how she wept, as they stuck up with wafers on the window, a paper notifying that the little rooms so long occupied were to let! They never would have such lodgers again, that was quite clear. After-life proved the truth of this melancholy prophecy: and Mrs. Clapp revenged herself for the deterioration of mankind by levying the most savage contributions upon the tea-caddies and legs of mutton of her *locataires*. Most of them scolded and

坐在马车的倒座上陪着。有时候赛特笠老头儿和他女儿也使那辆马车。克拉浦小姐时常陪她朋友出去;她披着那块有名的黄披肩坐在马车里,瞧见医生诊所里的小后生在对她看,心里非常得意。每逢她坐在马车里走过,小后生总是在诊所的百叶窗上面探头出来张望。

乔斯到白朗浦顿去过之后不久,住在赛特笠他们小屋里的人大家都伤心了一场。赛特笠一家在这所简陋的房子里已经住了十年。那天,乔斯派了马车(暂时租来的一辆,不是正在打造的大马车)——乔斯派了马车来接赛特笠和他女儿。他们离开之后当然不再回来了。房东太太和她女儿那一回倒是真心难受,这本历史里面无论什么人的眼泪都不能比她们的更真诚。她们和爱米丽亚从认识到相熟,那么长的一段时期里面,从来没有听见她说过一句伤人的话。她温柔近情,待人和气,得了一点好处就感谢不尽,甚至于在克拉浦太太发脾气逼着要房钱的时候也不变原来的态度。房东太太眼看着这好人儿从此一去不返,想起以前对她很不客气,心里悔之无及。她一面在窗口张贴招租条子,想法子把一向有人住的房子再租出去,一面伤心落泪。很明显的,他们以后再也找不着这么好的房客了。后来的日子证明这惨痛的预言一些也不错。克拉浦太太怨恨世道人心越来越堕落,只好在供应茶箱和羊腿的当儿狠狠地问房客多收点儿钱,借此出口气。大多数的房客都爱骂人,爱

grumbled; some of them did not pay; none of them stayed. The landlady might well regret those old, old friends, who had left her.

As for Miss Mary, her sorrow at Amelia's departure was such as I shall not attempt to depict. From childhood upwards she had been with her daily, and had attached herself so passionately to that dear good lady, that when the grand barouche came to carry her off into splendour, she fainted in the arms of her friend, who was indeed scarcely less affected than the good-natured girl. Amelia loved her like a daughter. During eleven years the girl had been her constant friend and associate. The separation was a very painful one indeed to her. But it was of course arranged that Mary was to come and stay often at the grand new house whither Mrs. Osborne was going; and where Mary was sure she would never be so happy as she had been in their humble cot, as Miss Clapp called it, in the language of the novels which she loved.

Let us hope she was wrong in her judgment. Poor Emmy's days of happiness had been very few in that humble cot. A gloomy Fate had oppressed her there. She never liked to come back to the house after she had left it, or to face the landlady who had tyrannized over her when ill-humoured and unpaid, or when pleased had treated her with a coarse familiarity scarcely less odious. Her servility and fulsome compliments when Emmy was in prosperity were not more to that lady's liking. She cast about notes of admiration all over the new house, extolling every article of furniture or ornament; she fingered Mrs. Osborne's dresses and calculated their price. Nothing could be too good for that sweet lady, she vowed and protested. But in the vulgar sycophant who now paid

抱怨；有些人不付房租；没有一个住长了的。怪不得房东太太想念走掉的老朋友。

玛丽小姐和爱米丽亚分手的时候有多么伤心，我简直说不上来。她从小到大，天天跟那位亲爱的好太太在一起，倒是一片热心和她好。她眼看着漂亮的马车来接她朋友去过好日子，伤心得晕倒在朋友的怀里。爱米丽亚差不多跟这好性子的姑娘一样感动。十一年来，玛丽一直是她的朋友，她的伴侣，她把玛丽就当做自己的女儿一样，临别的时候真是割舍不下。她们俩当然早已约好，奥斯本太太在漂亮的新房子里住定以后，常常接玛丽去住。玛丽说爱米丽亚住了大房子一定没有在他们"寒微的茅舍"里快活。她爱看小说，所以模仿小说的语气，管自己的家叫"茅舍"。

希望她猜测得不对，因为可怜的爱米在那"寒微的茅舍"里并没有过了几天快乐的日子。她的坏运气一直在折磨她。离了那屋子，她再也不愿意回去了。碰上房东太太脾气不好或是收不着房租的当儿，她恶狠狠地欺负爱米；到她一高兴，又亲昵得叫人肉麻，那腔调也一样可厌。如今她见爱米日子过得顺利，一味的拍马屁讨好，爱米也并不喜欢。克拉浦太太在新房子里一片声奉承，不论看见什么家具和摆设，都不住口的赞叹。她抚弄着奥斯本太太的衣服，估计它们值多少钱。她赌神发誓地说，像爱米这样的好人，什么讲究东西都配使。虽然她说了一大堆寒碜的奉承话

court to her, Emmy always remembered the coarse tyrant who had made her miserable many a time, to whom she had been forced to put up petitions for time, when the rent was overdue; who cried out at her extravagance if she bought delicacies for her ailing mother or father; who had seen her humble and trampled upon her.

Nobody ever heard of these griefs, which had been part of our poor little woman's lot in life. She kept them secret from her father, whose improvidence was the cause of much of her misery. She had to bear all the blame of his misdoings, and indeed was so utterly gentle and humble as to be made by nature for a victim.

I hope she is not to suffer much more of that hard usage. And, as in all griefs there is said to be some consolation, I may mention that poor Mary, when left at her friend's departure in an hysterical condition, was placed under the medical treatment of the young fellow from the surgery, under whose care she rallied after a short period. Emmy, when she went away from Brompton, endowed Mary with every article of furniture that the house contained: only taking away her pictures (the two pictures over the bed) and her piano—that little old piano which had now passed into a plaintive jingling old age, but which she loved for reasons of her own. She was a child when first she played on it: and her parents gave it her. It had been given to her again since, as the reader may remember, when her father's house was gone to ruin, and the instrument was recovered out of the wreck.

Major Dobbin was exceedingly pleased when, as he was superintending the arrangements of Jos's new house, which the Major insisted should be very handsome and comfortable, the cart arrived from Brompton, bringing

儿，爱米只记得她以前恶赖凶狠，自己时常受她欺负。每逢房租过了期没付，爱米得向她讨情；爱米买了些细巧的食品孝敬生病的父母，又得听她批评自己浪费。她曾经看着爱米失意，也曾经作践过她。

可怜的小爱米一辈子吃过不少这样的苦，可是没有人知道她的难处。这些话她从来不对父亲说，事实上她吃亏的原因多半是因为父亲糊涂。他干了坏事，女儿就得代他受罪。她这样温柔虚心，天生就是受人欺负的。

但愿她此后再不必受这样的糟蹋了。据说有痛苦就有跟着来的安慰，可怜的玛丽在朋友离开之后悲伤得眼泪鼻涕的哭闹，亏得医生诊所里的小后生来替她治病，才使她身体复原。爱米在离开白朗浦顿的时候把屋子里所有的家具都送给玛丽，只带走了床头的两张画像和她的钢琴。这架又小又旧的钢琴年代已经很久，发出来的声音叮叮咚咚的幽怨得很，不过她因为特别的原故，非常爱它。这钢琴原是当年她父母买给她的；她开始弹琴的时候，还是个孩子呢。读者想来还记得，后来她的父亲破产，有一个人特地从残余的家具里面把它买回来，重新送给爱米。

都宾少佐监督着布置乔斯的新房子，打定主意要把屋子里弄得又舒服又美观。正在忙碌的时候，一辆车子载着老房子里搬过来的箱子匣子，还有那架钢琴，从白朗浦顿来

the trunks and band-boxes of the emigrants from that village, and with them the old piano. Amelia would have it up in her sitting-room, a neat little apartment on the second floor, adjoining her father's chamber: and where the old gentleman sate commonly of evenings.

When the men appeared, then, bearing this old music-box, and Amelia gave orders that it should be placed in the chamber aforesaid. Dobbin was quite elated. "I'm glad you've kept it," he said in a very sentimental manner. "I was afraid you didn't care about it."

"I value it more than anything I have in the world," said Amelia.

"Do you, Amelia?" cried the Major. The fact was, as he had bought it himself, though he never said anything about it, it never entered into his head to suppose that Emmy should think anybody else was the purchaser, and as a matter of course he fancied that she knew the gift came from him. "Do you, Amelia?" he said; and the question, the great question of all, was trembling on his lips, when Emmy replied—

"Can I do otherwise? —did not he give it to me?"

"I did not know," said poor old Dob, and his countenance fell.

Emmy did not note the circumstance at the time, nor take immediate heed of the very dismal expression which honest Dobbin's countenance assumed; but she thought of it afterwards. And then it struck her, with inexpressible pain and mortification too, that it was William who was the giver of the piano; and not George, as she had fancied. It was not George's gift; the only one which she had received from her lover, as she thought—the thing she had cherished beyond all others—her dearest relic and

了，都宾看了满心喜欢。爱米丽亚吩咐把钢琴抬到三层楼上那间整齐的起坐间里搁好。那起坐间连着她父亲的卧房，老头儿后来一到黄昏便坐在里面歇息。

都宾看见扛伕抬着钢琴，爱米丽亚又叫他们抬到她的起坐间，心里得意，多情地说道："你还把它留着，我真高兴。我还以为你对它满不在乎。"

爱米丽亚道："在我眼睛里，它比世界上一切东西都宝贵。"

都宾虽然并没有把买钢琴的事跟别人说起，可是也没有想到爱米会以为钢琴是别人买的。他想爱米当然知道这是他送的礼。因此他叫起来说："真的吗，爱米丽亚？真的吗，爱米丽亚？"最重要的大问题已经到了他的嘴边，哪知道爱米答道：

"我怎么能够不宝贝它？这不是他给我的吗？"

可怜的都宾垂头丧气地答道："我倒没有知道。"

当时爱米并没有留心，也没有注意到忠厚的都宾那嗒丧的脸儿，后来她回想那时的情形，忽然明白过来，原来她以前弄错了，送钢琴给她的是威廉，不是乔治。这么一悟过来，她心里说不出的难受和懊恼。原来钢琴并不是乔治给的，她一向总以为它是爱人送给她的唯一的纪念品，把它当做宝贝，看得比一切都重。她对它谈起乔治；用它弹奏乔治

prize. She had spoken to it about George; played his favourite airs upon it: sate for long evening hours, touching, to the best of her simple art, melancholy harmonies on the keys, and weeping over them in silence. It was not George's relic. It was valueless now. The next time that old Sedley asked her to play, she said it was shockingly out of tune, that she had a headache, that she couldn't play.

Then, according to her custom, she rebuked herself for her pettishness and ingratitude, and determined to make a reparation to honest William for the slight she had not expressed to him, but had felt for his piano. A few days afterwards, as they were seated in the drawing-room, where Jos had fallen asleep with great comfort after dinner, Amelia said with rather a faltering voice to Major Dobbin,—"I have to beg your pardon for something."

"About what?" said he.

"About—about that little square piano. I never thanked you for it when you gave it me; many, many years ago, before I was married. I thought somebody else had given it. Thank you, William." She held out her hand; but the poor little woman's heart was bleeding; and as for her eyes, of course they were at their work.

But William could hold no more. "Amelia, Amelia," he said, "I did buy it for you. I loved you then as I do now. I must tell you. I think I loved you from the first minute that I saw you, when George brought me to your house, to show me the Amelia whom he was engaged to. You were but a girl, in white, with large ringlets; you came down sining—do you remember? —and we went to Vauxhall. Since then I have thought of but one woman in

最喜欢的曲子；在漫长的黄昏里坐在它旁边，尽她所能，在琴键上奏出忧郁的歌儿，一面悄悄地掉眼泪。既然它不是乔治的东西，还有什么价值呢？有一回赛特笠要她弹琴，她推说钢琴已经走了音，她自己又头痛，不高兴弹。

然后她又像平常一样，责怪自己小器没良心，决意要给老实的威廉一些补偿，因为她虽然没有明白表示瞧不起他的钢琴，心里却是那样想。几天之后，他们饭后都聚在客厅里，乔斯怪舒服地睡着了，爱米丽亚便吞吞吐吐地对都宾说："我得向你赔个不是才好。"

他说："赔什么不是呢？"

"就是为那架——那架小方钢琴。那还是好多年前我结婚以前你送给我的，我一直也没有给你道谢。我以为是另外一个人给我的。谢谢你，威廉。"可怜的爱米伸出手来给他拉手，心里却像刀绞的一样痛，她的眼睛当然也没有闲着。

威廉再也忍不住了。他说："爱米丽亚，爱米丽亚，我的确是为你才把它买下来的。那时候我就爱你，现在也是一样。这话我非告诉你不可。那会儿乔治把我带到你家里，要我认认他的未婚妻，大概我一看见你就爱上了你。你还是个小姑娘，穿了白衣服，头发梳成大圈儿。你还记得吗？你一边下楼一边唱歌，后来咱们还一起上游乐场来着。从

the world, and that was you. I think there is no hour of the day has passed for twelve years that I haven't thought of you. I came to tell you this before I went to India, but you did not care, and I hadn't the heart to speak. You did not care whether I stayed or went."

"I was very ungrateful," Amelia said.

"No; only indifferent," Dobbin continued, desperately. "I have nothing to make a woman to be otherwise. I know what you are feeling now. You are hurt in your heart at that discovery about the piano; and that it came from me and not from George. I forgot, or I should never have spoken of it so. It is for me to ask your pardon for being a fool for a moment, and thinking that years of constancy and devotion might have pleaded with you."

"It is you who are cruel now," Amelia said with some spirit. "George is my husband, here and in heaven. How could I love any other but him? I am his now as when you first saw me, dear William. It was he who told me how good and generous you were, and who taught me to love you as a brother. Have you not been everything to me and my boy? Our dearest, truest, kindest friend and protector? Had you come a few months sooner perhaps you might have spared me that—that dreadful parting. O, it nearly killed me, William —but you didn't come, though I wished and prayed for you to come, and they took him too away from me. Isn't he a noble boy, William? Be his friend still and mine"—and here her voice broke, and she hid her face on his shoulder.

The Major folded his arms round her, holding her to him as if she was a child, and kissed her head. "I will not change, dear Amelia," he said. "I ask for no more than your love. I think I would not have it otherwise. Only let

那时候起，我心眼儿里就只有一个姑娘，就是你。这十二年来，我可以说没有一时一刻不在惦记着你。到印度之前，我就想来告诉你。可是你心里没有我，我也没有勇气开口。我走开，我留下，你压根儿没有在乎。”

爱米丽亚道：“这是我没有良心。”

都宾不顾一切地说道：“不是没有良心，只是不关心。我也没有什么长处可以叫女人爱我。我知道你的心里。这会儿你心里很难受，因为你发现钢琴是我送的，而不是乔治送的。我也是一时忘情，不然我绝不会跟你那么说。所以还是应该我向你道歉。我不该一时糊涂，不该以为多少年来不变的忠心能够叫你同情我。”

爱米丽亚倔强地说道：“这会儿是你的心肠硬呀。不管在这儿还是在天堂上，乔治永远是我的丈夫。除了他，我怎么还能够爱上别的人呢？亲爱的威廉，我到今天还是他的人，就跟你当初看见我的时候一样。你有多少好处，你做人多么慷慨大量，也都是他告诉我的。他叫我把你像哥哥一样待。你对我和我的孩子可不是仁至义尽吗？你是我们最亲近、最忠诚、最仁慈的朋友和保护人。如果你早回来几个月，也许我不用和孩子分手，不用受这些罪。威廉，那一回我伤心得差点儿死了。我祷告，我希望你会回家，可是你不来，结果他们把他抢去了。威廉，他真了不起，是不是？求你还像从前一样照顾他，也照顾我——”她说到这里，哽咽起来，伏在他肩膀上遮着脸。

少佐伸出手来把她当小孩儿似的搂着，吻着她的头说：“亲爱的爱米丽亚，我不会变的。我只求你心上有我，别的也不想了。要不然的话，你根本不喜欢我了。我只希望常

me stay near you, and see you often."

"Yes, often," Amelia said. And so William was at liberty to look and long: as the poor boy at school who has no money may sigh after the contents of the tart-woman's tray.

常在你身边,常常看见你。”

爱米丽亚说:“好的,常常来吧。”这样,威廉算是得到许可,能够干瞧着得不到手的东西,好像学校里的穷孩子没钱买糕饼,只能看着甜饼小贩的盘子叹气。

Which Contains Births, Marriages, and Deaths

Whatever Becky's private plan might be by which Dobbin's true love was to be crowned with success, the little woman thought that the secret might keep, and indeed, being by no means so much interested about anybody's welfare as about her own, she had a great number of things pertaining to herself to consider, and which concerned her a great deal more than Major Dobbin's happiness in this life.

She found herself suddenly and unexpectedly in snug comfortable quarters: surrounded by friends, kindness, and good-natured simple people, such as she had not met with for many a long day; and, wanderer as she was by force and inclination, there were moments when rest was pleasant to her. As the most hardened Arab that ever careered across the Desert over the hump of a dromedary, likes to repose sometimes under the date-trees by the water; or to come into the cities, walk in the bazaars, refresh himself in the baths, and say his prayers in the Mosques, before he goes out again marauding; Jos's tents and pilau were pleasant to this little Ishmaelite. She picketed her steed, hung up her weapons, and warmed herself comfortably by his fire. The halt in that roving, restless life, was inexpressibly soothing and pleasant to her.

So, pleased herself, she tried with all her might to please everybody; and we know that she was eminent and successful as a practitioner in the art of giving pleasure. As for Jos, even in that little interview in the garret at

有人出生，有人结婚，有人去世

蓓基本来有心帮助都宾，使有情人能够遂心如意，可是究竟用什么计策，她却没有说出来。反正她对于别人的幸福都不如对于自己的前途那么关心。眼前有许多需要考虑的切身问题，比都宾少佐一生的快乐重要很多。

她忽然来到舒服的环境里，连自己也觉得突兀。现在她身边有的是朋友，对她非常体贴。四周围这种仁厚老实的好人，她已经好些时候没有接触过了。她对流浪生活很习惯，一则因为天性好动，二则也是出于不得已。话虽这么说，她有时候也很希望能够休息一下。哪怕是最不怕艰苦的阿拉伯人，惯会骑在骆驼背上在沙漠里奔驰，有时也爱在水草旁边枣树底下歇脚，或是进城逛逛市场，在澡堂里洗洗澡提提神，到教堂里做做祷告，然后再出外去干抢家劫舍的营生。同样的，蓓基一向被放逐在外面，现在住到乔斯的篷帐里面吃他的比劳[①]，觉得真是高兴。她拴好了马，放下兵器，怪受用地在他火旁边取暖。经过了漂泊不定的生涯，一旦安定下来，真有说不出的恬静愉快。

她自己觉得满意，便努力巴结这家子所有的人。讲到讨好别人这项本事，我们都知道她出人头地地能干。她和乔斯在大象旅社阁楼上谈了一席话，便哄得他回心转意了

---

① 印度的一种肉饭。

the Elephant inn, she had found means to win back a great deal of his good will. In the course of a week, the Civilian was her sworn slave and frantic admirer. He didn't go to sleep after dinner, as his custom was, in the much less lively society of Amelia. He drove out with Becky in his open carriage. He asked little parties and invented festivities to do her honour.

Tapeworm, the Chargé d'Affaires, who had abused her so cruelly, came to dine with Jos, and then came every day to pay his respects to Becky. Poor Emmy, who was never very talkative, and more glum and silent than ever after Dobbin's departure, was quite forgotten when this superior genius made her appearance. The French Minister was as much charmed with her as his English rival. The German ladies, never particularly squeamish as regards morals, especially in English people, were delighted with the cleverness and wit of Mrs. Osborne's charming friend; and though she did not ask to go to Court, yet the most August and Transparent Personages there heard of her fascinations, and were quite curious to know her. When it became known that she was noble, of an ancient English family, that her husband was a Colonel of the Guard, Excellenz and Governor of an island, only separated from his lady by one of those trifling differences which are of little account in a country where "Werther" is still read, and the "Wahlverwandtschaften" of Goethe is considered an edifying moral book, nobody thought of refusing to receive her in the very highest society of the little Duchy; and the ladies were even more ready to call her *du*, and to swear eternal friendship for her, than they had been to bestow the same inestimable benefits upon Amelia. Love and Liberty are interpreted by those

好些。她住下不到一星期，那印度官儿已经成了她忠心的奴才，发狂似的爱她。爱米丽亚比不上蓓基有趣，乔斯和她在一起的时候，吃过饭之后照规矩总得打个盹儿。利蓓加一来，他宁可不睡了，常常坐着敞车和她一同出去兜风，并且特地找些寻欢作乐的由头，为她请了好几次客。

代理公使铁泼窝姆本来恶毒毒地说蓓基的坏话，自从到乔斯家里吃过一餐饭之后，天天来拜访她。可怜的爱米向来不大说话，都宾走后，更加怏怏不乐，寡言罕语，因此这位高她一等的仙子一到，大家简直把她忘了。法国公使对于蓓基倾倒的程度，竟也不比他的英国对手差什么。至于德国的太太们呢，本来没有什么谨严的道德观念，对于英国人尤其另眼相看，所以瞧着奥斯本太太可爱的朋友那么机智聪明，都非常喜欢。蓓基虽然没有要求进宫，可是大公爵和他夫人听说她妩媚动人，很想见见她。后来大家知道她出身高贵，属于英国的旧世家，她丈夫是禁卫军里的上校，又是某某岛的总督大人；他们夫妻因为小事情不和，所以分居。在英国，大家仍旧看《少年维特之烦恼》，歌德的《选择的亲和力》也被公认为对于身心有益的读物，在这样的国内，夫妻分居算不了什么，所以公国里最高尚的人士都愿意招待她。太太们从前对爱米丽亚十分亲热，发誓始终如一地爱她；现在她们见了蓓基，更密切了一层，更愿意给她这

simple Germans in a way which honest folks in Yorkshire and Somersetshire little understand; and a lady might, in some philosophic and civilized towns, be divorced ever so many times from her respective husbands, and keep her character in society. Jos's house never was so pleasant since he had a house of his own, as Rebecca caused it to be. She sang, she played, she laughed, she talked in two or three languages; she brought everybody to the house: and she made Jos believe that it was his own great social talents and wit which gathered the society of the place round about him.

As for Emmy, who found herself not in the least mistress of her own house, except when the bills were to be paid, Becky soon discovered the way to soothe and please her. She talked to her perpetually about Major Dobbin sent about his business, and made no scruple of declaring her admiration for that excellent, high-minded gentleman, and of telling Emmy that she had behaved most cruelly regarding him. Emmy defended her conduct, and showed that it was dictated only by the purest religious principles; that a woman once, and to such an angel as him whom she had had the good fortune to marry, was married for ever; but she had no objection to hear the Major praised as much as ever Becky chose to praise him; and indeed brought the conversation round to the Dobbin subject a score of times every day.

Means were easily found to win the favour of Georgy and the servants. Amelia's maid, it has been said, was heart and soul in favour of the generous Major. Having at first disliked Becky for being the means of dismissing him from the presence of her mistress, she was reconciled to Mrs. Crawley subsequently, because the latter became

些无上的好处。这些单纯的德国人对于爱情和自由的看法是约克郡和索默塞脱郡的老实人所不懂的。在德国好些文明的城市里，居民的见解很通达，他们认为一个女人尽管离过好几次婚，可是在社会上的地位却一点不受影响。乔斯自从自立门户之后，家里的气氛从来没有像现在这么愉快。这全是利蓓加的功劳。她唱歌弹琴，有说有笑，会说两三国语言，把所有的人都引到家里来，并且使乔斯相信本地上流人士所以爱同他们往来，都是因为他善于应酬，口角俏皮的缘故。

爱米现在在家里什么事都不能做主，只有付账的时候才去向她要钱。可是蓓基不久就想出法子来讨好她安慰她。她不断地和爱米讲到都宾给撵走的事情，毫不顾忌地称赞他是个人品高贵的君子，表示十分佩服他，而且责备爱米对他太不近人情。爱米为自己辩护，说她不过是遵照基督教的教义行事，又说一个女人应该从一而终，她既然侥幸嫁过像天神一般的好丈夫，无论如何不愿意再嫁了。话虽这么说，蓓基称赞少佐，她听了一些不生气，蓓基爱夸他多少回都没有关系。不但如此，她自己常常把话题转到都宾身上，一天不下二十来次。

讨好乔杰和用人们是不难的。上面已经说过，爱米丽亚的贴身女用人全心全意赞赏慷慨大度的都宾少佐。起先她讨厌蓓基，怪她离间了少佐和女主人，可是后来看见她那么佩服少佐，为他辩护的时候口气那么热烈，气也平了。每

William's most ardent admirer and champion. And in those mighty conclaves in which the two ladies indulged after their parties, and while Miss Payne was "brushing their 'airs," as she called the yellow locks of the one, and the soft brown tresses of the other, this girl always put in her word for that dear good gentleman Major Dobbin. Her advocacy did not make Amelia angry any more than Rebecca's admiration of him. She made George write to him constantly, and persisted in sending Mamma's kind love in a postscript. And as she looked at her husband's portrait of nights, it no longer reproached her—perhaps she reproached it, now William was gone.

Emmy was not very happy after her heroic sacrifice. She was very *distraite*, nervous, silent, and ill to please. The family had never known her so peevish. She grew pale and ill. She used to try and sing certain songs ("Einsam bin ich nicht alleine," was one of them; that tender love-song of Weber's, which, in old-fashioned days, young ladies, and when you were scarcely born, showed that those who lived before you knew too how to love and to sing);—certain songs, I say, to which the Major was partial; and as she warbled them in the twilight in the drawing-room, she would break off in the midst of the song, and walk into her neighbouring apartment, and there, no doubt, take refuge in the miniature of her husband.

Some books still subsisted, after Dobbin's departure, with his name written in them; a German Dictionary, for instance, with "William Dobbin, —th Reg.," in the fly-leaf; a guide-book with his initials, and one or two other volumes which belonged to the Major. Emmy cleared these away, and put them on the drawers, where she

逢请客以后，两位太太晚上在一处相聚，配恩小姐给她们刷头发（一位太太是淡黄头发，另外一位是软软的栗色头发）——配恩小姐一面刷，一面总为那位亲爱的好先生都宾少佐说几句好话。爱米丽亚听了并不着恼，就好像她听见利蓓加夸奖他不觉得生气一样。她催着乔治经常写信给他，而且总不忘记叫他在信后写上妈妈嘱笔问候等等字样。到晚上她望望丈夫的遗像，觉得它不再责备自己。现在威廉走掉之后，说不定她反而有些怨怪它的意思。

爱米不顾一切地牺牲了自己之后，心上很不快活。她精神恍惚，不言不语，情绪非常不安，左也不是，右也不是的，家里人从来没有看见她脾气那么大。渐渐的她脸色青白，身上老是不快。她时常挑了几支歌儿自己弹唱，全是少佐以前喜欢听的——威勃所作的温馨的情歌《虽不是独自一个儿，我也寂寞》就是其中之一。小姐们啊，由此可见你们的前辈虽然老派，也知道怎么恋爱，怎么唱歌，那时候你们还没有出世呢。到傍晚，她在朦朦胧胧的客厅里唱歌，往往唱到一半，忽然停下来走到隔壁屋子里，想来总是瞧着丈夫的遗像找安慰去了。

都宾走了之后，还留下几本书，里面写着他的名字。一本是德文字典，空白页上写了“第×联队威廉·都宾”，一本是旅行指南，上面有他姓名的第一个字母，此外还有一两本别的书，都给爱米收起来搁在她卧房里的柜子上。这衣柜

placed her work-box, her desk, her Bible, and Prayer-book, under the pictures of the two Georges. And the Major, on going away, having left his gloves behind him, it is a fact that Georgy, rummaging his mother's desk some time afterwards, found the gloves neatly folded up, and put away in what they call the secret drawers of the desk.

Not caring for society, and moping there a great deal, Emmy's chief pleasure in the summer evenings was to take long walks with Georgy (during which Rebecca was left to the society of Mr. Joseph), and then the mother and son used to talk about the Major in a way which even made the boy smile. She told him that she thought Major William was the best man in all the world; the gentlest and the kindest, the bravest and the humblest. Over and over again, she told him how they owed everything which they possessed in the world to that kind friend's benevolent care of them; how he had befriended them all through their poverty and misfortunes; watched over them when nobody cared for them; how all his comrades admired him, though he never spoke of his own gallant actions; how Georgy's father trusted him beyond all other men, and had been constantly befriended by the good William. "Why, when your papa was a little boy," she said, "he often told me that it was William who defended him against a tyrant at the school where they were; and their friendship never ceased from that day until the last, when your dear father fell."

"Did Dobbin kill the man who killed papa?" Georgy said. "I'm sure he did, or he would if he could have caught him; wouldn't he, mother? When I'm in the

正在两个乔治的肖像底下，上面摆着她的针线盒子、小书台、《圣经》、圣书。少佐临走的时候忘了把手套带去，后来乔杰在他妈妈书台里找东西，发现这副手套给整整齐齐地叠好了藏在大家所说的“秘密抽屉”里。这也是事实。

爱米不喜欢应酬，心绪又不好，夏天傍晚唯一的消遣就是和乔杰出去散步，一直走得老远，把利蓓加撇在家里陪着乔斯先生。娘儿两个老是谈起少佐，妈妈的口气叫那孩子忍不住微笑。她告诉乔杰说她觉得威廉少佐是全世界最好、最温和、最慈厚、最勇敢同时又是最谦虚的人。她反复告诉他，说他们现在的一切，都是这位好朋友的恩赐，他们穷愁交逼的时候，全靠他照应；别人不理睬他们的时候，也亏他帮助。她说少佐的同事没一个不佩服他，虽然他本人从来不提到自己的功绩；乔杰的父亲最相信他，他从小到大，都亏得好威廉看顾他。爱米说：“你爸爸小时候常常告诉我说他们学校里有个恶霸欺负他，幸而有威廉保护着才没有吃亏。从那天起，他们两个就做了好朋友，一直到你亲爱的爸爸打仗死去为止。”

乔杰说：“都宾有没有把害死爸爸的敌人杀掉呢？我想他准已经把他弄死了，反正如果他把那人拿住以后，绝不饶他，是不是，妈妈？将来我进了军队，我跟那些法国人誓不

army,won't I hate the French? —that's all."

In such colloquies the mother and the child passed a great deal of their time together. The artless woman had made a confidant of the boy. He was as much William's friend as everybody else who knew him well.

By the way, Mrs. Becky, not to be behind-hand in sentiment, had got a miniature too hanging up in her room, to the surprise and amusement of most people, and the delight of the original, who was no other than our friend Jos. On her first coming to favour the Sedleys with a visit, the little woman, who had arrived with a remarkably small shabby kit, was perhaps ashamed of the meanness of her trunks and band-boxes, and often spoke with great respect about her baggage left behind at Leipzig, which she must have from that city. When a traveller talks to you perpetually about the splendour of his luggage, which he does not happen to have with him, my son, beware of that traveller! He is, ten to one, an impostor.

Neither Jos nor Emmy knew this important maxim. It seemed to them of no consequence whether Becky had a quantity of very fine clothes in invisible trunks; but as her present supply was exceedingly shabby, Emmy supplied her out of her own stores, or took her to the best milliner in the town, and there fitted her out. It was no more torn collars now, I promise you, and faded silks trailing off at the shoulder. Becky changed her habits with her situation in life —the rouge-pot was suspended—another excitement to which she had accustomed herself was also put aside, or at least only indulged in in privacy; as when she was prevailed on by Jos of a summer

两立！这是我的话。”

娘儿两个这样谈体己，一谈就是好些时候。心地单纯的女人把孩子当做心腹朋友。他呢，跟一切深知威廉的人一般，非常喜欢他。

顺便再说一句。蓓基太太在待人多情多义这方面不甘后人，在卧房里也挂起一张肖像来。许多人看见了都觉得又纳闷又好笑。肖像上不是别人，正是我们的朋友乔斯。他见蓓基屋里挂了自己的肖像，心中大喜。这小女人最初住到赛特笠家里来的时候，只带了一只旧得不像样的小箱子，后来的大箱子和纸盒子也破烂不堪。大概她觉得很不好意思，便时常谈起她留在莱比锡的行李，仿佛这些东西非常贵重，总说要想法把它们运来才好。我的孩子，如果出门旅行的人身边没有行李，而不断地跟你谈起他的行李怎么讲究，千万小心在意。这个人十分之九是个骗子。

乔斯和爱米都不懂得这重要的公理。蓓基的没现形的箱子里究竟是不是真有许多漂亮的衣服，他们并不放在心上。可是她眼前的衣着非常破旧，爱米只好把自己的供给她用，或是带她到本城最好的衣装店里去添置新衣服。我可以肯定地说一句，现在她不穿撕破领子的衣服了，也没有肩膀那里拖一块挂一块的褪色绸衫子了。环境一变，蓓基少不得把自己的习惯也改掉些。胭脂瓶暂时给藏了起来，另外一种习以为常的刺激也只能放弃，或者只能私底下享受一下，譬如像爱米娘儿俩夏天傍晚出去散步，有乔斯劝

evening, Emmy and the boy being absent on their walks, to take a little spirit-and-water. But if she did not indulge—the courier did: that rascal Kirsch could not be kept from the bottle; nor could he tell how much he took when he applied to it. He was sometimes surprised himself at the way in which Mr. Sedley's cognac diminished. Well, well; this is a painful subject. Becky did not very likely indulge so much as she used before she entered a decorous family.

At last the much-bragged about boxes arrived from Leipzig;—three of them, not by any means large or splendid;—nor did Becky appear to take out any sort of dresses or ornaments from the boxes when they did arrive. But out of one, which contained a mass of her papers (it was that very box which Rawdon Crawley had ransacked in his furious hunt for Becky's concealed money), she took a picture with great glee, which she pinned up in her room, and to which she introduced Jos. It was the portrait of a gentleman in pencil, his face having the advantage of being painted up in pink. He was riding on an elephant away from some cocoa-nut trees, and a pagoda: it was an Eastern scene.

"God bless my soul, it is my portrait," Jos cried out. It was he indeed, blooming in youth and beauty, in a nankeen jacket of the cut of 1804. It was the old picture that used to hang up in Russell Square.

"I bought it," said Becky, in a voice trembling with emotion; "I went to see if I could be of any use to my kind friends. I have never parted with that picture—I never will."

"Won't you?" Jos cried, with a look of unutterable rapture and satisfaction. "Did you really now value it for

着，她才喝些掺水的白酒。她并不放量痛饮；他家的向导，那混蛋的基希，就不同了，老是尽着肚子灌，简直离不开酒瓶子，而且一开了头就闹不清自己喝过多少。有的时候他发觉乔斯先生的哥涅克酒消耗得那么快，连自己也觉得糊涂。好了，好了，这些话叫人怪不好意思的，反正蓓基自从进了上等人家之后，一定没有以前喝得那么多。

形容得天花乱坠的箱子终于从莱比锡来了，一共有三只，既不华丽，也不怎么大，而且蓓基似乎并没有从箱子里拿出什么衣服首饰来用。一只箱子里装了许多纸张文件，——以前罗登·克劳莱发狠搜查蓓基的私房钱，抄的就是这一个箱子。她嬉皮笑脸地从这个箱子里拿出一张肖像钉在墙上，叫乔斯来看。这是一张铅笔画，画着一位先生，两腮帮子涂得红粉粉的非常好看。他骑在大象身上，远处有几棵椰子树和一座塔，正是东方的景色。

乔斯叫道："求老天保佑我的灵魂吧！这是我的画像！"这正是他的像，画得又年轻又俊美，上身穿着一件黄布衣服，还是一八〇四年的款式。这幅肖像从前一向挂在勒塞尔广场老房子里。

蓓基感动得声音发抖，说道："是我把它买下来的。那时候我去看看到底有没有法子帮忙我的好朋友们。我一直把这幅画儿好好藏着——我以后也要把它好好藏着。"

乔斯脸上说不出的高兴得意，说："真的？你真的为我才看重它吗？"

my sake?"

"You know I did, well enough," said Becky; "but why speak,—why think,—why look back? It is too late now!"

That evening's conversation was delicious for Jos. Emmy only came in to go to bed very tired and unwell. Jos and his fair guest had a charming *têteà-tête*, and his sister could hear, as she lay awake in her adjoining chamber, Rebecca singing over to Jos the old songs of 1815. He did not sleep, for a wonder, that night, any more than Amelia.

It was June, and, by consequence, high season in London; Jos, who read the incomparable *Galignani* (the exile's best friend) through every day, used to favour the ladies with extracts from his paper during their breakfast. Every week in this paper there is a full account of military movements, in which Jos, as a man who had seen service, was especially interested. On one occasion he read out—"Arrival of the —th regiment.—Gravesend, June 20.—The Ramchunder, East Indiaman, came into the river this morning, having on board 14 officers, and 132 rank and file of this gallant corps. They have been absent from England fourteen years, having been embarked the year after Waterloo, in which glorious conflict they took an active part, and having subsequently distinguished themselves in the Burmese war. The veteran colonel, Sir Michael O'Dowd, K. C. B., with his lady and sister, landed here yesterday, with Captains Posky, Stubble, Macraw, Malony; Lieutenants Smith, Jones, Thompson, F. Thomson; Ensigns Hicks and Grady; the band on the pier playing the national anthem, and the crowd loudly cheering the gallant veterans as they went

蓓基道："你明明知道我心里的确是这样。可是何必多说，何必多想，何必回顾往事呢？现在已经来不及了。"

那天晚上的谈话，乔斯听来真觉得滋味无穷。爱米回家的时候又疲倦又委顿，立刻上床睡觉，只剩乔斯跟他美貌的客人对坐谈心，彼此谈得很畅快。他妹妹在隔壁躺着睡不着，听得利蓓加把一八一五年流行的歌曲唱给乔斯听。当晚乔斯和爱米丽亚一样，也睡不着，真是希罕事儿。

当下已到六月，正是伦敦最热闹的时候。乔斯每天把《加里涅尼报》上的新闻细细看一遍，早饭的时候挑几段读给太太们听。这份天下无双的报纸真是国外旅行者的好伴侣，上面每星期都登载着军队调动的详细消息。乔斯也算在军队里混过的，所以对于这种消息特别关心。有一回他念道："第×联队士兵回国。格拉芙生特六月二十日电：英勇的第×联队士兵今晨乘东印度商船拉姆轻特号抵达此地，船上共计军官十四人，兵士一百三十二人。第——联队曾经参加滑铁卢大战，为国增光，一年后外调，在缅甸战役又大显身手，迄今已有十四年未曾回国。久经战阵的统领麦格尔·奥多爵士已在昨日登陆。同行的除奥多夫人和爵士的妹妹奥多小姐之外，有波斯基上尉、斯德卜尔上尉、马克洛上尉、玛洛内上尉、斯密士中尉、琼斯中尉、汤姆生中尉、弗·托母森中尉、赫格思少尉、格拉弟少尉。勇士们上岸的时候，乐队奏出国歌，观者欢声雷动，一路送他们到伟

into Wayte's hotel, where a sumptuous banquet was provided for the defenders of old England. During the repast, which we need not say was served up in Wayte's best style, the cheering continued so enthusiastically, that Lady O'Dowd and the Colonel came forward to the balcony, and drank the healths of their fellow-countrymen in a bumper of Wayte's best claret."

On a second occasion Jos read a brief announcement—Major Dobbin had joined the —th regiment at Chatham; and subsequently he promulgated accounts of the presentations at the Drawing-room, of Colonel Sir Michael O'Dowd, K. C. B., Lady O'Dowd (by Mrs. Malloy Malony of Bally malony), and Miss Glorvina O'Dowd (by Lady O'Dowd). Almost directly after this, Dobbin's name appeared among the Lieutenant-Colonels: for old Marshal Tiptoff had died during the passage of the—th from Madras, and the Sovereign was pleased to advance Colonel Sir Michael O'Dowd to the rank of Major-General on his return to England, with an intimation that he should be Colonel of the distinguished regiment which he had so long commanded.

Amelia had been made aware of some of these movements. The correspondence between George and his guardian had not ceased by any means: William had even written once or twice to her since his departure, but in a manner so unconstrainedly cold, that the poor woman felt now in her turn that she had lost her power over him, and that, as he had said, he was free. He had left her, and she was wretched. The memory of his almost countless services, and lofty and affectionate regard, now presented itself to her, and rebuked her day and night. She brooded over those recollections according to her

德饭店进餐。伟德饭店为招待各位卫国英雄起见，特备上等筵席，酒菜十分丰盛。进餐时群众继续在外面热烈欢呼。奥多上校和奥多夫人特地出席到阳台上，举杯满饮伟德饭店最贵重的红酒祝群众‘身体健康’。”

又有一次，乔斯读出一段简短的新闻，说是都宾少佐已经到达契顿姆，重新回到第×联队里原有的岗位上。后来他又读到下级骑士麦格尔·奥多爵士、奥多爵士夫人，以及葛萝薇娜·奥多小姐进宫觐见的情形。奥多夫人的引见人是葛兰曼洛内的玛洛哀·玛洛内太太，奥多小姐的就是奥多夫人。这项消息刊登出来不久，都宾的名字就在陆军少将的名单上出现。原来铁帕托夫老将军在第——联队从玛德拉斯回国的时候死在半路。军队回国以后，国王特将麦格尔·奥多上校升为陆军中将，并且下旨任命他为团长总指挥，正式统带向来在他属下的出众的士兵。

关于这些事情，爱米丽亚已经听说过一点儿。乔治和他保护人之间信来信去，一直没有间断。威廉离开之后，甚至于还写过一两封信给爱米丽亚本人，可是口气老实不客气地冷淡，因此这一回轮到可怜的女人心里气馁，觉得已经失去了控制威廉的力量。正是他说的，他如今是自由身子了。威廉离开了她，又叫她心酸。她想到以前他一次又一次地替自己当差，不知帮了多少忙，而且对自己又尊重又体贴；这一切都涌到眼前，日日夜夜使她不得安宁。她依照向来的习惯，暗底下难过，想起从前把他的爱情不当一回事，

wont: saw the purity and beauty of the affection with which she had trifled, and reproached herself for having flung away such a treasure.

It was gone indeed. William had spent it all out. He loved her no more, he thought, as he had loved her. He never could again. That sort of regard, which he had proffered to her for so many faithful years, can't be flung down and shattered, and mended so as to show no scars. The little heedless tyrant had so destroyed it. No, William thought again and again, "It was myself I deluded, and persisted in cajoling; had she been worthy of the love I gave her, she would have returned it long ago. It was a fond mistake. Isn't the whole course of life made up of such? and suppose I had won her, should I not have been disenchanted the day after my victory? Why pine, or be ashamed of my defeat?" The more he thought of this long passage of his life, the more clearly he saw his deception. "I'll go into harness again," he said, "and do my duty in that state of life in which it has pleased Heaven to place me. I will see that the buttons of the recruits are properly bright, and that the sergeants make no mistakes in their accounts. I will dine at mess, and listen to the Scotch surgeon telling his stories. When I am old and broken, I will go on half-pay, and my old sisters shall scold me. I have 'geliebt und gelebet' as the girl in Wallenstein says. I am done.—Pay the bills, and get me a cigar: find out what there is at the play to-night, Francis; to-morrow we cross by the 'Batavier.'" He made the above speech, where of Francis only heard the last two lines, pacing up and down the Boompjes at Rotterdam. The 'Batavier' was lying in the basin. He could see the place on the quarter-deck, where he and Emmy had sate

现在才明白这种感情的纯洁和美丽。只怪自己不好，轻轻扔掉了这样的珍宝。

威廉的爱情真的死了，消耗尽了。他心里觉得自己对她的爱情已经一去不返，而且以后也不可能重新爱她。多少年来他忠忠心心献给她的一片痴情给她扔在地下摔得粉碎，即使修补起来，裂痕总在，爱米丽亚太轻率，太霸道，生生地把它糟蹋了。威廉反复寻思道："只怪我痴心妄想，一味自己哄自己。如果她值得我这么爱她，一定早已报答我的真情。这都是我心地糊涂，才会误到如今。人生一辈子，不就是一错再错地错下去吗？就算我赢得了她的爱情，看来也会立刻从迷梦中醒过来。何必灰心丧气，因为失败而觉得害臊呢？"他仔细咀嚼半生追求爱米丽亚的过程，越想得透，就越看得穿，明白自己受了骗。他说："还是回去干我的老本行吧！天既然派我过那种生活，我就好好地尽我的本分。我的任务就是督促新来的弟兄们把制服上的纽扣擦亮，教导军曹们把账目记清。我以后在大饭堂吃饭，听那苏格兰医生讲故事。到我年老力衰的时候，就领个半俸告老，我的老妹妹们嘴碎，正好骂骂我。正像《华伦斯坦》[①]里的女孩子说的：'我曾经恋爱过，也领略过人生。'这会儿可觉得累了。弗兰西斯，把账付了，给我拿一支雪茄烟来。再看看今儿晚上有什么戏。明天咱们乘'巴达维埃'号过海。"他一面在罗脱达姆的旅馆里踱来踱去，一面说了上面的一篇话，可是弗兰西斯听见的却只有最后的两句。"巴达维埃"号邮船泊在船坞里，当初出国的时候，他和爱米同坐在那艘船的后甲板上，大家欢天喜地；现在他还看得见那块地方。

① 德国大诗人席勒(Schiller，1759—1805)所著历史悲剧，1799年出版。

on the happy voyage out. What had that little Mrs. Crawley to say to him? Psha! to-morrow we will put to sea, and return to England, home, and duty!

After June all the little Court Society of Pumpernickel used to separate, according to the German plan, and make for a hundred watering-places, where they drank at the wells; rode upon donkeys; gambled at the *redoutes*, if they had money and a mind; rushed with hundreds of their kind, to gormandise at the *tables-d'hôte*; and idled away the summer. The English diplomatists went off to Töplitz and Kissengen, their French rivals shut up their *chancellerie* and whisked away to their darling Boulevard de Gand. The Transparent reigning family took, too, to the waters, or retired to their hunting-lodges. Everybody went away having any pretensions to politeness, and, of course, with them, Doctor von Glauber, the Court Doctor, and his Baroness. The seasons for the baths were the most productive periods of the Doctor's practice—he united business with pleasure, and his chief place of resort was Ostend, which is much frequented by Germans, and where the Doctor treated himself and his spouse to what he called a "dib" in the sea.

His interesting patient, Jos, was a regular milch-cow to the Doctor, and he easily persuaded the Civilian, both for his own health's sake and that of his charming sister, which was really very much shattered, to pass the summer at that hideous seaport town. Emmy did not care where she went much. Georgy jumped at the idea of a move. As for Becky, she came as a matter of course in the fourth place inside of the fine barouche Mr. Jos had bought: the two domestics being on the box in front. She might have some misgivings about the friends whom she

他想:克劳莱的女人不知道究竟有什么话跟我说?管它!明天我们就动身过海,回英国,回家,回本行!

一过六月,本浦聂格尔的贵族按照德国的风俗,分散到许多矿泉浴场去避暑。他们喝矿水,骑驴子,如果又有钱又有兴致,还可以上赌场赌钱。他们成群结队地去吃客饭,吃得狼吞虎咽。一夏天就这样闲闲散散地过去。英国外交官有的到托百利兹,有的上基新根。他们的法国对头也关了公使馆匆匆忙忙地住到他们最喜欢的特·刚大道去。大公爵一家到温泉避暑,或是住在猎屋里过夏。凡是有资格自称上流人物的,没一个留在本国。御医冯·格劳白先生和他的男爵夫人少不得也跟着大伙儿一起走。上温泉避暑的时候,医生的收入最多,可算是一面干正经事,一面寻欢作乐。他经常避暑都到奥斯当。那边德国人多,医生和他太太又可以洗海澡。

那怪有趣的病人乔斯现在成了他最靠得住的一头奶牛。医生对乔斯说,他自己身子不结实,他可怜的妹妹更是虚弱得厉害,两个人都应该休养。这样一说,就毫不费力地打动了乔斯,把他带着一同到那可厌的海口去过夏天。爱米无可无不可,不管到哪里都行。乔杰听得有机会旅行,高兴得直跳。蓓基当然也跟着一起走,在乔斯新买的大马车里占了第四个位子。两个用人坐在马车外面的座位上。蓓基想到在奥斯当可能遇见的熟人,心里大概有些不安,害怕

should meet at Ostend, and who might be likely to tell ugly stories—but, bah! she was strong enough to hold her own. She had cast such an anchor in Jos now as would require a strong storm to shake. That incident of the picture had finished him. Becky took down her elephant, and put it into the little box which she had had from Amelia ever so many years ago. Emmy also came off with her Lares,—her two pictures,—and the party, finally, were lodged in an exceedingly dear and uncomfortable house at Ostend.

There Amelia began to take baths, and get what good she could from them, and though scores of people of Becky's acquaintance passed her and cut her, yet Mrs. Osborne, who walked about with her, and who knew nobody, was not aware of the treatment experienced by the friend whom she had chosen so judiciously as a companion; indeed, Becky never thought fit to tell her what was passing under her innocent eyes.

Some of Mrs. Rawdon Crawley's acquaintances, however, acknowledged her readily enough,—perhaps more readily than she would have desired. Among these were Major Loder (unattached), and Captain Rook (late of the Rifles), who might be seen any day on the Dyke, smoking and staring at the women, and who speedily got an introduction to the hospitable board and select circle of Mr. Joseph Sedley. In fact, they would take no denial; they burst into the house whether Becky was at home or not, walked into Mrs. Osborne's drawing-room, which they perfumed with their coats and mustachios, called Jos "Old Buck," and invaded his dinner-table, and laughed and drank for long hours there.

"What can they mean?" asked Georgy, who did not

这些人会散播不好听的谣言。她想:管它呢!反正她有能耐,站得定脚跟。现在乔斯是拿得稳的,除非是疾风暴雨般的大变卦才拆得开他们俩。自从那幅画像挂出来之后,他就掉在她手掌心里了。蓓基把她的一幅大像拿下来藏在许多年以前爱米丽亚送给她的小箱子里。爱米也把两幅天神的真容收拾起来,一家人都来到奥斯当,租了一宅又贵又不舒服的房子住下来。

爱米丽亚开始在温泉里洗澡,尽量利用温泉来恢复健康。她和蓓基一同进出。蓓基碰见的老相识不下几十个,大家不睬她,爱米丽亚反正不认得他们,根本不知道她选中的好伴侣受到怎样的怠慢。蓓基觉得不好把实情告诉给她听,让她蒙在鼓里。

罗登·克劳莱太太有几个朋友倒是很愿意跟她来往,——说不定她本人却有些嫌他们。这些人里面有楼德少佐(目前不属于任何部队)和以前在火枪营任职的卢克上尉。他们两个差不多天天站在堤岸上,一面抽烟,一面光着眼看女人。不久他们踏进了乔瑟夫·赛特笠先生高尚的圈子里。赛特笠先生十分好客,他们便常在他家吃饭。事实上他们根本不容许主人拒客,不管蓓基在家不在家,自己冲到屋里,闯进奥斯本太太的客厅,衣服上和胡子上的香水味儿熏得满屋都是。他们管乔斯叫"老家伙",占住了他的饭桌子嘻嘻哈哈地喝酒,一坐就是好半天。

乔杰不喜欢这些人。他问道:"他们说的话我不懂。昨

like these gentlemen. "I heard the Major say to Mrs. Crawley yesterday, 'No, no, Becky, you shan't keep the old buck to yourself. We must have the bones in, or, dammy, I'll split.' What could the Major mean, Mamma."

"Major! don't call him Major!" Emmy said. "I'm sure I can't tell what he meant." His presence and that of his friends inspired the little lady with intolerable terror and aversion. They paid her tipsy compliments; they leered at her over the dinner-table. And the Captain made her advances that filled her with sickening dismay, nor would she ever see him unless she had George by her side.

Rebecca, to do her justice, never would let either of these men remain alone with Amelia; the Major was disengaged too, and swore he would be the winner of her. A couple of ruffians were fighting for this innocent creature, gambling for her at her own table; and though she was not aware of the rascals' designs upon her, yet she felt a horror and uneasiness in their presence, and longed to fly.

She besought, she entreated Jos to go. Not he. He was slow of movement, tied to his Doctor, and perhaps to some other leading-strings. At least Becky was not anxious to go to England.

At last she took a great resolution—made the great plunge. She wrote off a letter to a friend whom she had on the other side of the water; a letter about which she did not speak a word to anybody, which she carried herself to the post under her shawl, nor was any remark made about it; only that she looked very much flushed and agitated when Georgy met her; and she kissed him and hung over him a great deal that night. She did not

天我听见少佐对克劳莱太太说：‘蓓基，你把那老家伙一个人霸占了可不行啊。咱们把骰子拿进屋吧。要不，有什么咱们对半分。’妈妈，少佐的话究竟是什么意思呢？”

爱米说：“少佐！他也配叫少佐！这些话我也不懂。”她一看见他和他的朋友，心里说不出多少害怕和嫌恶。他们嘴里操着醉话奉承她，隔着饭桌子乜斜着眼睛色眯眯地看她。上尉向着她动手动脚，慌得她心里作恶。若是乔杰不在身旁，她从来不肯露脸。

说句公平话，这两个人来他们家的时候，利蓓加从来不让爱米丽亚独自陪客。少佐也是单身，赌神发誓说要把她弄到手。两个恶棍都馋涎这个不懂世事的女人，相争不下，在她自己的桌子上赌赛，把她作赌注。她虽然不知道两个坏蛋背地里怎么算计她，可是见了他们就害怕，战战兢兢的只想逃走。

她苦苦央求乔斯赶快离开当地。可是他不肯。他行动迟慢，离不开医生，说不定还受另外一个人的牵制。反正蓓基并不着急要回英国。

最后爱米狠下心不顾一切冒了一个大险。她写了一封信给海外的一个朋友。关于这件事她对家里的人一个字不提，把信藏在披肩下面走到邮局寄出去。乔杰去接她的时候看见她两腮通红，样子很激动。她吻了乔杰，那天晚上一直守着他。散步回家之后，她就留在卧房里没有出来。蓓

come out of her room after her return from her walk. Becky thought it was Major Loder and the Captain who frightened her.

"She mustn't stop here," Becky reasoned with herself. "She must go away, the silly little fool. She is still whimpering after that gaby of a husband—dead (and served right!) these fifteen years. She shan't marry either of these men. It's too bad of Loder. No; she shall marry the bamboo cane, I'll settle it this very night."

So Becky took a cup of tea to Amelia in her private apartment, and found that lady in the company of her miniatures, and in a most melancholy and nervous condition. She laid down the cup of tea.

"Thank you," said Amelia.

"Listen to me, Amelia," said Becky, marching up and down the room before the other, and surveying her with a sort of contemptuous kindness. "I want to talk to you. You must go away from here and from the impertinences of these men. I won't have you harassed by them: and they will insult you if you stay. I tell you they are rascals; men fit to send to the hulks. Never mind how I know them. I know everybody. Jos can't protect you, he is too weak, and wants a protector himself. You are no more fit to live in the world than a baby in arms. You must marry, or you and your precious boy will go to ruin. You must have a husband, you fool; and one of the best gentlemen I ever saw has offered you a hundred times, and you have rejected him, you silly, heartless, ungrateful little creature."

"I tried—I tried my best, indeed I did, Rebecca," said Amelia, deprecatingly, "but I couldn't forget—;" and she finished the sentence by looking up at the portrait.

基以为是楼德少佐和那上尉把她吓着了。

蓓基自己肚里思忖道："她不应该留在这儿。这小糊涂虫！她非得离开这儿不可。她那个没脑子的丈夫，死了十五年了，（死了也是活该！）她还在哼哼唧唧的舍不得他。这两个男人是不能嫁的。楼德太坏了。不行，还是叫她嫁给那竹子拐棍儿吧。今天晚上我就得把这件事办好。"

蓓基端了一杯茶到爱米丽亚的房里，看见她愁眉苦脸地瞧着两幅画像，仿佛是坐立不安的样子。她放下茶杯。

爱米丽亚说："谢谢你。"

蓓基在爱米面前来回踱步，一半轻蔑一半怜惜地瞧着她说道："爱米丽亚，听我说，我想跟你谈谈。你得离开这儿才好。这些人太混账，你不能跟他们在一起。我不愿意看见他们折磨你。如果你再不走的话，他们就该侮辱你了。告诉你吧，他们都是流氓，应该进监牢的。至于我怎么认得他们的，你不必管。我是什么人都认识的。乔斯不能保护你。他太无能，自己都需要别人来保护。你跟手里抱着的奶娃娃一样，哪儿配在外面混！你还是赶快结婚吧，要不然你和你那宝贝儿子准遭殃。傻瓜，你非有个丈夫不行。有一位百里挑一的君子人已经再三向你求婚，而你却回绝了他。你这糊涂、没心肝、没天良的小东西！"

爱米丽亚为自己辩护道："我——我也很想答应他。这是真话，利蓓加。可是我忘不了——"她抬头看看画像，代替了说话。

"Couldn't forget *him*!"cried out Becky;"that selfish humbug,that low-bred cockney dandy,that padded booby,who had neither wit,nor manners,nor heart,and was no more to be compared to your friend with the bamboo cane than you are to Queen Elizabeth. Why,the man was weary of you,and would have jilted you,but that Dobbin forced him to keep his word. He owned it to me. He never cared for you. He used to sneer about you to me,time after time;and made love to me the week after he married you."

"It's false! It's false! Rebecca,"cried out Amelia, starting up.

"Look there, you fool," Becky said, still with provoking good-humour;and taking a little paper out of her belt,she opened it and flung it into Emmy's lap. "You know his hand-writing. He wrote that to me—wanted me to run away with him—gave it me under your nose,the day before he was shot—and served him right!" Becky repeated.

Emmy did not hear her;she was looking at the letter. It was that which George had put into the bouquet and given to Becky on the night of the Duke of Richmond's ball. It was as she said: the foolish young man had asked her to fly.

Emmy's head sank down, and for almost the last time in which she shall be called upon to weep in this history,she commenced that work. Her head fell to her bosom,and her hands went up to her eyes;and there for a while,she gave way to her emotions,as Becky stood on and regarded her. Who shall analyse those tears,and say whether they were sweet or bitter? Was she most grieved,because the idol of her life was tumbled down

蓓基嚷道："忘不了他！他是个自私自利的骗子，土头土脑下流没教养的纨绔子弟，是个草包，是个蠢东西，又没有脑子，又没有心肝，又不懂规矩！他压根儿不配和你那拿竹子拐棍儿的朋友相提并论，等于你不配跟伊丽莎白女王相提并论一样。什么呀，他对你早就腻味了。要不是都宾逼着他履行婚约，他准会丢了你。这话是他自己对我说的。他向来没爱过你，几次三番在我面前拿你取笑。你们结婚以后一个星期，他就跟我谈情说爱。"

爱米丽亚霍地坐起来嚷道："你胡说！你胡说！利蓓加。"

蓓基的好脾气叫人看着冒火。她从腰带底下掏出一张小纸，打开之后扔在爱米身上，说道："你这傻瓜，瞧瞧这个吧。你认得出他的笔迹。这是他写给我的，要我跟他一起私奔。这还是他给打死的前一天当着你的面给我的呢。他死也是活该！"

爱米没有听见她的话。她正在看那封信——原来就是里却蒙公爵夫人开跳舞会的那天晚上乔治藏在花球里递给蓓基的便条。蓓基说的不错，糊涂的小伙子果然约她私奔。

爱米低下头哭起来——这恐怕是她在这本小说里面最后一次伤心落泪。她把头越垂越低，抬起手来遮着眼睛哭了一会儿，让郁结在心里的感情奔放发泄，蓓基站在旁边瞧着她。谁能够揣摩这些泪珠儿的含义呢？谁能够断定它们是苦是甜呢？她是不是因为崇拜了一辈子的偶像现在倒坍

and shivered at her feet, or indignant that her love had been so despised, or glad because the barrier was removed which modesty had placed between her and a new, a real affection? "There is nothing to forbid me now," she thought. "I may love him with all my heart now. Oh, I will, I will, if he will but let me, and forgive me." I believe it was this feeling rushed over all the others which agitated that gentle little bosom.

Indeed she did not cry so much as Becky expected—the other soothed and kissed her—a rare mark of sympathy with Mrs. Becky. She treated Emmy like a child, and patted her head. "And now let us get pen and ink, and write to him to come this minute," she said.

"I—I wrote to him this morning," Emmy said, blushing exceedingly. Becky screamed with laughter—"*Un biglietto*," she sang out with Rosina, "*eccolo quà!*"—the whole house echoed with her shrill singing.

Two mornings after this little scene, although the day was rainy and gusty, and Amelia had had an exceedingly wakeful night, listening to the wind roaring, and pitying all travellers by land and by water, yet she got up early, and insisted upon taking a walk on the Dyke with Georgy; and there she paced as the rain beat into her face, and she looked out westward across the dark sea-line, and over the swollen billows which came tumbling and frothing to the shore. Neither spoke much, except now and then, when the boy said a few words to his timid companion, indicative of sympathy and protection.

"I hope he won't cross in such weather," Emmy said.

"I bet ten to one he does," the boy answered.

下来滚在脚边给摔得粉碎而伤心呢？还是因为丈夫小看她的痴情而气愤呢？还是因为世俗礼仪所竖起的障碍已经去除，可以得到一种新的、真正的感情而欣喜呢？她想："现在我可以全心全意地爱他了。只要他肯原谅我，给我机会补过，我一定掏出心来爱他。"我想在她温柔的心里，这种感情一定淹没了其他许多使它激动的感情。

出于蓓基意料之外，她只哭了一会儿。蓓基吻着她，用好言好语安慰她。这样慈悲的行为，在蓓基是少有的。她把爱米当做小孩子，拍拍她的头，说道："咱们现在拿出墨水和笔来，写信叫他立刻回来。"

爱米满脸通红，答道："我——我今天早上已经写信给他了。"蓓基听说，尖声大笑起来。她用萝茜娜[①]的词句唱道："这里有一封信！"屋子里上下都听得见她的刺耳的歌声。

这件事情过去两天之后，爱米丽亚一早起来。外面路上风风雨雨，她一夜没有好睡，耳朵听着大风怒号，心里想着在陆上水上的行人该多么可怜。话虽如此说，她仍旧再三要和乔杰一起散步到堤岸上去。她在那儿来回地踱着，让雨水淋在脸上，眼光越过汹涌奔腾、向岸上冲击得浪花四溅的波涛，向西望着黑沉沉的水平线。两个人都不大开口，孩子偶然对他怯生生的同伴说几句话，表示对她同情，给她保护。

爱米说："我希望他不要挑这样坏的天气过海。"

孩子答道："我跟你打赌，十分之九他会来的。妈妈，你

---

① 法国戏剧家博马舍（Beaumarchais，1732—1799）的《塞维勒的理发师》一剧中的女主角。剧本曾由意大利音乐家改编成歌剧。

"Look, mother, there's the smoke of the steamer." It was that signal, sure enough.

But though the steamer was under weigh, he might not be on board: he might not have got the letter; he might not choose to come.—A hundred fears poured one over the other into the little heart, as fast as the waves on to the dyke.

The boat followed the smoke into sight. Georgy had a dandy telescope, and got the vessel under view in the most skilful manner. And he made appropriate nautical comments upon the manner of the approach of the steamer as she came nearer and nearer, dipping and rising in the water. The signal of an English steamer in sight went fluttering up to the mast on the pier. I daresay Mrs. Amelia's heart was in a similar flutter.

Emmy tried to look through the telescope over George's shoulder, but she could make nothing of it. She only saw a black eclipse bobbing up and down before her eyes.

George took the glass again and raked the vessel. "How she does pitch!" he said. "There goes a wave slap over her bows. There's only two people on deck besides the steersman. There's a man laying down, and a—chap in a—cloak with a—Hooray! —It's Dob, by jingo!" He clapped-to the telescope and flung his arms round his mother. As for that lady, let us say what she did in the words of a favourite poet—Dakruoen gelasasa. She was sure it was William. It could be no other. What she had said about hoping that he would not come was all hypocrisy. Of course he would come: what could he do else but come? She knew he would come.

The ship came swiftly nearer and nearer. As they

看，那是汽船的黑烟。”这个信号果真出现了。

虽然汽船向这边行驶，他也许不在船上呢？说不定他没有收到信，说不定他不高兴回来呢？爱米的心里有千百样的恐惧在七上八下，翻翻滚滚的像正在向堤岸奔腾的波浪。

跟着黑烟，船身也出现了。乔杰有一架很花哨的望远镜，他拿起来很熟练地从望远镜里找着了汽船。他看见那船越驶越近，在浪里一起一伏地颠簸，很内行地批评了几句。码头上扯起旗子，报告有一艘英国汽船将要靠岸。那小旗子上升的时候簌簌地抖——我想爱米的一颗心也跟它一样簌簌地抖。

爱米想法在乔杰后面从望远镜里张望，可是什么也看不清，只看见一块黑影在眼前一起一伏。

乔杰把望远镜拿回去细细地向汽船看着。他说：“瞧它颠簸得多厉害！我看见一个浪头砰的打在船头上。甲板上除了舵手之外只有两个别的人。一个人躺在那儿。还有一个人——穿了一件大衣——还有——好哇！他正是都宾！”他收起望远镜，一把搂着母亲的脖子。至于那位太太呢，我们只能借用大家爱好的那位诗人的话来说：她“喜欢得落泪”了。[①] 她心里知道船上的人准是威廉。难道还能是别的人不成？她刚才说什么希望他不要来的话全是装腔。他当然会来。除了赶回来之外他还有什么别的路走？她知道他会回来的。

汽船驶得很快，越来越近。他们到码头上船只靠岸的

① 荷马史诗《伊利亚特》第四卷海克多(Hector)和安特罗马克(Andromache)分别的一幕。

went in to meet her at the landing-place at the quay, Emmy's knees trembled so that she scarcely could run. She would have liked to kneel down and say her prayers of thanks there. Oh, she thought, she would be all her life saying them!

It was such a bad day that as the vessel came alongside of the quay there were no idlers abroad; scarcely even a commissioner on the look-out for the few passengers in the steamer. That young scapegrace George had fled too: and as the gentleman in the old cloak lined with red stuff stepped on to the shore, there was scarcely any one present to see what took place, which was briefly this:

A lady in a dripping white bonnet and shawl, with her two little hands out before her, went up to him, and in the next minute she had altogether disappeared under the folds of the old cloak, and was kissing one of his hands with all her might; whilst the other, I suppose, was engaged in holding her to his heart (which her head just about reached) and in preventing her from tumbling down. She was murmuring something about—Forgive—dear William—dear, dear, dearest friend—kiss, kiss, kiss, and so forth—and in fact went on under the cloak in an absurd manner.

When Emmy emerged from it, she still kept tight hold of one of William's hands, and looked up in his face. It was full of sadness and tender love and pity. She understood its reproach, and hung down her head.

"It was time you sent for me, dear Amelia," he said.

"You will never go again, William?"

"No, never," he answered, and pressed the dear little soul once more to his heart.

地方去迎接它的时候，爱米的两条腿软绵绵的跑也跑不动。她恨不得就地跪下来感谢上天。她想："啊，今后得一辈子感谢天恩才对！"天气那么坏，船靠岸的时候周围一个看热闹的闲人都没有，连等着照看船上那几个旅客的管理员也不见。乔杰那不长进的小子也溜掉了。穿红里子旧大衣的先生上岸的时候，旁边没一个人看见当时发生的事情。大致的情形是这样的——

一位戴白帽子围白披肩的太太，身上滴滴答答的淌着雨水，张开两臂，一直向他走去。一眨眼的工夫，她就给卷在他的大衣褶裥里面，用尽力气吻他的手。他另外一只手大概一面要扶着她防她跌倒，一面又要紧紧搂着她。她的头只到他胸口。她嘴里喃喃呐呐，说什么原谅——亲爱的威廉——亲爱的，最亲爱的，最最亲爱的朋友——吻我，吻我，吻我——这等等的话。大衣底下的情形真是荒谬得不成话。

爱米从大衣底下走出来的时候，一手还紧紧攥着威廉的手，一面抬起头看着他。他脸上有深情，怜悯，也有伤感的成分。她懂得他的责备，把头低了。

他说："亲爱的爱米丽亚，你早该来叫我回来了。"

"你从此不走了吗，威廉？"

"从此不走了，"说着，他重新把亲爱的小人儿搂在胸口。

As they issued out of the Custom-house precincts, Georgy broke out on them, with his telescope up to his eye, and a loud laugh of welcome; he danced round the couple, and performed many facetious antics as he led them up to the house. Jos wasn't up yet; Becky not visible (though she looked at them through the blinds). Georgy ran off to see about breakfast. Emmy, whose shawl and bonnet were off in the passage in the hands of Mrs. Payne, now went to undo the clasp of William's cloak, and—we will, if you please, go with George and look after breakfast for the Colonel. The vessel is in port. He has got the prize he has been trying for all his life. The bird has come in at last. There it is with its head on his shoulder, billing and cooing close up to his heart, with soft outstretched fluttering wings. This is what he has asked for every day and hour for eighteen years. This is what he pined after. Here it is—the summit, the end—the last page of the third volume. Good-bye, Colonel—God bless you, honest William! —Farewell, dear Amelia—Grow green again, tender little parasite, round the rugged old oak to which you cling!

Perhaps it was compunction towards the kind and simple creature, who had been the first in life to defend her, perhaps it was a dislike to all such sentimental scenes,—but Rebecca, satisfied with her part in the transaction, never presented herself before Colonel Dobbin and the lady whom he married. "Particular business," she said, took her to Bruges, whither she went; and only Georgy and his uncle were present at the marriage ceremony. When it was over, and Georgy had rejoined his parents, Mrs. Becky returned (just for a few days) to

他们走出海关的时候，乔杰向他们冲过来，一面从望远镜里看着他们，一面大笑着表示欢迎。他在他们两人旁边手舞足蹈，做出种种滑稽顽皮的把戏，一路把他们引到家里。乔斯还没有起身，蓓基也不露脸，只在百叶窗后面看着他们。乔杰跑去吩咐厨房里预备早饭。爱米自己的帽子和披肩已经给配恩小姐拿到过道里去，现在上前来帮忙解开威廉大衣上的搭扣——如果你不反对，咱们还是跟着乔杰去给上校预备早饭吧。船已经泊岸。想望了一辈子的宝贝已经到手。小鸟儿终究飞进来了。它的头枕着他的肩膀，张开颤抖的翅膀，依依地偎在他的胸口。这是他十八年来日夜盼望的，苦苦思慕的酬报；现在已经得到了。这就是顶峰，就是终点，就是最后的一页。再见了，上校。愿天保佑你，忠厚的威廉！再见了，亲爱的爱米丽亚！你这柔弱的寄生藤啊，愿你绕着粗壮坚实的老橡树重新抽出绿叶子来！

利蓓加呢，也许是有些内疚，觉得自己对不起心地忠厚、头脑简单的爱米，她有生以来第一个恩人，也许是嫌这些多情的场面太肉麻，总之，她认为在这次纠葛里已经尽了本分，从此没有去见都宾上校和他太太。她动身到白吕吉恩去，说是有要紧事情得办理。婚礼举行的时候，只有乔杰和他舅舅在场。这以后，乔杰和父母在一起团聚，蓓基太太重新回来安慰那寂寞的单身汉子，乔瑟夫·赛特笠。她说

comfort the solitary bachelor, Joseph Sedley. He preferred a continental life, he said, and declined to join in housekeeping with his sister and her husband.

Emmy was very glad in her heart to think that she had written to her husband before she read or knew of that letter of George's. "I knew it all along," William said; "but could I use that weapon against the poor fellow's memory? It was that which made me suffer so when you—"

"Never speak of that day again," Emmy cried out, so contrite and humble, that William turned off the conversation, by his account of Glorvina and dear old Peggy O'Dowd, with whom he was sitting when the letter of recall reached him. "If you hadn't sent for me," he added with a laugh, "who knows what Glorvina's name might be now?"

At present it is Glorvina Posky (now Mrs. Major Posky): she took him on the death of his first wife; having resolved never to marry out of the regiment. Lady O'Dowd is also so attached to it that, she says, if anything were to happen to Mick, bedad she'd come back and marry some of'em. But the Major-General is quite well, and lives in great splendour at O'Dowdstown, with a pack of beagles, and (with the exception of perhaps their neighbour, Hoggarty of Castle Hoggarty) he is the first man of his county. Her Ladyship still dances jigs, and insisted on standing up with the Master of the Horse at the Lord Lieutenant's last ball. Both she and Glorvina declared that Dobbin had used the latter *sheamfully*, but Posky falling in, Glorvina was consoled, and a beautiful turban from Paris appeased the wrath of Lady O'Dowd.

When Colonel Dobbin quitted the service, which he

她过几天就要走的。乔斯表示宁可在欧洲住下去，不愿意和妹夫妹妹并家。

爱米想起自己总算在看见乔治那封信以前已经写信给她丈夫，心上很安慰。威廉说："我老早知道这件事。可是我怎么能够利用这样的手段，叫那可怜家伙身后的名誉受累呢？也就是为这个原因，我听了你的话心里真是难受——"

爱米嚷道："再别提那天的话儿了！"她的样子那么谦虚，那么懊丧，威廉便把话锋转到葛萝薇娜和佩琪·奥多那亲爱的老太太身上去。爱米信到的一天，他正和这两个女人坐在一起。他笑道："如果你不来叫我的话，谁也断不定葛萝薇娜将来姓什么。"

现在她的姓名是葛萝薇娜·波斯基，也就是波斯基少佐太太。她打定主意，只嫁部队里的军官；波斯基的第一个妻子一死，她就嫁了他。奥多太太对于部队的感情也很深厚。她说如果密克有个三长两短，她准会回来在其余的军官里面挑一个丈夫。可是中将身体健得很。他住在奥多镇，养着一群猎狗，排场很阔。除掉他的邻居霍加抵堡的霍加抵之外，区里没人比得上他的地位。奥多夫人仍旧跳急步舞，副省长上次开跳舞会的时候，她还再三要和管马大臣比赛谁的气长。她和葛萝薇娜都说都宾对待葛萝薇娜太不应该。幸而有波斯基凑上来，葛萝薇娜才有了安慰。奥多太太收到一块从巴黎寄去的美丽的包头布，气也平了。

都宾上校结婚以后立刻退休，此后在汉泊郡离开女王

did immediately after his marriage, he rented a pretty little country place in Hampshire, not far from Queen's Crawley, where, after the passing of the Reform Bill, Sir Pitt and his family constantly resided now. All idea of a Peerage was out of the question, the baronet's two seats in Parliament being lost. He was both out of pocket and out of spirits by that catastrophe, failed in his health, and prophesied the speedy ruin of the Empire.

Lady Jane and Mrs. Dobbin became great friends—there was a perpetual crossing of pony-chaises between the Hall and the Evergreens, the Colonel's place (rented of his friend Major Ponto, who was abroad with his family). Her Ladyship was godmother to Mrs. Dobbin's child, which bore her name, and was christened by the Rev. James Crawley, who succeeded his father in the living: and a pretty close friendship subsisted between the two lads, George and Rawdon, who hunted and shot together in the vacations, were both entered of the same college at Cambridge, and quarrelled with each other about Lady Jane's daughter, with whom they were both, of course, in love. A match between George and that young lady was long a favourite scheme of both the matrons, though I have heard that Miss Crawley herself inclined towards her cousin.

Mrs. Rawdon Crawley's name was never mentioned by either family. There were reasons why all should be silent regarding her. For wherever Mr. Joseph Sedley went, she travelled likewise; and that infatuated man seemed to be entirely her slave. The Colonel's lawyers informed him that his brother-in-law had effected a heavy insurance upon his life, whence it was probable that he had been raising money to discharge debts. He procured

的克劳莱不远的地方租了一宅漂亮的房子住下来。自从改革议案通过之后,毕脱爵士一家一直住在乡下过日子。从男爵在国会的两个议员席都已经失去,加爵是没有希望的了。经过这次灾难,他手头拮据,总是无精打采的,身体也不好,时常预言英帝国不久便会垮台。

吉恩夫人和都宾太太成了极好的朋友。克劳莱大厦和上校的常绿庐之间(这房子是向他的朋友邦笃少佐租来的,目前邦笃和他一家都在外国)——克劳莱大厦和常绿庐之间马车来,马车去,来往得很频繁。吉恩夫人是都宾太太女儿的教母,小女孩儿就用了她的名字。执行洗礼的就是詹姆士·克劳莱牧师,自从他爹死后,由他接手做了本区的牧师。乔治和罗登这两个小后生交情很深,两个人在假期里一块儿打猎骑射,后来读大学,也是进的剑桥同一个学校。他们当然都爱上了吉恩夫人的女儿,两人争风吃醋。两个太太心坎儿上老早有个打算,要把小姐和乔治结为夫妇,不过我听说克劳莱小姐本人倒是对于堂哥哥更有意。

两家都不提起克劳莱太太的名字。他们对她的事缄口不言是有原因的。因为不论乔斯·赛特笠到哪里,她总跟着走。那着了迷的乔斯彻头彻尾成了她的奴隶。上校的律师告诉他说他大舅子保了一大笔人寿险,看来他正在筹款子还债。他向东印度公司请了长假,身体一天比一天虚弱。

prolonged leave of absence from the East India House, and indeed his infirmities were daily increasing.

On hearing the news about the insurance, Amelia, in a good deal of alarm, entreated her husband to go to Brussels, where Jos then was, and inquire into the state of his affairs. The Colonel quitted home with reluctance (for he was deeply immersed in his "History of the Punjaub," which still occupies him, and much alarmed about his little daughter, whom he idolizes, and who was just recovering from the chicken-pox), and went to Brussels and found Jos living at one of the enormous hotels in that city. Mrs. Crawley, who had her carriage, gave entertainments, and lived in a very genteel manner, occupied another suite of apartments in the same hotel.

The Colonel, of course, did not desire to see that lady, or even think proper to notify his arrival at Brussels, except privately to Jos by a message through his valet. Jos begged the Colonel to come and see him that night, when Mrs. Crawley would be at a *soirée*, and when they could meet *alone*. He found his brother-in-law in a condition of pitiable infirmity; and dreadfully afraid of Rebecca, though eager in his praises of her. She tended him through a series on unheard-of illnesses, with a fidelity most admirable. She had been a daughter to him. "But—but—oh for God's sake, do come and live near me, and—and—see me sometimes," whimpered out the unfortunate man.

The Colonel's brow darkened at this. "We can't, Jos," he said. "Considering the circumstances, Amelia can't visit you."

"I swear to you—I swear to you on the Bible," gasped out Joseph, wanting to kiss the book, "that she is

爱米丽亚听见他保寿险的消息，十分放心不下，求她丈夫到布鲁塞尔去看看乔斯，查个明白。上校离家出国的时候很不愿意，一则他正在聚精会神地写《旁遮普历史》[①]（到目前为止还没有写完），二则他心爱的小女儿出水痘刚痊愈，他还是不大放心。他到了布鲁塞尔，发现乔斯住在本城的一家大旅馆里。克劳莱太太住的就是同一旅馆的另外一套房间。她有自备马车，也常常请客，过活得很有气派。

上校自然不想碰见这位太太。他甚至于没有让别人知道他已经到达布鲁塞尔，只叫用人悄悄地送了个信给乔斯。乔斯央告上校当夜就去看他。那天晚上克劳莱太太出门做客，他们两个可以私下见见。上校发现大舅子虚弱得可怜，而且他虽然没口地称赞利蓓加，可是对于她真是战战兢兢。据说他害了一大串的病，全亏她看护。这些病名儿是以前没人听见过的，她对朋友的忠诚也是令人敬佩的。她伺候乔斯简直像女儿伺候父亲。那倒霉的家伙哼哼着说道："可是——可是——唉，看老天面上，搬到这儿来住在我近旁吧。有的——有的时候你们可以来瞧瞧我。"

上校听了这话，皱眉说道："那不行的，乔斯。在这样的情形之下，爱米丽亚不能来看你。"

"我向你起誓，我拿《圣经》起誓，"乔瑟夫一面气喘吁吁地说话，一面准备吻圣书，"她跟孩子一样纯洁，跟你的太太

① 旁遮普是印度的一省。

as innocent as a child, as spotless as your own wife."

"It may be so," said the Colonel, gloomily; "but Emmy can't come to you. Be a man, Jos: break off this disreputable connexion. Come home to your family. We hear your affairs are involved."

"Involved!" cried Jos. "Who has told such calumnies? All my money is placed out most advantageously. Mrs. Crawley —that is—I mean,—it is laid out to the best interest."

"You are not in debt, then? Why did you insure your life?"

"I thought—a little present to her—in case anything happened; and you know my health is so delicate—common gratitude you know—and I intend to leave all my money to you—and I can spare it out of my income, indeed I can," cried out William's weak brother-in-law.

The Colonel besought Jos to fly at once—to go back to India, whither Mrs. Crawley could not follow him; to do anything to break off a connexion which might have the most fatal consequences to him.

Jos clasped his hands, and cried—"He would go back to India. He would do anything: only he must have time: they mustn't say anything to Mrs. Crawley:—she'd—she'd kill me if she knew it. You don't know what a terrible woman she is," the poor wretch said.

"Then, why not come away with me?" said Dobbin in reply, but Jos had not the courage. "He would see Dobbin again in the morning: he must on no account say that he had been there. He must go now. Becky might come in." And Dobbin quitted him full of forebodings.

He never saw Jos more. Three months afterwards Joseph Sedley died at Aix-la-Chapelle. It was found that

一样清白。”

上校没精打采地答道：“也许你说的不错，可是爱米不能来。乔斯，做个男子汉大丈夫，把这个不名誉的关系斩断了吧！你回家来住得了。我们听说你的经济情况很糟。”

乔斯嚷道：“很糟！谁在造谣伤人？我所有的钱都好好儿的存在外面，利息大着呢！克劳莱太太——我的意思是——我是说——我的钱处置得非常好。”

“你没有借债吗？那么干什么保寿险呢？”

“我本来想——送她一份小小的礼——说不定我有个三长两短。你知道我身子很弱——一个人总得拿出良心待人。我的钱准备都留给你们——钱我可以省得出来，真的省得出来，”威廉的意志薄弱的大舅子叫叫嚷嚷地这么说了一篇话。

上校求他赶快逃走，如果乔斯回到印度，克劳莱太太绝不能跟着去。他说把这样的关系维持下去，可能造成最严重的后果，所以无论如何先得和她脱离。

乔斯这可怜虫把两只手紧紧捏在一起叫道：“我就到印度去。随便要我怎么都行。可是得慢慢儿来啊。咱们绝不能把这话告诉克劳莱太太。她——她知道了准会把我杀死。你不知道她多可怕！”

都宾答道：“那么干吗不跟着我回家呢？”可是乔斯鼓不起这勇气。他说他第二天早上再跟都宾见面；都宾可不准说他隔夜已经来过了的。他又催都宾快走，因为蓓基也许就要回来。都宾回去的时候，觉得这件事凶多吉少。

他从此没有看见乔斯。三个月之后，乔瑟夫·赛特笠在埃克斯·拉·夏北尔地方去世。大家发现他所有的财产都在各种投机事业里闹掉了，剩下的只有几家滑头公司发

all his property had been muddled away in speculations, and was represented by valueless shares in different bubble companies. All his available assets were the two thousand pounds for which his life was insured, and which were left equally between his beloved "sister Amelia, wife of, and his friend and invaluable attendant during sickness, Rebecca, wife of Lieutenant-Colonel Rawdon Crawley, C. B.," who was appointed administratrix.

The solicitor of the Insurance Company swore it was the blackest case that ever had come before him; talked of sending a commission to Aix to examine into the death, and the Company refused payment of the policy. But Mrs., or Lady Crawley, as she styled herself, came to town at once (attended with her, solicitors, Messrs. Burke, Thurtell, and Hayes, of Thavies Inn), and dared the Company to refuse the payment. They invited examination, they declared that she was the object of an infamous conspiracy, which had been pursuing her all through life, and triumphed finally. The money was paid, and her character established, but Colonel Dobbin sent back his share of the legacy to the Insurance Office, and rigidly declined to hold any communication with Rebecca.

She never was Lady Crawley, though she continued so to call herself. His Excellency Colonel Rawdon Crawley died of yellow fever at Coventry Island, most deeply beloved and deplored, and six weeks before the demise of his brother, Sir Pitt. The estate consequently devolved upon the present Sir Rawdon Crawley, Bart.

He, too, has declined to see his mother, to whom he makes a liberal allowance; and who, besides, appears to be very wealthy. The Baronet lives entirely at Queen's

行的股票，全无价值。二千镑寿险是唯一能兑现的遗产。这笔钱一半给他妹妹爱米丽亚，一半给“他的朋友利蓓加，下级骑士罗登·克劳莱少将之妻，因为他病中多承她照顾，给他的帮助难以估计”。同时，利蓓加又是遗嘱的执行人。

保险公司的律师赌神发誓，说他一辈子没有见过这样不明不白的案件，应该派专员前来调查死亡的原因；保险公司也拒绝付款。克劳莱太太（她自称克劳莱爵士夫人）立刻带着泰维斯法学院的白克、德脱尔、海斯几位律师赶到伦敦来办交涉。保险公司敢不付钱吗？律师们欢迎公司方面调查真相，他们声称有人阴谋陷害克劳莱太太，已经不是一朝一夕的事了。结果她大获全胜，银钱到手，又保全了好名声。都宾上校把他的一份钱退还保险公司，并且斩钉截铁地拒绝和利蓓加通信或来往。

虽然她继续自称克劳莱爵士夫人，其实她是没有这种资格的。他大人罗登·克劳莱上校在考文脱莱岛害黄热病去世，比他哥哥毕脱爵士早死一个半月。群众对于他非常爱戴，听了他的死讯万分哀痛。克劳莱的庄地由现在的从男爵罗登·克劳莱爵士承继。

他也拒绝和他母亲见面，不过给她一份丰厚的生活费。除了这笔钱，他母亲似乎还有许多别的财源。从男爵一年到头住在女王的克劳莱，和吉恩夫人和她女儿在一起。利

Crawley, with Lady Jane and her daughter; whilst Rebecca, Lady Crawley, chiefly hangs about Bath and Cheltenham, where a very strong party of excellent people consider her to be a most injured woman. She has her enemies. Who has not? Her life is her answer to them. She busies herself in works of piety. She goes to church, and never without a footman. Her name is in all the Charity Lists. The Destitute Orange-girl, the Neglected Washerwoman, the Distressed Muffin-man, find in her a fast and generous friend. She is always having stalls at Fancy Fairs for the benefit of these hapless beings. Emmy, her children, and the Colonel, coming to London some time back, found themselves suddenly before her at one of these fairs. She cast down her eyes demurely and smiled as they started away from her; Emmy scurrying off on the arm of George (now grown a dashing young gentleman), and the Colonel seizing up his little Janey, of whom he is fonder than of anything in the world—fonder even than of his "History of the Punjaub."

"Fonder than he is of me," Emmy thinks, with a sigh. But he never said a word to Amelia that was not kind and gentle; or thought of a want of hers that he did not try to gratify.

Ah! *Vanitas Vanitatum!* which of us is happy in this world? Which of us has his desire? or, having it, is satisfied? —Come, children, let us shut up the box and the puppets, for our play is played out.

蓓加呢（她也是爵士夫人），大多的时候在温泉和契尔顿纳姆两边住住。在这两个地方有许多极好的人都帮她说话，认为她一辈子受尽了冤屈。她也有冤家。这也是免不了的。对于这等人，她目前的生活方式就是一个回答。她热心宗教事业，经常上教堂，背后总有听差跟着。在所有大善士的名单上，总少不了她的名字。对于穷苦的卖橘子女孩儿，没人照顾的洗衣服女人，潦倒的煎饼贩子，她是一个靠得住的、慷慨的施主。为这些可怜人开的义卖会上，她总有份，每回守着摊子帮忙。不久以前爱米和她的儿女，还有上校，一起到伦敦来，在一个义卖会上出其不意地和她打了个照面。他们慌慌张张地跑了，她只低下眼睛稳重地笑了一笑。爱米勾着乔治的胳膊仓皇逃走（乔治现在已经长成了一个漂亮潇洒的小伙子）；上校抱起小吉内跟着。他看着吉内比世界上一切的东西都重——甚至于比他的《旁遮普历史》还重。

爱米叹口气想到："也比我重。"可是他对爱米丽亚总是温柔体贴，千依百顺。

唉，浮名浮利，一切虚空！我们这些人里面谁是真正快活的？谁是称心如意的？就算当时遂了心愿，过后还不是照样不满意？来吧，孩子们，收拾起戏台，藏起木偶人，咱们的戏已经演完了。